THE
SAFFRON PATH

THE
SAFFRON PATH

trekking the globe with
THE WALKING MONK

BHAKTIMARGA SWAMI

The Saffron Path
Trekking the Globe with The Walking Monk
By Bhaktimarga Swami (John Vis)

Copyright © 2022 The Walking Monk
All rights reserved.

ISBN: 9798807152664

– – First Edition 2022 – –

Developmental Editors:
Wade Wilson
Jennifer Layne Bortnak (Nitai Priya Devi Dasi)

Line Editors:
Jennifer Layne Bortnak (Nitai Priya Devi Dasi)
Wade Wilson
V.L. Murray

Copy Editors:
Jennifer Layne Bortnak (Nitai Priya Devi Dasi)
V.L. Murray

Cover Design / Layout / Photo Editing:
Jennifer Layne Bortnak (Nitai Priya Devi Dasi) of Neat Eye Design

Photographers:
Quidam Photography (Daruka Das) – Including original photo for back cover
Vitaliy Grytsyuk (Vivasan Das)
Gaurav Agarwal – Including original photo for front cover

Photographs from Bhaktivedanta Archives courtesy of The Bhaktivedanta Book Trust International, Inc. Used with permission.
The author has made every effort to obtain permission from and credit contributors for photos used in this publication. In the event of omission, please contact the author and credit(s) will be amended in future editions.

The conversations in this book come from the author's own recollections and do not necessarily represent word-for-word transcripts; the essence and meaning of any dialogue remains correct.

The information presented is the author's opinion and does not constitute health or medical advice. The content of this book is for entertainment purposes only and is not intended to diagnose, treat, cure, or prevent any physical or mental condition or disease. The author holds no liability for any actions taken by the reader, or the results of those actions, that are inspired by any part of this book's content; all such actions and results are the sole responsibility of the reader.

Website: www.thewalkingmonk.net

This book is dedicated to my teacher and guide, Srila Prabhupada, who took that brisk walk every morning setting the tone for pilgrimage.

TABLE OF CONTENTS

Foreword **i**   A Walking Prayer **v**   Introduction **vii**   A Note to the Reader **xi**

CANADA

CHAPTER 1
Why I Took a Fancy to Walking — 1

CHAPTER 2
I Don't Like Cars — 8

CHAPTER 3
Beginnings — 14

CHAPTER 4
Finding Our Way Through — 19

CHAPTER 5
Focus and Determination — 24

CHAPTER 6
Porridge or Forage: Food on the Road — 30

CHAPTER 7
In the Thick of the Mountains — 36

CHAPTER 8
A Prayer and a Bear — 40

CHAPTER 9
Apprehension in the Darkness of Night — 44

CHAPTER 10
A Slice of Alberta and Freaks of Nature — 49

CHAPTER 11
The Silky Way — 55

CHAPTER 12
Close Calls and the Log Man — 61

CHAPTER 13
Highway Bullies — 67

CHAPTER 14
You Can't Judge a Biker by His Colours — 72

CHAPTER 15
Jazz on the Road — 77

CHAPTER 16
Reincarnation: Walking from Body to Body   82

CHAPTER 17
Getting Noticed as a Moving Traffic Cone!   87

CHAPTER 18
Beware of Dog   93

CHAPTER 19
The Times I Laughed on the Road   97

CHAPTER 20
To Serve and Protect   101

CHAPTER 21
Mild to Mean Attacks   107

CHAPTER 22
By George!   112

CHAPTER 23
I Believe in Everyday Miracles   115

CHAPTER 24
Roadspill or Roadkill   119

CHAPTER 25
Many Returns to a Familiar Door   124

CHAPTER 26
Indigenous Goodness   129

CHAPTER 27
Lessons in Lust and Love   134

CHAPTER 28
Helpful Hugs   137

CHAPTER 29
My Longest Day   141

CHAPTER 30
The Times I Cried on the Road   147

CHAPTER 31
To Dad with Love   152

CHAPTER 32
Random Roadside Prayers   158

CHAPTER 33
The Misunderstood Monk   162

CHAPTER 34
Monk for a Minute   167

CHAPTER 35
Endings and the Ghost on the Rock   171

ACROSS THE WATER

CHAPTER 36
Ireland and Rain the Ripper   178

CHAPTER 37
Trinidad: Trekking for the Destitute   182

CHAPTER 38
Delicious Mauritius   188

CHAPTER 39
Angels and Gangsters in Guyana   193

CHAPTER 40
Fantastic Fiji   198

CHAPTER 41
Israel: Why Not?   205

UNITED STATES

CHAPTER 42
A Slice of New England: Massachusetts and Connecticut   211

CHAPTER 43
Hail Mary and Hare Krishna! Pennsylvania, New Jersey, New York   219

CHAPTER 44
The Great Midwest! Hello Ohio!   231

CHAPTER 45
The Three 'I's: Indiana, Illinois, and Iowa   239

CHAPTER 46
Big Long Nebraska   248

CHAPTER 47
Colorado Cool – Switching Roads   254

CHAPTER 48
Ups and Downs in Utah   261

CHAPTER 49
Nevada – and a Pooch Pooja   269

CHAPTER 50
California: It's Smoking!   278

AFTERWORD
My Walking Compadres   287

FOREWORD

I first encountered Bhaktimarga Swami in the mid-1980s. It was a fleeting meeting with quite a few others also present, but I remember being most struck by his enthusiasm for life, his very jolly, if not joyous disposition, and if I may say, the very pure and angelic vibration he exuded.

It would be a little over a decade before we met again, and this time it was the dawn of a blossoming, and ultimately very rich and sweet friendship.

By this time, Bhaktimarga Swami had embarked on using his unique and very natural artistic and creative abilities in conceiving, writing, producing, and directing many impressive plays depicting some of the profound and inspirational stories of ancient India. Indeed, he was doing the very same on many contemporary topics, too. I remember when acting in some of those plays being mesmerized as to how he could pull everything together and master all the different skill sets required. I think I would have to admit to being a little envious of him!

The next remarkable venture that Bhaktimarga Swami embarked on was walking! I say remarkable because what's the big deal about walking? However, any illusions I may have had about this venture were blown out of the water when I learned that his first walking project was a mere 7,000-kilometre expedition across the whole of Canada! Initially, I thought he was being fanciful in the extreme, but some weeks later after he had achieved his goal, I realized the extraordinary commitment, determination, and courage of this man. It was not only I who found that an astonishing feat, but the National Film Board of Canada featured him in a documentary, entitled *The Longest Road*. Lo and behold, it did not stop there, not at all. In fact, he has practically never stopped walking since that first journey, and each time huge distances and tracts of land are being traversed. Such ambitious walking trips across the United States, Ireland, the Fiji Islands, Mauritius, Trinidad, Guyana, and Israel. I joined him for a fraction of his walk in my home country of Ireland for some forty-eight kilometres (thirty miles), and that greatly deepened my appreciation for his extraordinary endeavours. Boy, can this man walk fast—pedestrians beware! Some ten years his junior, I simply couldn't keep up, but my competitive nature dictated that I at least try to. What a mistake that proved to be!

In my attempt to keep up with this professional walker, who'd probably qualify for the Olympics, I sustained an unusual injury. After some miles of straining every muscle to keep up while pretending my gait was comfortable, I noticed a little discomfort emanating from my left big toe. By the time it got to the point of unendurable pain and I stopped to check the damage, it was too late. As I took my shoe off, and then my sock, I saw my toenail was all but detached from my toe! But no worries, the job was complete the next morning when I woke up. The bed sheets had done the rest and I no longer had a big toenail. If only I could be as detached as my toenail was, revelling in its new-found independence from my foot!

As I write, our professional walker, Bhaktimarga Swami, has now traversed Canada four times, and all his toenails remain in place! Can you imagine? That is some 28,000 kilometres of walking just in Canada alone! And just as with his plays, he touches the hearts of everyone he meets on these epic treks with his infectious sharing of the spiritual secrets of ancient India in such a relevant and meaningful way.

The Saffron Path is a racy read, it walks apace through many intriguing and compelling subjects, and there is no one more suited or qualified than Bhaktimarga Swami to safely navigate us through that particular journey. He straddles between such topics as the environment, diet, health (both physical and spiritual), fear in all its guises (such as nature), other living beings, and our own mental wellbeing. Also, human nature, passion and desire, the power of prayer, and the compelling connection we all have with our karma and future existences.

Addressing these topics and more is a great and much-needed service to us all, and never more so given the world today where we seem to be ever rushing to stand still. The rate of knots the world is moving at can indeed be scary, and I know from time to time I contemplate jumping off the careering carousel that is the world we live in.

For the vast majority of us, we feel the constant pushing and pulling of modern life, so the attraction to pressing the stop button is often compelling, but hair raising in equal measure. Bhaktimarga Swami has a beautiful knack for putting all that in perspective, which offers us all a priceless solace.

Deep down, we know there must be more to life than rushing to grow old, and The Walking Monk gives us enormous pointers in *how* to grow old, not just gracefully, but with far-reaching insight into the purpose of our very existence.

Of course, there is many a slip between thinking and doing, and for some the doing never comes to pass. The ever-revolving carousel that is modern life spins so fast it often leaves us in state of constant flux with life's loose ends never being concluded.

We could ask that if time is an eternal phenomenon, why does it always seem we do not have enough of it?

Or why do we squander time when we often grumble its shortage? One thing is for sure, in this world what lies ahead for us may be as clear as mud, but rest assured the end is ever near!

So, please enter the timeless and intriguing journey with Bhaktimarga Swami that is *The Saffron Path* and stride through life, as opposed to allowing it to walk all over you!

–Paul Murphy aka Praghosa Dasa

A WALKING PRAYER

Dear Creator,

I express my gratitude for the privilege to walk.
To move about and make friends along the way.
To feel the texture of the land and the touch of a hand.
To smell the scents of sweet blossoms and grass.
To be awed by nature's vistas and views.
To marvel at creatures of land, water, and sky.
To see both life and death and the struggle between.
To go through the rigors of pain in the legs.
To learn from it the qualities of detachment.
To gaze at the truth of duality in my face.
To feel the sun's warmth and the winter's embrace.
To step into the tall, to make me feel small.
To build physical strength, fortitude, character.
To help realize the world's fragility and whimsy.
To see the pillar of the Source behind the force.
To understand service as all that there be.
To share what I've learned and to pass it on.

–The Walking Monk

INTRODUCTION

"Grandma! Grandma!" said the frantic young passenger girl.
"What is it, dear?"
"There's three dead men in the ditch! I just saw them!"
"Are you sure?" said the grandparent, the driver of the car. "Where?"
"Back there" said the girl, pointing to the ditch and the tall grasses.
"Oh, my God" exclaimed Grandmother. "We better let the police know."
Convinced by the testimony of the young witness, Grandma headed in the direction of the nearest public phone at the general store in Echo Bay where she dialed 911 for emergency.
"Officer, I want to report something terrible that has happened out on Highway 17," she began. "I was driving with my granddaughter when she saw three corpses in the ditch on the side of the road."
While the woman was explaining the tragic situation, her conversation was overheard by a stockily-built British bloke by the name of Madhai. He was curious about the story because the three people could be his companions who had been walking along that very highway. He cautiously moved toward the six-year-old girl while her grandmother was on the phone with the police.
"Hello," said Madhai. "Was one of the men in the ditch wearing orange, maybe?"
The shy youngster moved closer to her grandmother without responding to the strange man. Madhai imagined the worst. *Could it be them? Are my friends really gone? They had been foraging for greens along the road. Maybe they picked the wrong plant or maybe they were struck by a big truck. Could this be the end of their adventure?* His mind turned to the *swami*, the monk in orange who walks around forty-two kilometres (twenty-six miles) a day.
Madhai was providing support for the *swami*. There had been dangerous encounters: attacks by aggressive birds in the Canadian Prairies, a threatening encounter with a grizzly bear in the Rocky Mountains, nasty wasps stinging his backside during a call of nature, and nearly falling into the path of oncoming traffic after suffering from delirious fatigue. These

were all dangerous scenarios. Everyday Madhai massaged the monk's swollen feet and delivered him to functions in the support van. He had become the navigator, camp locator, media liaison agent, and cook—services that he relished.

Madhai decided to go see for himself and left the general store, jumped into the old '79 Dodge van, and headed to the vicinity where he figured the walking party would be.

Now the truth of the matter was that the three men, including the monk, were lying in the grasses *dead tired*. It had been a long, hard, hot day of trekking, and they had decided to take a break in the shade and the softness of the grasses along the road's edge.

An officer dispatched from the Ontario Provincial Police was sent out to investigate. He arrived quickly to the scene and saw, as reported, three persons, all male (one of them in his teens), lying in the grass. The lightest of the sleepers, Garuda, woke up when the officer slammed his car door.

Incidentally, Garuda had taken a break from his day job to spend a few days on the road on a walking excursion. He was a Sheriff from Orangeville County, and he wasn't too impressed with the police officer's approach to handling the situation.

"You're not allowed to be here in the ditch; it is the property of the Department of Highways," the officer said. "Can I see your ID please?"

Reluctantly, Garuda submitted.

"I'd like to see your son's ID as well," the officer demanded.

It didn't sit well with Garuda in the least that Tulsi, his still sleeping teenage son, was, in Garuda's mind, about to be interrogated. Garuda took this opportunity to assert himself as Sheriff of Orangeville County. In other words, he was also part of the system to serve and protect. In fact, his primary function was to deliver legal papers to citizens being charged with felonies. Regardless of who held the superior rank, the tide of authority had turned.

"And just what is your name, officer?" demanded Garuda.

The officer answered.

"And what is your badge number?"

He answered that as well.

"We are doing nothing wrong, officer," said an excited Garuda. "I am assisting this monk who is walking across Canada for a cause—a cause promoting a simpler, healthier way of life." Garuda's voice was raised to a volume that woke the monk.

And that monk was me.

What's all the commotion about? I dissolved myself from a deep catnap and struggled to my feet. When I viewed Garuda chiding the policeman, I was concerned about his tactics. "Careful now with the authorities." But upon hearing his logic, I thought that perhaps the rude awakening for the officer's insensitivity was justified. Had we been in India (which I visit annually), an officer would have put palms together in respect upon seeing a *sadhu*, a holy man in saffron robes. And if by circumstance, a *sadhu* would walk on a farmer's field, the proprietor would say, "Thank you for blessing my land."

But this is not India.

It was interesting to see the uneasiness of the officer's eyes at Garuda's demands. The officer departed slightly more timid than when he first came to investigate. Perhaps he'd met his match. I did feel sorry for him, however, as he drove off.

Madhai eventually found us. We were alive and well. What a sigh of relief that was for him. We could now forge ahead with our trekking mission.

In as much as this passing of one hour or less contained an incident which held some drama and misunderstanding, it contributed to a pretty typical day on the road.

So, there I was, a pilgrim, a Caucasian in Indian orange garb, going through the rhythm of the day, taking in the good, the bad, and the ugly. But in truth, it is all good.

Om Tat Sat.

A NOTE TO THE READER

While planning how to detail my many walks (particularly the four across Canada), I decided to opt for a thematic approach as opposed to a linear one. In revisiting my journeys, I noticed there were several common themes and categories of events and adventures through each one. In a similar fashion to when I'm sharing my "Tales from Trails" presentation with live audiences, I resolved that sharing these themes together in their own chapters makes for far more captivating storytelling.

As you read on in these adventures, you may at one moment find yourself travelling with me from Canada's west coast to its east coast on my first walk, and in the next moment, walking in the opposite direction some years later—and in both, facing a related hilarity, fright, wonderment, or heartfelt connection.

–The Walking Monk

CHAPTER 1
WHY I TOOK A FANCY TO WALKING

"Habituate yourself to walk very far."

–Thomas Jefferson

Like most people, I started walking right around my first birthday. I can't remember those initial feeble attempts, but having watched other little ones begin the process, I can only imagine the joy I experienced with those first few shaky steps. My parents would know the actual details of my learning to walk, but they have peacefully moved on to those heavenly walking pastures. By my recollection, I was five when I made more serious and solemn solo walking excursions to school and back home each day. No bus, no car, no regrets.

That trek along Tecumseh Road was educational and memorable. The mile-long walk was curvy and twisty. A surprise awaited me around each bend presenting a fresh new view of magic for an inquisitive five-year old. Observing the trees, I saw how a mild breeze gently shook their leaves while wild winds bent their branches in a distorted way.

Seasonal changes from spring to summer to fall to winter painted the landscape in diverse colours. Birds would line up, perched on the hydro lines, to contribute their chorus of songs for the enjoyment of this solo stroller. Sparrows, doves, and crows filled the air with their chirping, cooing, and cawing. They were my feathered friends and provided company on those amazing little treks.

In the autumn a farmer's tractor with a plow hitched to it would overturn the clay soil exposing fat, juicy earthworms. This annual tilling of the soil attracted seagulls galore, flitting about in ecstasy, enjoying the newly exposed crawlers. The whitish seafowl were an eager bunch winging their way up into the sky only to descend and satisfy their pecking voraciousness. Farmers could never complain about being alone when plowing their recently harvested cornfields.

My walk to school would take me past our neighbours' homes. The first was a nicely kept house and a bright red barn with a sign that read, "Jack

Caron and Sons." I would continue past the more modest homes of the Larshes, Sullivans, and Goulets. They all had children my age or older, who had a shorter walk to school. S.S. #1 Harwich was a typical red brick, rural one-room schoolhouse which snugly accommodated eight grades. Our teacher, Mrs. Antaya, was elderly, sometimes feisty, but sweet.

Next to the school was a church, Saint Peter's Catholic, founded back in 1802. Those must have been exciting times. Canadians turned back an American invasion in The War of 1812. In 1813, Chief Tecumseh was killed by an American militia gunshot. The church is about an adult's one day, thirty-kilometre walk up the Thames River in southwestern Ontario, from where the great chief met his maker.

MEMORY LANE OF THE ONE-ROOM SCHOOLHOUSE. WALKED A MILE EVERY DAY AT AGE 5.

When I walked on that meandering road along the river, I often had two people in mind, apart from my parents and siblings. Those two people were God and Shawnee Chief Tecumseh. They were, and still are, my heroes. I remember praying for warmth to the Creator on some of those intensely cold Canadian winter days.

Walking was always an integral part of my life in those early years. Later on, a bicycle would become a faster form of transportation along my childhood road. I often rode with my younger sister Connie perched on the top bar of my bicycle. Once, while riding with reckless abandon, I lost control and jumped off my bike, watching it and poor Connie plunge into the ditch. It took a while, but she finally forgave me for that childhood event. I also remember dogs being an issue, as they would chase me and my bike, viciously snarling and barking.

Biking was okay, even though it was at times dangerous. But it was walking that really appealed to me. It just seemed the right pace and allowed me to dream. I wondered if I would ever have a barn with my name on it, 'and Sons' or 'Daughters'?

Walking also allowed me to be very much in the present moment. Only an occasional automobile or truck, always a 1950-something Dodge, Chevy, or Ford, would interrupt my flow of thought and movement. I would step aside as best I could on the shoulder-less road to make room. Everyone was friendly back then, and motorist and walker would always exchange a cordial wave of the hand.

Later on, our family moved to a home near the town of Blenheim which had a population of 3,000. I continued walking to elementary, and then high school.

I was soon off to a school of higher learning, where in 1973 I made a decision to terminate my student and college affairs for a renounced life. I truly believe my love of walking contributed to that decision. Don't get me wrong, I loved my fine arts courses at Cambrian College, and my professors were great. But this was the 1970s and Bob Dylan sang, "The times they are a changin'." I don't think Bob influenced me a whole lot, but I really felt I needed to undertake a radical lifestyle change.

PREPARING TO LEAVE THE WORLD OF SECULAR EDUCATION FOR THE EDUCATION OF THE SPIRIT.

Hitchhiking then became my favourite mode of transportation. I loved visiting my cousin, Andy, and his wife, Rose, and bumming a ride was my way of getting to their place. But, on the way home from one particular visit, I discovered I was getting tired of standing along the side of the road with my thumb out hoping a car would come along. I was restless due to the lack of interest on the part of the motorists failing to do me a favour by pulling over and offering this weary traveller a ride.

I remember clearly it was a gorgeous sunny April day. The spring thaw was underway with snow and ice melting and quickly disappearing. Despite the great weather and the optimism that often comes with it, no one was willing to play the Good Samaritan. It was Saturday and people seemed to be rushing off to go shopping or head to a party. They were too busy to bother with me and in some cases I am sure they didn't even notice this humble hiker.

I felt ambivalent. Half of me was aloof to the circumstance and I figured what the heck, why should this bother me? But the other half was resentful, feeling abandoned and wanting to curse the world. It was then I came to terms with the reality of the situation and figured if these reluctant motorists didn't want to give me a lift, I would hoof it.

So, I started with step number one on a nine-mile trek back to my apartment. During that troubled walk, my animosity toward a self-centred world gradually wore away. My deliberations led to a kind of liberation and feeling of relief which finally allowed me to cross a major threshold in my life. While rhythmically embracing the earth and stones with my feet, I also gained a certain level of acceptance. I would become a monk.

I had met five Hare Krishna monks the previous December. They shared many thoughts about vegetarianism, reincarnation, and chanting, during a brief overnight stay at my apartment. They really cared about my soul, and that moved me. They also had this blissful, joyful appearance, and it seemed to me they had discovered something that had given them inner peace. I had been contemplating a paradigm shift in my life for at least four months. Now, nearing the end of this nine-mile walk, my resolute purpose was to get back to the apartment and tell Michael, my roommate, about my decision.

"Michael, I'm giving up my art studies to practice higher consciousness," I boldly declared.

"Okay," said Michael, with a certain level of uncertainty. The expression on his face said, "Are you alright?"

In hindsight, I have to acknowledge the synchronicity of the situation. That nine-mile power walk, accompanied by aching calf muscles and a sensational spiritual awakening, became a meaningful coincidence. From that day on, I could not separate walking and praying. I felt a reunion with God, whom I had more or less put on the shelf during my high school years.

I was happy to hear from the Hare Krishna monks that their *guru*, Prabhupada, walked every morning, chanting with every step, and seeing sacredness everywhere. This great *guru* was incorporating those simple thoughts and techniques through the course of his sauntering.

Health experts are always beating the drum telling us about the benefits of walking. They claim walking refreshes the mind, reduces fatigue, increases energy, lowers blood pressure, improves digestion and evacuation, relieves stress and tension, and strengthens bones. It also strengthens the heart, lungs, and muscles, and reduces excess weight. Oh, it does at least one more thing, and that involves social interaction, encouraging us to communicate with our fellow humans and feel a part of the natural universe.

I agree with all of those proclamations, but when it comes to walking, there are more than physical benefits. Walking has helped me enhance sensitivity and soften my heart. Most of us, products of a hard-hearted society of consumer self-centeredness, are craving an outlet for deeper, more compassionate feelings. We require downtime, time to process, reflect, and step into the three phases of time—past, present, and future.

While solitude is a component of walking—the mere technique involves placing one's foot in front of the other, then lifting the back one to swing forward and repeat the process—there is also a need to break silence and interact, to meet the elements, and meet the people.

This anatomical movement of toes, feet, ankles, knees, hips, spine, arms, shoulders, neck, and head is a first-rate way of addressing life and participating in a superlative sport. But it is much more than that. Walking has allowed me to merge the physical with the spiritual.

After becoming a monk, I swiftly embraced my new way of life. I joined the International Society for Krishna Consciousness (ISKCON) centre in Toronto, Canada. I eventually discovered the numerous ravines running throughout the city and took advantage of their greenness and walkability. In the early years of monkhood, I wouldn't consider walking alone on such trails. It had nothing to do with fear of wild animals, but the culture of the early seventies in the monastic order generated the mood that if you were to stroll off by yourself, you would be a deviant; you'd be in *maya*, illusion.

MY GURU, PRABHUPADA, WAS A WALKING INSPIRATION.

We always had a companion, another *brahmachari* (student monk) with us. We didn't even leave the *ashram* at the temple unless we were participating in some 'authorized engagement'. These activities included distributing books and chanting Hare Krishna on the street, holding programs at someone's home, or engaging in *sangha*, spiritual teaching, at a public place.

After twenty-two years in the mission, I felt mature and confident enough to walk the trails in the ravine alone. These were peaceful, insightful walks, and I began having serious thoughts about doing something special as an offering to my *guru*, Prabhupada, who formally accepted me as his disciple in a traditional initiation ceremony six months after I joined the *ashram*. He was born in 1896 and left his physical body in 1977. His 100th birthday would be celebrated all over the world in 1996, and I wanted to do something for him that came from my heart.

An idea came to me one evening after seeing a skunk on one of those ravine trails. Indigenous belief has it that the skunk stands for humility and is also symbolic of power and strength. I felt some empowerment after that encounter, and the concept of walking the entire country came to me. I had been reading about Chaitanya, who lived during India's spiritual renaissance in the early 1500s, and how he had roamed to every town and village.

I liked that lifestyle, the idea of being a pilgrim, and the concept of freedom and adventure. After more than two decades in Toronto, I wanted, and perhaps even *needed*, a change. My body and mind were becoming antsy. I was involved in the administration of ISKCON Toronto, and while it was a vibrant community, the darker side of human interactions with its gossipy dynamics were becoming unpalatable. I required a change—a radical one—but not alien to that of a renunciant.

The idea of going on a major walk would mean moving about and seeing things up close, simplifying life and exploring new sights, sounds, and smells. It would also mean a simpler diet, abandoning the rich temple food I was accustomed to. I immediately became obsessed with the idea and longed to see the forests, lakes, rivers, mountains, and vast valleys. I dreamed of peaceful encounters with bear, moose, bison, and most of all—humans. It all seemed so enticing, auspicious, entertaining, and enlightening.

Maybe I could even reach the public through the media at various places in Canada to let people know that the Krishna people are still alive and kicking. We had appeared in numerous Hollywood films back in the seventies and eighties, but had now been off the radar screen for quite a while. People might be wondering where we had gone and what we were up to.

There was something else that inspired me to take on this cross-country walk. A political issue had dominated the Canadian landscape for much of the previous year. Quebec, our largest province and the predominantly French-speaking segment of the country, was voting in a referendum to either remain a part of Canada or to separate. I believed that we need not always think regionally, so perhaps a walk through the ten provinces would allow me to share an ancient wisdom focused less on patriotic and regional identities.

I wanted to encourage Canadians to see ourselves as members of the universe, all sharing the same oneness of spiritual dimension. Having been a student and teacher of the *Bhagavat* philosophy, I felt it important to convey the message of *aham brahmasmi*, "I am spirit, not this body." It is a profound message that has been obscured by the powers that be in our materialistic world. Perhaps sharing this message, while walking in my robes, could soften some hearts along the way. "Simple living, high thinking!" is a phrase Gandhi embraced. I wanted to live like that and encourage other folks to consider this lifestyle, too.

That's my early history of walking, from a baby in 1950s rural Ontario, to a Hare Krishna monk about to begin his first marathon trek across Canada. My hopes and aspirations were to be inspired by what I was about to see, hear, smell, taste, and touch along the trails and roads. Perhaps I might even be able to inspire a few folks along the way.

Walking really does cover a lot of territory. It heals wounds, ignites problem solving, invites dreams and provides visual entertainment.

But above all, it hardens the soles as it softens the heart.

CHAPTER 2

I DON'T LIKE CARS

"A business that makes nothing but money is a poor business."

–Henry Ford

Henry Ford was a great mechanical mastermind, perhaps the greatest industrialist of the twentieth century. Henry may not have invented the automobile, but his vision led to an assembly line that produced cars faster than anyone else and made them affordable to the masses. More cars required better roads and eventually highways. Construction workers, mechanics, parts suppliers and a whole host of other automobile related industries sprouted up to fuel the new economy.

Alfred Brush Ford, Henry's great-grandson, is a friend of mine. Both of us have been members of ISKCON since the 1970s. Not so long ago I ran into Alfred in Houston and had a frank discussion with him about cars. I expressed what was burning in my heart by saying, "I hope you don't take offense, but I don't like cars and what they've done to the world."

I felt a little guilty because I thought I may be embarrassing him by criticizing the Ford family business. Alfred is one of the nicest, most humble guys you'll ever meet and the last thing I wanted to do was insult him. How could I ever dare to question the dynasty of one of the greatest industrialists of all time?

But Alfred's response was a real stunner. "Don't worry, I don't like them either." He spoke almost apologetically.

I felt relieved about our mutual point of view. The odd thing is, neither of us entered into the rationale behind our shared opinion. We agreed with each other, and that seemed to be good enough.

You may wonder why I don't like cars. I grew up in the 1950s and '60s, a time when the automobile fascinated just about every young man. But as it turned out, I was different from most young men in several ways; after all, I became a monk. But that's another story. Getting back to cars, I still have some childhood flashbacks of auto-related incidents that laid the foundation for my negative opinion on the subject.

My personal disconnect with the automobile began back when I was celebrating those single digit birthdays. Dad would drive the family car, and I should point out, he was far from reckless when he got behind the wheel. As a matter of fact, he was one of the most cautious people I have ever driven with. But I had a weak stomach, especially on those winding rural Ontario roads of my youth. And if an exhaust pipe ever had the tiniest pinprick causing the slightest leak, those fumes would find my nostrils leaving me to gag in agony. Motion sickness is what they called it, and for me it was downright unpleasant.

Even back in those days I preferred walking my meandering Tecumseh Road in Essex County in southern Ontario. That road edged along the banks of the beautiful Thames River, and even as a kid, walking made more sense to me as long as distance and/or time weren't an issue.

Childhood memories get imprinted in our minds and in that same countryside, what was supposed to be a leisurely Sunday family drive turned into a shattering nightmare. My first memory of a car accident is a horrid one. Fortunately for us, no one in our family was physically hurt, although some of us were emotionally scarred as we witnessed the aftermath of a head-on collision. Blood and bodies were literally strewn by the side of the road and one of the drivers was still alive, trapped in a vehicle that looked more like a crushed accordion. I vividly remember the poor soul moaning in hellish agony.

That single incident burst the bubble of childhood innocence for my siblings and I. My heart went out to those who died and those who survived. I can't imagine the grief their families and friends must have experienced. I was ten years old at the time and I distinctly recall how it dawned on me that head-on collisions never happen to pedestrians. As you probably can see, I was beginning to believe the automobile was a culprit.

Moving quickly ahead six years, I came to the apex of male adolescence. Obtaining a driver's licence was a rite of passage for every sixteen-year-old Canadian boy. Remember earlier when I said I was different? Well, I held back a year and was apprehensive about getting my licence. But peer pressure was strong, and I didn't want to feel left out. All of the guys were getting theirs, so somewhat reluctantly, I thought I'd better give it a try. Well, I flunked my first test, but was too embarrassed to tell my friends. I tried again and was successful. In the beginning all went well, until calamity struck.

A young kid who was riding his moped at break-neck speed dashed out from behind the bushes onto a side street. As fate would have it, I was driving the family car and unceremoniously bashed into the moped. The boy was tossed into the air and hit the ground with a thud. It was quite a shock to the both of us and it was my second traumatic experience involving motorized vehicles. No serious damage was done to the lad, but the moped was a mangled mess. I was now thinking maybe I should dislike mopeds, scooters, and motorcycles, as well as cars.

I DON'T LIKE CARS

Let's fast-forward. It's about three years later and I guess that would make me twenty. As a product of the counter-culture sixties I fashioned myself, in some ways, to be a radical thinker. That eventually led me to becoming, of all things, a monk. But back in 1973 I was a fine arts student who was deliberating on who I was, what I was doing here, and what I was going to do with the rest of my life. I always had that strong, natural proclivity toward the spiritual, and at that time I was swept away by the lure of The Beatles' lyrics, especially those having to do with *mantras*. All of that eventually swayed me to the mission of the Hare Krishnas and Prabhupada, also known as Bhaktivedanta Swami, who had influenced George Harrison and the other Beatles.

Shortly after becoming a monk, I was sent 'on assignment', and since I had a licence, I was given the keys to a van and headed off with Jiva Mukta, another devotee. It was at night during the winter in the town of Belleville, Ontario, and we stopped at a train crossing. The warning lights were flashing, and the alarm bells were clanging. We looked both ways and there was no train in sight, but we continued to wait for what seemed like forever for the 'Iron Horse' to appear; still nothing was happening.

"We've been sitting here for an eternity. Do you see anything?" I asked Jiva.

It was dark and hard for him to see, but after peering out the window, he confirmed there was no train in sight.

We began to cautiously approach the crossing. All of a sudden, out of nowhere, a train whistle blared and then... BANG! The train's engine rammed into our van, ripping the bumper right off. And then...BANG...

BANG...BANG, every split second, the front end of our van was jolted as each train car made contact with us. Time seemed to stop and I was obviously in shock, but Jiva's instincts were sharp. He reached over, opened the driver door and pushed me out, before jumping out the passenger door. We landed just inches from the big steel rail. Jiva's quick response saved our lives.

I know this episode comes across as an act of human stupidity—especially on my part—but fortunately we emerged unscathed, as did the train. Our van, particularly the front end, was totalled. Another incident. Maybe I should dislike trains, too.

The next memory involving vehicles occurred on Canada's busiest highway, the 401, during a return trip from Detroit, known to many as The Motor City. This time I was a passenger heading back to Toronto with four other members of our community, including a handicapped fellow monk by the name of Dharma Prana.

Suddenly, and for no apparent reason, our vehicle veered out of control. The steering wheel started shaking from what was later determined to be a mechanical issue, and we found ourselves headed across the grassy median toward the two westbound lanes of oncoming traffic. The rollercoaster ride ended with a jolt and there we were, suspended upside down, held in place by our seat belts and cushioned by sleeping bags and other paraphernalia that monks pack for road trips.

The world stopped and there was silence, dead silence, but fortunately, we weren't dead.

We opened the doors and wiggled our way out. Anxious on-lookers rushed from all directions to the scene. A crowd formed just in time to see us emerge from the capsized car. They were astonished to see all of us, especially a *swami* with his *danda* (staff), coming out of the wreckage.

The whispers were aplenty. "How did they survive?" was the big question. It was indeed a narrow escape. The only injury was to the driver, who had a small cut on his forehead. We were safe and lucky to be alive. Krishna obviously spared us so we could carry on with our devotional services. After that wreck I started to realize there was no safe place in this world, especially when in a car.

Fast forward long past the 1970s to my sixty-first birthday. I had ridden in many cars over the years, mostly without further incident, but always maintained a dislike for them. A family from Florida came north to Canada to treat me to a special birthday gift. Since childhood I've admired Tecumseh, the Shawnee chief, who fought hard to save his people from the oppression of European settlers. We drove to an event held in celebration of the 200th anniversary of Tecumseh's death at the battle of Moraviantown.

So, there we were, en route to the historic re-enactment, when a major roadblock forced us to detour off the famous 401, the highway motorists love to hate. Was it construction? Could it be an accident? We were puzzled why all the lanes were closed and imagined something serious must have happened.

Eventually we made it to the celebration for Tecumseh (bravo to the actors!). Then, we went to my dear sister's place for dinner, a birthday dinner (I was born on the anniversary of Chief Tecumseh's death). Discussions went on with sister, Rose-Ann, and hubby, Jim, and the topic of the highway closure finally came up, but without conclusion.

The following day, a local newspaper, *The Sarnia Observer*, provided the inside story. Elgin Ontario Provincial Police said a west-bound tractor-trailer hit the south shoulder about 1.5 kilometres west of the Graham Road exit and rolled over blocking most of the west-bound lanes. A car with five occupants, an SUV with two, and several truck drivers stopped to help the male driver and male passenger of the disabled truck. Police said Robert McGuigan, a passenger in the car, and a female truck driver were on the road attempting to light flares when another west-bound tractor-trailer slammed into them, the rolled-over truck, and the parked car and SUV.

Robert had been a family friend and attended school with my brother, Jerry, and I. Over four decades ago he had given me a magazine about *dharma*, about righteous living. Those articles from the publication *Back to Godhead* helped form and shape my life, and directly led to me becoming a monk. And now he was gone.

It should be evident after this that I share no romance with the machines of madness. Princess Diana, and the iconic film star, James Dean, were both killed in car accidents. The Peace Pilgrim (Mildred Norman Ryder), a peace activist who put 25,000 miles under her feet walking the U.S. and Canada, ironically perished in a traffic accident.

According to the World Health Organization, over 1.3 million people on planet Earth die from traffic mishaps each year and twenty to fifty million are injured or disabled. For practicality's sake, we employ automobiles and other types of vehicles, and modern life seems to justify this necessary evil. I don't want to sound morbid, but I see a bright new car as just another shiny coffin.

Henry Ford was a brilliant man. His innovations changed the face of the earth forever. I'm sorry Mr. Ford, but I don't like cars, and when given the choice, I prefer to walk.

CHAPTER 3

BEGINNINGS!

"Do the difficult things while they are easy and do the great things while they are small. A journey of a thousand miles must begin with a single step."

–Lao Tzu

Whenever I begin one of these extreme marathon walking excursions, a certain excitement comes over my body and mind. My mind anticipates all of the places, people, and circumstances to come, and my body almost always shudders with the knowledge that aches, pains, and calluses are coming its way.

I've always enjoyed walking, but over the last two decades it has become more than a mere walk in the park. Yet all of this marathon walking had to start somewhere, and that somewhere was Victoria, British Columbia, which is about as far west as you can go in Canada. The date was April 12th, 1996.

The days leading up to that first walk were filled with anticipation and excitement. Not having attempted anything like this before, I was anxious and a little scared. My mind was racing when I went to bed the night before beginning that first Canadian walk. After a surprisingly decent night's sleep, I awoke, not to the crow of a rooster, but to the screech of a seagull.

Just before transforming into a fully conscious state, I remembered that I was near the ocean. I took the call of the gull as an affirmation, a good omen perhaps, to confirm I was doing the right thing. After all, I was walking for my *guru*—an 8,000-kilometre trek across Canada—so it had to be the right thing!

That first walk was something I had contemplated for years and planned for months. I anticipated more signs of encouragement, so I leaped out of bed, brushed my teeth, took a cool shower, and donned my saffron robes. I then applied the customary *tilak*, the clay markings Hare Krishna monks put on their foreheads and other upper body parts as a gesture for protection.

I was ready and set to go! Everything seemed dreamlike and almost perfect. The sun shone brightly, and when I arrived at the starting point, the local *brahmacari* monks were already there chanting sacred songs. The sounds of *mridanga* drums and *kartals* (small cymbals) welcomed me, and the local newspaper reporter for the *Times Colonist* was there to cover my departure. I interpreted these all as auspicious signs.

Here we were, standing at a monument in Beacon Hill Park which had a plaque reading, "0 Miles," marking the beginning of the world's longest road. Now, east coast Newfoundlanders will tell you the Trans-Canada Highway actually begins in their province and ends in British Columbia (but that's a debate for another time). A tiny procession began and I moved in sync with all of the well-wishers along Douglas Street, also the Trans-Canada Highway.

A Jehovah's Witness woman stood there with the iconic *Watchtower* magazine in her hand, also on a mission for God. As we passed by, I burst out with joyful enthusiasm saying, "I'm going to walk the whole country."

GETTING BLESSINGS FROM THE PACIFIC OCEAN, VANCOUVER ISLAND, BEFORE STARTING MY FIRST MARATHON.

"Well, yeah!" she responded, in a rather equivocal way.

One of the processional participants tapped me on the shoulder and pointed to a parked truck belonging to a moving company. On both sides of the vehicle it read, "Moving Monk." Another sign confirming my journey! It appeared to be 'thumbs up' all the way!

After a few kilometres of walking and chanting together, my companions sent me off waving gestures of farewell. The sun was still shining, and as I walked on, I watched the saffron-clad team of monks appear smaller and smaller, slowly becoming a distant reality.

It was now clearly obvious I was left to tackle the nation virtually alone and on foot. Dave Poirier, a support person from Vancouver Island, was there with his 1979 dark brown Dodge van. Dave's jalopy was going to carry our stuff: a Coleman stove, two cooking pots, utensils, our clothes, reading material, and sleeping satchels for the nightly rest. Dave would be a driver, errand boy, and friend. He was my physical and moral back-up.

But for the most part, I was to be alone.

My first day was also blessed by the presence of family. My sister, Rose Ann, and sister-in-law, Joyce with her son, John, were at the send-off ceremony. But it was Paul, my brother, and his daughter, Anne Marie, who trekked with me near the end of that first day. So, I wasn't completely by myself. It sure felt good to hit the trail and begin a journey across the second largest country on Earth.

We had a few laughs that day and Anne Marie got us going with the classic joke, "Why did the chicken cross the road?"

The rest of us replied, "To get to the other side! Everyone knows that one!" I appreciated that it was within the category of road jokes.

She continued, asking, "Why did the turtle cross the road? To get to the Shell station!"

And lastly, "Why didn't the dinosaurs cross the road? Because there weren't any roads!"

Anne Marie had us in giggles. Not to be outdone, I had to try to come up with a joke of my own.

"Why did the rooster cross the road? To prove he wasn't chicken!"

I believe laughter is a good way to start a project and so we laughed ourselves silly over those corny jokes. "Laughter is the instant vacation," said comedian, Milton Berle. I know it to be very healing, the best medicine, and a good release for pressure. My *guru* was a tremendous laughologist when an occasion called for humour, while also being a staunch *bhakti yogi*.

Anne Marie's jovial nature comes from her Dad, a member of the Canadian Naval Force. He's always been happy-go-lucky. I've always believed there are only two ways to be in life: upbeat or beat-up. Paul, my brother, is rather upbeat. As a naval officer at sea, he has plied through some dangerous waters. Having a naval officer and lighthearted family members with me that first day provided a sense of security.

The sun was still shining as I cantered off on the Galloping Goose Walking Route. But a little later, overcast conditions set in, then sprinkles, then rain, and finally hail. After trudging on for a few more hours the sun returned, and with it, a rainbow. It was right about then I had my first revelation of the trip.

I had often wondered why I'd been given the name Bhaktimarga when I was initiated into the Krishna consciousness movement. Even though I had been proudly carrying the name for twenty-three years, I still wasn't sure why. On day one of that first Trans-Canada walk, it struck me like a lightning bolt. My *guru*, Prabhupada, gave me the name, knowing all along there was an innate passion within me. The word *bhaktimarga* means 'the path of devotion', or 'one whose devotion is on the path'. I leaped into the air with elation having just been blessed with a little insight into my *guru*'s mystical mind. It was a resounding realization, a sensational sign, and a crystal-clear confirmation.

Much wonder filled my heart that day because you never know what you are going to be dealing with on a trip like this. I certainly didn't feel 'chicken'. I'd travelled forty-seven kilometres—a little over twenty-nine miles—a whopping number in my books. Only 7,953 kilometres to go! When and how much would fatigue play a role in walking across a big country? Would there be bigotry and prejudice lodged against me? Some folks might not like my robes or what they stand for. Would Dave and I have adequate accommodation along the way?

Of course, we were prepared to 'rough-it' by sleeping in a tent or in the van. What about bears, cougars, or wolves? And bugs? What about storms with relentless winds, rains, and possibly snow? What about loneliness? Dave was not always going to be nearby. He had chores to attend to. Despite there being so many questions left unanswered, I figured seeing wildlife along the way or just stepping into the unknown in general would be a good adventure. Whatever happened around the bend would be excitement in itself, and I've had plenty of excitement over the years.

I became a monk in March of 1973, and have travelled to India several times. I provided administrative leadership for a vibrant Toronto community for ten years. I had journeyed extensively in Canada and the United States on missionary duties. I'd done significant work in the culinary department of a temple, in addition to being engaged in script writing and directing theatre productions with Vedic themes, carried out janitorial services, and performed many other 'odds and sods' in the monastery. But now it was time for something different.

I was intrigued by how the world had changed since I became somewhat isolated in an *ashram* (monastery) environment. The culture I was blessed to be in was insular indeed. I missed out on the whole disco era of the seventies, and in the eighties, Michael Jackson's *Thriller* album and his iconic 'moon walk'. Computers and other technology came along and because of my monastic life I was sheltered from such things.

But now, all that was going to change. With this walk, I would maximize outdoor living and marginalize indoor confinement, having the sky as my roof, the trees as my walls, and actual earth, gravel, and grass as my floor. I would live the simple life and keep materialism at a minimum. I perceived all of this as a positive change.

I also learned, after the fact, that sixteen years earlier on this same day, April 12th, Terry Fox started his benevolent Marathon of Hope. That put me in very illustrious company in an ethereal kind of way. In spirit, I felt I was on a trail that he had already blazed.

I saw that first of many days on the road as very auspicious. Fortunate! Glorious! Victorious! A complete confirmation! One hundred percent! I was sure as I am of death (and taxes) that I was going in the right direction and I was ready for whatever lay in store.

CHAPTER 4

FINDING OUR WAY THROUGH

"The more I study science, the more I believe in God."

–Albert Einstein

When word got out that I was embarking on my very first marathon walk, a lot of folks wished me luck. Some people said I was crazy, and still others offered up a wide range of advice.

"You'll need an RV," advised a friend from Toronto.

"What's an RV?" I asked.

"A recreational vehicle; you know, something like a Winnebago," he replied. "The person driving it will always be behind you, and you'll also need a walkie-talkie." This was back in the mid-nineties before the use of cell phones became widespread. "And you'll also need…" he began to say before I gently cut him off.

"I have something else in mind, because I don't need to do this walk in the style of Terry Fox," I said. "After all, he had cancer and one artificial leg, so it was necessary for him to have extra assistance." I explained to my friend that I was thinking about walking along the road or maybe abandoned rail lines which were being turned into the new Trans-Canada Trail system. I wanted to walk freely and have the opportunity to talk to people along the way, including other walkers, motorists, cyclists, townsfolk, country people, and anyone else I happened to meet. I liked the idea of living at the mercy of others and nature.

My friend couldn't believe I was prepared to head out on the lengthy roads and trails of Canada without a huge support team and vehicle. I wanted to be like Chaitanya, a famous renounced monk born in fifteenth century India. I wanted to be like a *sannyasi* and let things happen of their own accord. A little less organized and a little dreamier was what I was after. I figured I would backpack it. On second thought, I realized it might be a good idea to have a partner along, especially when I remembered Chaitanya had an assistant as he visited every town and village.

Come to think of it, I likely would need some help with food preparation, since mine was a vegetarian diet. The last thing I wanted was to succumb to eating from convenience stores or a *depanneur* (the Quebec version). I refer to these places as infamous sugar-and-salt shacks.

Diet was going to be important. Wholesome food was required to keep a marathon walker's body fuelled. So, after thinking things over I decided one companion in a humble vehicle would be able to provide all the support I needed. We could keep our supplies in the vehicle and he (well, it would never be a 'she' as I'm a monk) would drop me off, go about his errands, and just check on me once in a while. More care-free, but not quite car-free.

It happened that I settled for a divine arrangement—or intervention—that was in sync with my wishes. Balabhadra, a fine *bhakti yogi* from the west coast, who heard about my project, informed me just two weeks before I embarked on that first journey, that he had found a prospective helper.

"I found a support guy for you. Remember Dave from the early days of the Toronto temple?" he asked. "Well, he's got a van and is looking forward to an adventure."

In April of 1996, I rendezvoused with my support person after arriving in Victoria, British Columbia, on Canada's west coast. Dave Poirier was part First Nations and part French—amongst other ethnicities—and a resident of Nanaimo on Vancouver Island. He had time off from work and remembered me from when I was leaner in flesh and wisdom back in the early days of the Toronto temple. In those days I was a novice in Krishna consciousness.

Perfect. Let's go Dave!

What began was a journey of whims and woes, like a page torn out of the ancient song, *Bhagavad-gita*, where all is told of this world of dual realities: the good, the bad, and the way to learn about detachment.

The first day was moist with spring rain. Tires from trucks reconfigured the rain puddles, causing mean splashes that leaped out of ruts on the road and flew a good three metres through the air. Anything by the roadside—especially me—was a natural target. Dave was dry having shelter in his van. When Dave was off doing errands, I was left to solo along alone. Other than being splashed by trucks, it was great!

I decided to walk toward the oncoming traffic, as you are supposed to, but soon experimented, and eventually took to walking on the side of the road going with traffic. This somehow proved successful. Motorists dislike turning around, but because I was on their side of the road, they could stop with some ease. It just meant slowing down, pulling over to the right, stopping, and rolling down the window.

"Would you like a ride?" became the common *mantra*. Of course, I refused, although most always had pleasant exchanges with folks.

The consequence of walking on one side of a highway becomes problematic. Like walking along a beach, the endless slope of the highway becomes a painful, unforgiving experience. Roads are highest in the middle and slope both ways allowing rainwater to drain off to the sides. After a week or so of walking nine-to-ten-hour days, a piercing sciatic nerve started to pinch my left thigh. This issue haunted me for much of the 8,000-kilometre walk.

Had I done the wise thing and spent part of each day walking on both sides of the road, I might have avoided the problem. That method would have evened out the length of my legs, which were being seriously challenged by the endless slope of the road's shoulder. But I was obstinate as an ox and figured being accessible to motorists was my top priority. By the time I reached the end of the first walk, I accepted reality and decided I'd likely walk again, full steam ahead, but this time against traffic. And guess what? It worked.

Back then I decided to tough it out and implement, as best as possible, a self-healing approach. I pressed hard

WALK THE LINE.

with my left ring finger and sometimes thumb, in an acupressure fashion on the agitated nerve. It gave relief. I would press and then release slowly.

God knows, I was doing this all for my *guru*. The sacrifice itself, for all intents and purposes, was a personal consolation. Sacrifice is a healthy challenge.

A pinched nerve wasn't my only challenge, however. I was walking west to east in Canada, and it became cold, especially when we got into the mountains. By the time we left the early wet spring of the lower mainland of British Columbia, winter stared us straight in the face when we reached the mountains at the town of Hope. Fortunately, Dave and I had both taken to the austerities quite well. We would sleep in the van nestled in our sleeping bags, and then rise for the compulsory monk's morning bath. But where in such wilderness can you bathe? Glacial-fed water was plentiful, so we would find a snowy, ice-free zone, dip our bucket in frigid water, dump the contents on our 98-degree Fahrenheit bodies and watch the clouds of steam ascend. Then we would dash to the van after quickly drying off with a towel. Dave and I both insisted on being clean, even if it meant taking a frigid shower.

When the weather warmed and the spring thaw was over, a tent at campsites became our norm for sleeping. Dave would cook, feeling it was his responsibility, which I'll discuss a little more later on.

Fatigue was another issue. It could strike at any time of the day. A cat nap was a daily routine but had no set time, and usually occurred only sporadically when I found an appropriate location. When I'd grow weary from walking, I'd look for somewhere quiet, where I could rest for a short time, undisturbed.

Believe it or not, old Scottish cemeteries often provided the best sanctuary. I would comfortably lie down next to the reclining Scottish lads and lassies. If not there, then behind a rock or a tree, and if it were a tree-cleared zone, I would lie down directly on the dry soil of soybean fields, hoping not to be detected by motorists or farmers.

There were times when the sun would drain my energy. I'd feel like I was dragging, but was determined to keep up the pace. Once, I was so tired that I almost fell directly into the path of traffic. It was then, in the Prairies, that I implemented yogic *pranayama* (a breathing technique). With this method, oxygen becomes comfortably distributed to one's head. It was very rejuvenating and brought life back to my tired body, allowing me to regain consciousness, composure, and momentum.

Word about my walk got out to the Hare Krishna community at large, and one of our monks from the U.K. was inspired to join our team and help out. Madhai flew to Winnipeg to join Dave and I. Madhai proved to be a competent cook and helped with driving and other chores, including contacting members of the local media.

He was great, but unlike Dave, persisted in always being in the vehicle and rarely taking time to trek with me or participate in *mantra* meditation. I recall becoming frustrated and losing my cool once. I figured an occasional walk would help him keep in shape. Overall, I appreciated his participation; he was a trooper, for the most part.

Dave eventually left and went back home. I appreciated Dave, and will always remember him. I guess I impressed upon him a part of my personality.

"Are you a Libra?" he once asked me.

"Yes, as a matter of fact, I am," I replied.

"You remind me of my wife. She always worries," he said.

Dave was probably right. I do sometimes worry too much. To tell the truth, I'm a worry wart, but part of that worry is because I'm concerned about people. I want to see them better off and suffering less. I'm always concerned about how people are affected, impacted, and oppressed by consumerism, which has gotten worse over the years. The sad thing is most folks aren't even aware of how they are being manipulated by big business and government. People also suffer through tough times in their relationships. Many families are dysfunctional and are often plagued by addictions. We could do better. We should work together to deal with these things and improve our lives.

That was part of the reason for my walk. By ambling on and interacting daily with travellers and local nesters, I hoped to offer an alternative. I would encourage people to lead a more balanced life through a marriage of the practical and the spiritual.

CHAPTER 5
FOCUS AND DETERMINATION

"Our greatest weakness lies in giving up. The most certain way to succeed is always to try just one more time."

–Thomas Edison

Harakumara, one of my colleagues, and a monk residing in our Toronto *ashram*, has a natural gift for astrological reading. I tease him sometimes for being a Woody Allen look-alike. He is also our local conspiracy-theorist (every *ashram* seems to have one).

One day, before I embarked on my first walk across Canada, Harakumara presented me with a personal astrological chart reading. It suggested I could actually be a good astrologer, if I set my mind to it. The chart also indicated my needs would be met and money wouldn't be a problem. It also claimed I had a natural proclivity for being focused and determined. I figured that last one was likely true, based on my life experiences. I grew up in the country with a garden to tend and other chores that gave me a good work ethic at an early age. I credit my Dad for securing summer jobs for me on nearby farms, which entailed long hours of hard physical work. It helped me value perseverance and determination. Life on a family farm was like that because 'chores give you scores'.

Rural farm life as a youngster is not the only thing that has contributed to who I am today. I have been a life-long celibate and am determined to keep it that way. This restraint might seem incomprehensible to some folks, but I'm pretty happy with my decision.

"You mean ya never had sex?" asked a member of a group of people in a bar in a small town in Saskatchewan. What was I doing in a bar? Well, it was my fourth trek across Canada, and I was invited inside for an ice-cold glass of water. I accepted the invitation to quench my thirst, only to be gently grilled by a curious bunch of patrons. They had questions about my monastic lifestyle.

"Well, as a teen I came very close one time with a girl my age," I explained. "Then just before intimate contact, God whispered in my ear,

'Don't do it.'" My audience hung on every word, as I told my story, and you could hear a pin drop in that dimly lit place. But everyone broke out in hysterical fits of laughter when I said God told me not to do it. "The Catholic in me said it wasn't the right time because I wasn't married," I clarified. "I just wasn't ready to compromise my values."

The stance I took at this adolescent junction of my life leaves me somewhat surprised when I reflect on it now. And that brings me to a story I found in the purports of the *Bhagavad-gita* about determination. It's a beautiful story about a sparrow that constructed a nest and laid her eggs inside. Being in close proximity to the ocean, the nest was swept away by a humongous wave.

"Give me back my eggs or I will dry you up!" the distraught sparrow challenged the ocean in her most stern tone.

The ocean laughed at the threat and paid no attention to the sparrow's words. The little bird took up the project, as she had threatened, and relentlessly began to take a few drops of water in her beak, drop it on the shore, and return to the ocean for more.

The ocean continued laughing at the impossible efforts, but the sparrow stayed busy with her work. Meanwhile, Garuda, a much larger bird who was the famed carrier of Lord Vishnu, was soaring about in the area and looked down when he heard the commotion. He landed on the beach and asked his sister bird what was going on.

"The ocean has taken my eggs. I demanded their return, but he doesn't take me seriously," said the sparrow.

The imposing Garuda stood strong at the ocean's edge. "Bring those eggs back or I'll take up the work of the sparrow and together we'll dry you up!" he stated.

The ocean was fearful of Garuda and with one glorious swoop returned the eggs. All this was accomplished because the mother sparrow was so determined.

I told this charming story to a small group in Victoria, British Columbia, just before commencing the first seven-and-a-half-a-month walk across Canada. Just talking about determination fuelled me for what lay ahead.

When I look at a road, a trail, or a path, its very presence is welcoming and automatically invites me to seek out a new adventure. When it is one of those car-friendly, asphalt highways, it sends an obvious message with its striped line down the centre. It is a determined message saying, "Let's go!"

In most cases, the road is a well-travelled public domain and speaks its own language. The roads, streets, trails, and highways have their own personalities and, for me at least, they have become a travelling companion, an amigo, a friend.

"I'll be with you every step of the way," they seem to say.

Undertaking these marathon treks is a big commitment. I quietly take time to think about them, plan for them, and prepare for the physical and mental challenges they present. Then and only then do I let folks know I've decided to hit the road again, and once I announce plans for another marathon trek, I just can't back out.

"We can stick this out together," the road seems to say when I begin a new journey.

These walks take their toll, especially when you are out on the road for weeks and months at a time. I've learned to take on the spirit of a warrior, commanding an unswerving aim for the target—the finish line—wherever that predetermined bullseye may be.

There's an inspiring story from the Vedic epic, *The Mahabharata*, which addresses the passion of a warrior and a friend. Arjuna was an archer who had an incredible aim and unwavering determination. No matter what, he could not be distracted. At one training session, his martial arts *guru*, Drona, asked his students to shoot the eye of a bird decoy suspended in a tree.

"What do you see?" he asked as they prepared to shoot their arrows.

"The bird, its feathers, its beak, its feet, the sky, the clouds, another bird in flight," they replied.

Drona rejected their responses and asked Arjuna to come forward.

"What do you see?"

"I see the eye of the bird," said Arjuna.

"You don't see anything else?" asked Drona.

"No, only the eye of the bird," replied Arjuna.

"Then shoot," the teacher said.

Arjuna released his arrow; it flew straight through the air, piercing the eye of the bird. He displayed his skill with determination and precision which pleased his *guru* very much. This story is an inspiration, and often comes to mind when I am out alone trudging across the tundra.

However, sometimes our minds play games with us and we become skeptical of our commitment to our goals. Such an incident occurred one night on that 1996 walk while I was trying to have a rest in Calgary, Alberta. Tossing, turning, and unable to sleep, I switched on the light and reached for a map of Canada, curious to see what I had achieved after a month on the road. Seeing what I had done and what was still left to do caused a serious doubt to come over me.

What have I gotten myself into? There is so much distance yet to cover. Will I ever be able to complete this gruelling walk? My doubtful mind was so demanding.

"I've met lots of people who have tried cross-country walking but most of them usually peter out by the time they hit the Prairies," a journalist told me once, during an interview.

That remark continued to haunt me, especially once I had trekked through the Rockies and was about to forge ahead over the foothills of Alberta, and then on to the expansive flatlands.

I figured I would be alright if my feet and legs held up and as long as I remained determined with the conviction of a warrior and a sparrow. I didn't want to quit after telling everyone I was doing this trek. But most of all I couldn't let down my *guru* in whose honour I was walking. Prabhupada, who is formally known as His Divine Grace A.C Bhaktivedanta Swami, would have been 100 years old in 1996. I was celebrating his life and his service by walking in an easterly direction toward his birthplace, Kolkata, India. My indebtedness to my teacher became a major motivating factor and driving force. When ambition is strong, you can be unstoppable.

When I first embark on pilgrim treks I find the initial days to be like moving on 'cloud nine'. There is this high energy and adrenalin-powered enthusiasm. Days one, two, three, and four of that first walk had flown by as if moving on wings. A group of cheerleading *brahmacharis* (monks) saw me off. My brother Paul and family were there, and members of the Vancouver ISKCON community walked along with me as well. All that support, camaraderie, and company enhanced my focus and determination.

STAY ON TRACK.

On day five, reality started to kick in. My well-wishers had departed, and there I was—trudging along alone. The novelty and glamour of becoming, perhaps, a man of steel, a monk championing mind over matter, slowly diminished, only to be replaced by aching feet and blisters. On top of that, a planter's wart had manifested itself on the ball of my right foot. My agility was waning and stiffness was setting in. If my legs could have spoken, they would have been screaming in protest.

My mind was also rather demanding. *What the hell are you doing to this body?*

But I wasn't about to turn back. "Carry on, persevere, and prevail" was the *mantra* that came with every breath. Once you stop listening to the complaints of the body and mind, and let them know you are the boss, things change. They just had to get used to it! A line was stepped over once I had that realization. Apprehension and hesitation ended.

I continued on with renewed vigour, but at one point a serious problem with my left ankle emerged. It looked and felt as if something was dislocated. I was in pain and hobbled along using a perfect walking stick I had found in a nearby forest. The broken tree branch served me well, but one day I only managed two and a half kilometres. At that rate I would never reach the eastern shores of Canada, and I became a bit disheartened.

"What's going to happen tomorrow?" I wondered out loud.

Dave, my support person, and I were in Ashcroft, British Columbia, staying overnight at the home of Harvey and Mary Ellen. We were relaxing in the comfort of their living room after another long day on the road. I looked over at their personal stockpile of movies and saw a video of the feature film *Forrest Gump*. Dave had mentioned it several times on our walk.

"You've just got to see it; it's very inspirational. It's about this guy, an American Vietnam veteran, who runs across the United States," Dave said.

"But I haven't seen a movie in years," I replied. "I haven't had much opportunity or desire, since most Hollywood flicks aren't very 'monk friendly'."

"That's okay," said Dave, "I'll fast-forward through the things that a *swami* shouldn't be looking at."

It was a deal. I watched Forrest as a youngster being chased by a group of bullies. He was running awkwardly as best he could with metal leg braces. His handicap put him in great danger, when suddenly, a miracle occurred. The braces came undone; he outran the bullies and grew up to become a remarkable long-distance runner. Forrest became a hero.

Inspired, I returned to the road with steadfastness of mind. I called on Krishna to help my aching ankle. I kept the fictional Forrest in my mind as well. The discoloured and perhaps dislocated ankle began to look and feel better. I picked up the pace and soon was back to my normal forty kilometres a day.

Perhaps you won't take to the roads and embark on an 8,000-kilometre trek across Canada, but we all have everyday challenges, large and small, in our lives. My advice is stay focused and determined by taking one step at a time, and never give up. Or, as Thomas Edison proclaimed, "If we did all the things we are capable of, we would literally astound ourselves."

CHAPTER 6

PORRIDGE OR FORAGE: FOOD ON THE ROAD

"Shall I not have intelligence with the earth? Am I not partly leaves and vegetable mould myself?"

–Henry David Thoreau

People often ask about my eating habits when I'm out on the road. And it's a good question because when you walk over forty kilometres (twenty-five miles) a day, you need to make sure you are getting the appropriate nutrition to sustain your body. There's no doubt in my mind that suggesting a veggie-based diet cannot provide a person with enough strength is a complete myth. After all, some of the most robust mammals on the planet are herbivores, like the elephant, rhino, hippo, and even our North American bison, muskox, and moose. A good meal helps your mind and spirit when you are out there for weeks on end.

Food plays a major role in sustaining marathon walkers and everyone else who participates in extreme physical activities. I once met a man, on a drenching, wet spring day at a road construction site in Vancouver. When I told him about my cross-country trek, his jovial response was, "By the time you get to the other end of here, there'll be nothing left of you!"

"Not if I eat well!" I responded.

But eating well is not easy. These cross-country jaunts are a frugal undertaking. I have to be budget conscious and stretch a dollar to its limits. Luckily, Krishna looks after me (and my support person) and often provides sustenance from unlikely sources.

My normal eating habits on the road have evolved into a daily schedule built around two major meals. Meal one: wraps made with a combination of tortillas or chapatis, with hummus, fresh peppers, kale or spinach, olives, and avocado (a bit of a luxury item). Meal two: *kichari* with cooked rice, *dhal* beans, and vegetables, all spiced with ginger, cumin, turmeric, and asafoetida (also called *hing*—an essential ingredient in

Indian vegetarian cooking). Fresh herbs are a nice addition, too, if they are available.

Dave, my first support person on my premiere walk, figured that he and I ought to consume some of the herbs and other plants we saw growing in the wild. I had just finished walking across Vancouver Island, entered the mainland at Horseshoe Bay, passed the dynamic city of Vancouver, and entered the region near Chilliwack when Dave suggested we keep our eyes open for food. I liked the idea and thought it would be delectable, *maybe*. Since we both were vegetarians, roadkill was totally out of the question!

"Just look, there's lots of food out here," Dave said, as he scanned the wild greens beginning to grow in the ditch along the road. I was seeing weeds, but he obviously saw something else.

Dave has an interesting ancestral background. He has some Indigenous blood, and as most of us know, the First Peoples of the Americas are often well-experienced in the art of identifying wild edible plants. Many of them were nomads, and as a result of all that travelling they became experts at foraging for food. I was enthused, but Dave soon admitted he knew very little about all of that, even though he was still very inquisitive.

I liked the idea but hoped Dave wasn't suggesting that we live only on 'weeds'. In my deliberation on the word 'weed' I realized I had been raised with some prejudice toward plants I hadn't personally sown into the ground. 'Weed' has become a convenient word to describe a plant whose good properties one is unaware of.

Dave claimed that ditches, fallow fields, and forests could yield delicious, nutritious foods, some of which are miraculously medicinal. After all, *yogis* in India could survive in the wild largely on the roots, shoots, and fruits of the forest. And as we've read in the tale, *The Ramayana*, the herculean monkey, Hanuman, fetched *sanjeevani*, an herbal cure from a mountain in the Himalayas, for his injured companion, Lakshman.

"Perhaps Mother Earth and Father Time really do contribute to the world in ways we are not aware," I told Dave. "Maybe you're onto something, and maybe we can add a unique culinary dimension to the whole walking experience."

But it was April, and there wasn't a whole lot of produce growing just yet. So, we carried on and didn't think much more about it until we reached Northern Ontario. That was almost 3,500 kilometres from Vancouver. By then it was July, and all kinds of plants were in full bloom, so once again I began to wonder if there were really things I could pick out in the wild and incorporate into our cooking regimen. I figured this whole walking thing was an adventure, so why not be a daredevil and give some of these plants a try? I remembered reading that wetlands provide some really wholesome green food, such as cattails, those bountiful cigar-shaped vertical flowering spikes that spring upward out of flat-bladed leaves.

Apparently, they are one of the most versatile veggies of all; but it's a challenge to harvest them.

What the heck, I was prepared to get wet and maybe even a little muddy after entering a swampy marshland. I managed to find a young plant and pulled out the inner leaves, which revealed a lighter white-to-yellow tone. I ate some raw, and it had a flavour which reminded me of a cool cucumber. That was my first delicious surprise.

IN THE VAN. IT WAS DAVE'S IDEA THAT WE TRY FORAGING.

Later, while walking with Garuda, Tulsi, and Madhai, some friends from the shores of Lake Superior, I found more cattails. More confident now, I plopped these mature plants onto a picnic table right next to the Coleman stove. We peeled the leaves from the beautiful plant, revealing the most tender part of its white stalk. Amazingly, Garuda had also found some wild sweet peas growing in the ditch which we also harvested. What did not require foraging were the farm-fresh potatoes we bought which were added to our stew. These three veggies were sautéed in light vegetable oil with crushed coriander seeds, turmeric powder, asafoetida powder, and just a pinch of salt. I occasionally gave this wild gourmet creation a quick stir, but mostly kept the lid on to keep the contents moist.

Soon the veggies were soft and almost ready to eat, but first I carried out a simple devotional procedure I have maintained over the years, even during these marathon walks. Onto a small metal plate, reserved exclusively for offerings to Krishna, I spooned out a small portion of the veggies and some cooked rice (not wild rice, unfortunately). I then placed a small, framed picture of Krishna—which I carry during my travels—before the preparations and began ringing a small brass bell with my left hand as I chanted *mantras*. This simple, yet effective procedure, is a divine gesture of expressing gratitude to the Creator.

Probably not since the days of the Ojibwe, the original people of the area, had a ritual of this sort taken place along the shores of *Gitchigoomee* (Lake Superior). And just as they had gracefully carried out their offerings centuries ago in the great outdoors, we presented this humble offering of love to Krishna. The sun was shining in the midst of favourable breezes on a sandy beach near this large body of fresh water.

Anyone who wants to implement this method can chant the great *mantra* called the *Maha-mantra*: Hare Krishna, Hare Krishna, Krishna Krishna, Hare Hare, Hare Rama, Hare Rama, Rama Rama, Hare Hare. This invokes the subtle presence of God. It's as if you're saying, "Please partake with pleasure." Once the *mantras* are completed, in the manner of *bhakti* (devotional mindfulness), the food is consecrated (blessed) and becomes *prasadam*, which literally means 'mercy'.

Those of us who assembled the meal now indulged. It was a feast for a weary group, who were as passionate about the *prasadam* as we were about our walking adventures. Walkers need their nutrition and now we had that plus *bhakti* (devotion), a form of mindfulness injected into the foraged food. *Bon appétit*!

The meal was very flavourful, well-received, and a resounding success. What nature had provided was quite astounding. After a long walk, a plentiful harvest, and a colossal meal, we realized we had experienced a joyful day!

Light humour and a good dinner go hand in hand, but this meal really inspired us. Deep inside our inquisitive minds, we wondered what other delightful things were growing out there in the wilderness that we could forage and offer back to the Divine. We anticipated the dawn of a new morning that would allow us to see what other food options were available in the U-Pick organic produce section along the roadside, fields, and forest.

Over many years, during my marathon walks, I have plucked and pulled greens of all sorts out in the wild. Cooked fiddleheads from the fern plant are a great natural food. Lambsquarters are as delicious as spinach when cooked or eaten raw. The marvelous dandelion greens, mustard leaves, and the dock herb are terrific in a salad.

Although I'm not a fan of deep frying, I did try my hand at making dandelion flower fritters with chickpea batter. I have shared this dish with others, and without telling them what they were eating, watched it melt in their mouths.

"What do you think it is?" I ask.

When they give up guessing, they are absolutely stunned to find out this delectable entrée, with the buttery taste and tantalizing texture, contains flower-heads from the dandelion. Many people don't believe it and accuse me of pulling their leg.

Now you know there are a variety of edible greens and veggies out in the wild, but you are probably more familiar with wild fruit. Along the road I've become a taste-tester for berries—my favourite being blueberries. Other wild berries included in my marathon walking diet are blackberries, salmonberries, strawberries, cranberries, and raspberries.

I always leave enough of this delectable fruit for bears to consume before they begin their long winter hibernation. The one thing about wild berries that attracts me is their intense flavour, much more vibrant than their cultivated cousins.

Have you heard of the sumac shrub? Its cousins are the cashew, mango, pistachio, and poison ivy. And that reminds me to issue a disclaimer right here and now. It's very important to learn plant identification before gathering and eating from the wild. There are over thirty-five variations of sumac world-wide, so do your research if you choose to use it. Some versions make a delicious drink that tastes a lot like pink lemonade. Others can make you very sick. Be careful which one you pick.

Some folks say sumac is nature's tea, but you need to sweeten it a bit. My favourite sweetener is maple syrup. Canada is the land of the maple tree, and we even have a maple leaf on our flag. The sap is collected in the early spring and boiled down until it turns into a succulent syrup. The white birch, prevalent in many parts of Canada, also produces a sweet sap.

I'm often asked if I get bored or tired of walking for endless days. The answer is a resounding 'no', because foraging occupies some of my precious time and cooking is something that needs to be done daily.

And that brings me back to Dave. Early on, during that first cross-Canada marathon, he had been cooking for the two of us. Before we began eating wild plants, he would go to the local grocery store and see what he could find to suit our vegetarian diet. Dave has a good heart and is always well intentioned, but I found his cooking left something to be desired. After a few weeks on the road, I came to the conclusion that something had to change, so I decided to take over the culinary duties. Unfortunately, his curried veggies, which I refer to as *subjee*—a generic Hindi word for vegetables or vegetable entrées—were bland and saltless. Dave was on this salt-free kick, totally abstaining from it. I frankly needed the stuff and before the walk my *Ayurvedic* doctor had even told me to make sure I included some salt in my diet.

"Just a little, please?" I pleaded with Dave. My rationale was that walking an average of forty-two kilometres a day made me perspire excessively, causing my saffron *kurta* (shirt) to sometimes get encrusted with salty stains.

After a while this became a mild bone of contention. I hate to complain when someone takes the time and effort to cook for me, but Dave's attempt at *chapatis*, a flatbread made with whole wheat grain, was also failing on a daily basis. They were turning out like crusty crackers instead of the soft, pliable delicacies I was accustomed to.

"Dave, I learned from some of the best cooks back in the Toronto temple kitchen, especially Mother Subuddhi, a talented lady from northern India," I explained. "So, you take a break, just relax and sit this one out. I'll cook and that will give me a little diversity in my service to *guru* and God."

Dave, who was already doing so much to support my walking mission, agreed to give me a chance to work at the Coleman stove. While I chopped the vegetables and cooked up a wholesome creation, including my beloved chapatis, Dave read to me about *bhakti* (devotion) from my *guru*'s books. This was a real source of inspiration and certainly helped my meditation while cooking. I loved hearing about the lives of *yogis*, *maharajas* (kings), and *avatars*, and how devotion to the Great Spirit evolved for them.

Our new method worked wonders and the results were immediate. I was getting my salt and the chapatis were nice and soft.

The ditches, fields, valleys, mountains, and forests yield wild edibles that are there for the taking. My eyes have become opened to the wonders of the world in the form of natural food alternatives, and I have become delightfully surprised at the outcome. These days, when walking, my mix of wild and domestic food is a practical reality, and I no longer have to feel that breakfast means just a bowl of porridge.

A happy walker should have a happy stomach. A happy stomach and a happy conscience are everything.

Thank you, Dave!

CHAPTER 7

IN THE THICK OF THE MOUNTAINS

"The more I see of this country, the less I know about it. There is a saying that after five years in the north every man is an expert; after ten years, a novice."

–Pierre Berton

I often ponder how those who came before us found routes to travel when the bush was thick and the mountains, humungous hurdles. We are the lucky ones, since travel today, even on foot, has become relatively easy because of the blood, sweat, and tears others invested to make a clear path. They are the heroes who toiled and sacrificed to make it possible for us to enjoy the trails they blazed.

The Rocky Mountains are a nature-made barrier between the Canadian Prairies and the Pacific Ocean. Today there are rail lines, roadways, and hiking trails which allow us to cross over and through the mountains. Can you imagine what it must have been like for the First Peoples who lived there, and then the first European explorers who came to the Rockies?

The Rocky Mountain Nakoda are an Indigenous people whose vast ancestral homeland includes the Rocky Mountains in Alberta. Since ancient times, they have lived along the eastern slopes of the Rockies and their oral history confirms they are the original and genuine Mountain People. The Kootenay and Secwépemc (Shuswap) First Nations Peoples also populated the Rocky Mountain region and travelled the southern mountain passes to hunt bison on the Prairies.

Much later, European explorers approached the massive mountains from the north. In 1793, Alexander Mackenzie became the first of the newcomers to cross the Rockies. Mackenzie took the Peace River to get through, the same route later used by Simon Fraser, who established the first Rocky Mountain trading post at Hudson's Hope in 1805.

Kicking Horse Pass was chosen in 1882 for the Canadian Pacific Railway link between the Prairies and coastal British Columbia. Construction of the railroad was relatively easy for the 900 miles across the Prairies, between Winnipeg and the Rocky Mountains. But laying rails through the mountains for the next 724 kilometres (450 miles) was difficult, and completing the railroad was one of the most amazing feats of the nineteenth century.

Later on, just before the First World War, a rail line was pushed through at Yellowhead Pass, southwest of Edmonton. The railways opened up the west for settlers and established a Canadian nation before the expansionist Americans could claim that part of the Great White North.

The railway led to the development of mountain resorts at Banff, Lake Louise, Jasper, and other new towns in the Rockies. Banff, Jasper, Kootenay, and Yoho form the largest range of mountain parkland on earth, and in 1984 was proclaimed a World Heritage Site.

So, with these things in mind and a great respect for the First Nations Peoples and their Rocky Mountains, I stepped into the dense portion of the Selkirk Mountain range, elevation 1,300 metres (over 4,000 feet) at Rogers Pass. It was late May of 1996, and after a month or so on the road, I approached the peaks, the most difficult physical challenge of any cross-Canada walk.

The steep, unforgiving elevations also challenged rail and road engineers. Carving out a passageway for travellers was no easy task in this region. Without the technology and equipment we take for granted today, the Canadian Pacific Railway penetrated the rough terrain. It was a colossal effort, where even now avalanches are common, and massive snowslides stop traffic from passing through during the winter.

Statistics show that around 15,000 Chinese labourers were employed to construct the CPR railroad. Over 600 of these migrant workers died, mostly from frostbite and scurvy, in these harsh mountain conditions. It was tough, dangerous work, even though the rate of pay was a dollar a day (good wages for the time).

Highway construction came a century later and was completed in the Rogers Pass area in 1962. Dynamite was used and fewer lives were lost because improved living conditions and safety measures were the order of the day. The tunnels the workers constructed are a sensation to walk through.

In 2003, Canada's National Film Board made a documentary about the history of the Trans-Canada Highway called *The Longest Road*. I was with the film crew for a month and had the good fortune to be used as 'the thread' to tell the story of the TCH, by way of reenacting my 1996 walk.

During the production of the film, I met one of the major road engineers responsible for cutting through the mountains and laying the pavement at

Rogers Pass. He was a fabulous guy, from Selkirk, Manitoba, who loved talking about the project. When the highway was completed, the engineer said, with well-earned pride, that it was like winning hockey's Stanley Cup. He told me his team could practically build a road on the flat Prairies in their sleep, but the real challenge came when they arrived at the Rockies.

The Trans-Canada Highway is a ribbon of road that stretches for 7,821 kilometres (4,860 miles). It became my lifeline for a good five months in 1996. It was at Rogers Pass, located on that great highway, that Dave and I made our way through this mountainous wonderland. Dave was not so inclined to walk but preferred to drive on ahead, park his vehicle and wait for me to catch up.

IN THE THICK OF THE MOUNTAINS.

It was an old Dodge almost two decades old, and not in the greatest shape. Its patchy paint job in various shades of chocolate brown was also not very glamorous. Yet, beggars can't be choosers, and Dave's old van was all we had, and for the most part, served us well. It was not only our vehicle, but also became our house and home. We slept in it at night and saw it as our shelter. We would dash to the comfort of the heated van after early morning baths in glacial-fed, icy-cold water, dumped by buckets onto our shivering bodies, causing clouds of steam to ascend toward the heavens. Those showers were the swiftest wash-and-towel-dry routines of the century. The water was frigid, and it was often tough to find a clearing of open water through the patches of snow and ice along those mountain creeks. Ugly or not, the van was our refuge, and we came to appreciate the shelter it provided us.

One day, while Dave was waiting for me along the Pass, a Royal Canadian Mounted Police officer pulled up behind the van. He was suspicious because of the shady outward appearance of our vehicle, the relative quiet of the highway, and the fact that Dave appeared to be just hanging around. The RCMP were working on a case and Dave suddenly became a potential suspect in a break and enter theft which had occurred at the nearby Glacier Lodge Park Resort. The officer began to question the suspected criminal and even frisked him.

"So what are you doing here at Rogers Pass?" said the officer, asking the obvious question.

"I'm waiting for The Walking Monk to catch up to me because I'm looking after him on the road," replied a worried Dave.

"Oh, you mean that guy with the long orange robes down the road in the other valley?"

"Yes!" answered Dave.

"What's he doing?"

"He's walking across Canada."

"What for?"

"For the spiritual healing of the nation."

The officer paused a bit. "Well, is it working?"

"Sure, can't you feel it?"

The officer eventually was satisfied that Dave was no petty criminal and went on his way. I had a good chuckle when I was told about this encounter with Canada's national constabulary. I thought it was precious, but not as precious as the dedicated trail blazers who forged their way through Rogers Pass and the great Rocky Mountains.

CHAPTER 8
A PRAYER AND A BEAR

"The best way of being kind to bears is not to be very close to them."

–Margaret Atwood

I offered a special prayer to Krishna as I was trekking through splendorous mountain country in British Columbia, Canada's westernmost province. There were not any buildings, shelters, or homes on today's forty-kilometre stretch. It was pure, raw countryside, protected land, something we call conservation wilderness.

My prayer kind of went like this, "Krishna, this is my third walk across Canada. The whole world knows this land for its wilderness and beauty. I'm in bear country and I haven't seen a single one since I started doing this extreme walking. If You would show me Your form as some bear *avatar*, I would appreciate You even more. It's just a wish."

I have a lot of faith in prayer, and I usually ask Krishna to allow me to render service to Him and His devotees. But this time I sincerely asked Him for something for my own enjoyment or satisfaction. I was curious, and knowing bears are sometimes big and dangerous, I still thought it would be great to see one…from a distance, in its natural habitat.

My support person on this trip was Garuda (not the bird), and we were doing our regular morning walking routine. He would drop me off at the exact spot where the walk had ended the previous day. Then he would drive ahead, pull over right around the five-kilometre mark, park the vehicle, and walk back to me. When we would meet, he'd do an about-face, and we'd proceed to walk to the vehicle once again. When we reached it, we would repeat the whole process again.

We were making our way along the famous Crowsnest Pass, headed toward the town of Castlegar on a quiet, lonely-looking road. Nature's gorgeousness was in full display in that early morning setting, and we were taking it all in, one fresh breath after another.

I am used to walking alone and experiencing the sounds, sights, and smells of the trail. Garuda has a tendency to chat quite a bit. He's a good walker, though perhaps an even better talker. In his usual loveable and loquacious way, he was going on about something or other when I noticed this ape-like creature roaming around a curve on this serene mountain road.

"Garuda, look ahead, do you see him?" I asked.

Speechless for once, Garuda nodded his head as his jaw dropped open.

There he was, a chunky and stocky specimen walking toward us. In the middle of the two-lane road this furry creature with sandy dark brown coloured hair had a huge hump on his back. Surely, this was no gorilla because we don't have them in Canada. He was prowling west while we were walking east, and we were bound to meet at some point. As we got closer it became clearly apparent that this creature was a giant grizzly bear.

Right around 1805, the explorers, Lewis and Clark, came across this animal's ancestor during their famous Expedition and labeled him, 'grizzly'. A decade later, the beast was formally classified by naturalist George Ord as *Ursus horribilis*, which means 'terrifying bear'.

Okay, so we weren't *quite* terrified, but we were a bit concerned—not overly, not at first sight, at least. We felt confident because we were on a road that was made by man, and for some reason that made us feel somewhat safe. We also felt almost adventurous out here, alone, and nearly eye to eye with this solitary and majestic symbol of the wild.

Garuda and I became a bit confused, because instead of darting off the road and into the safety of his forest, this bear kept trekking along, coming right down the middle of the road. It was so quiet we could hear ourselves breathing. Just fifty metres away now and we realized that he hadn't yet seen us and was totally unaware of our existence in his habitat. All of a sudden, he paused, stuck his nose straight up into the air and sniffed loudly, perhaps detecting our presence. Bears compensate for their poor eyesight with a sharp sense of smell. With his snout flung into the air and twitching his head this way and that, it became obvious he had finally picked up our scent. Instead of backing off, or fleeing into the woods, he forged on toward us.

Now what?

We had no place to run; no place to hide. With thick forest on either side, the road seemed to be the safest place for us to be. But there he was, his nose distorted trying to determine whether we were food or foe. Suddenly, almost heaven-sent, a motorist came up behind our grizzly. At the sound of a blaring horn, the killer bear fled full throttle straight into the woods.

Wow, what a relief!

We had been more than a little anxious with this close encounter, but now, Garuda and I heaved sighs of relief.

We ambled along, too stunned to say much. About fifteen minutes later, our reprieve was short-lived, when we heard a sudden snort behind us. We turned in unison and there he was—one of the biggest predators on Earth! He had circled around behind us and was hot on our trail, only twenty metres away and closing in fast.

Garuda and I were shocked by this turn of events but in awe of his mighty frame, roundish head, and protruding dark snout. He was extremely bulky. Not knowing what to do next, Garuda and I started loudly chanting a protective Sanskrit song, "*Namaste Narasimhaya*," a prayer to the Creator in the form of a lion.

What were we going to do? Our vehicle was at least two kilometres away. There was no use running for our lives because this fellow can cover fifty metres in less than five seconds and reach a top speed of seventy kilometres an hour! Again, what were we going to do? No people. No bear spray. Our *mantras* continued, and we even tried communicating with him, telling him he was so big and strong. Garuda and I figured we were 'bear smart', but now we were put to the test.

"Raise your arms. Stand tall. His eyesight is poor. Height can intimidate him!" I blurted out. This was the advice I recall reading in a "Protect Yourself from Grizzlies" brochure.

Suddenly, down toward the valley and coming up the road, we heard the echo of grinding gears. *What a racket!* A transport truck, the source of this joyful sound, was slowly coming up behind the bear. The eighteen-wheeler seemed small in the distance, but he was growing in size and volume as he approached our Mister Bear. As the driver urged on his diesel-belching machine, the sound of the hard-working engine reverberated throughout the cavernous mountain valley. The burly bear was just four metres from us and still coming our way. We could hear him breathing as he uttered a ghastly growl. He then perked up his ears, and his head swayed from side-to-side as he seemed unsure of the source of the noisy commotion. By now the truck was closing in on the bear's heels. The grizzly finally turned his large head and looked back, only to come face to face with that giant metal monster. With the transport truck almost on top of him and quickly realizing his plans were dashed, he ran off once again, into the safety of his lovely wilderness, never more to be seen.

At least, not by us.

Normally, I am somewhat appalled by the sound of an eighteen-wheeler shattering the quiet, peaceful sound of the trail. But this was one time when I was happy to see and hear a truck, and I waved in gratitude to the driver as he slowly overtook us, working his way up the mountain.

The moral of the story is, 'Be careful what you pray for!'

But there is a little more to the story. Not but an hour later when Garuda drove off to seek out a lodge—if there were any—for our overnight stay, I forged on alone to cover my day's distance. A smaller black bear came into my view. It was a mama bear, and lo and behold, she had her cub with her—a young energetic cub who was climbing up a nearby coniferous tree.

The road I tread was actually a form of embankment, and I was at a higher elevation in position to the bear and her cub. She spotted me suddenly. I must have looked intimidating to her. With a sound much like that of a cow, she cried out an alarm to her cub, who quickly made his way to the base of the tree and fled along with his mother.

EYE TO EYE WITH A MAJESTIC SYMBOL OF THE WILD- BE CAREFUL WHAT YOU WISH FOR!

In this case, I was the fearsome grizzly.

On the day's topic of 'bear', I surely had my share.

CHAPTER 9

APPREHENSION IN THE DARKNESS OF NIGHT

"A person can hurry through or sleepwalk through life, but whenever they stop to catch their breath or awaken from a long nap, they will find apprehension, disquiet, and fretfulness waiting their directed attention."

–Kilroy J. Oldster, Dead Toad Scrolls

After three hours of sleep in a cozy room at Radha Madhava's Cultural Centre in Calgary, I suddenly awoke for no apparent reason. Could it be that little demon, insomnia, who comes to attack me now and then? Or had my bodyguard, melatonin, gone on vacation, leaving me alone without protection?

My sleeping patterns had improved substantially since commencing this first marathon walk. After pushing so many kilometres a day, I would become naturally fatigued. But despite the daily workouts, some nights were still troublesome when the demonic insomnia paid a visit. That nasty little guy comes to haunt older people. But wait a minute, that first Trans-Canada marathon walk began in April of 1996, and I was only forty-three, which isn't very old at all, so my bouts of insomnia were something of a mystery.

"Stress can cause lack of sleep," advised Dave. "You're a Libra, just like my wife, and you always worry just like she does."

Some people believe the astrological signage reveals much about the nature of a person, so perhaps he was right. There's also something else to consider. The cause of stress for many people who minister to spiritual communities can come from the pain they absorb from the people they advise and assist. That kind of shared anxiety adds up and can create restless nights. I'm in that category; but in this case, I had been on the road for days, and basically alone, so I should have been more relaxed.

For whatever reason, some impulse triggered an internal and premature wake-up call. It was midnight, and I wanted to get a full night's rest to prepare for what lay ahead. I anticipated a good day and was hoping to cross the entire length of the city of Calgary from west to east. However, lying there on that comfy mattress with eyes wide open, I felt defeated. I was concerned I would not return to the restful slumber my body craved.

"The best cure for insomnia is to get a lot of sleep," said W.C. Fields.

As a kid, I used to get a kick out of the old vaudeville comedian's one liners. His take on insomnia was almost as funny as one of his other lines about why he never consumed water and only drank liquor.

"Water—fish copulate in it," Fields said.

But comedy wasn't my remedy that night, and recalling W.C.'s one liners wasn't helping. I really just wanted to go back to sleep, and I needed something stronger to help me cope with this anguish over that lack of sleep. Drugs and alcohol were out of the question, so I did what I often do and that was to call upon the Divine.

"Bless me with some more rest, so I can perform well for You," I prayed, thinking this was the better option.

Still unable to sleep, I pulled off the bed covers, turned on a light and pulled out my trusty map of Canada. Perhaps peering over the territory yet to cover would enthuse and appease me.

Unfortunately, looking at the map had the opposite effect. I was dismayed and felt as if struck by a ton of bricks. I looked at British Columbia and the slice of Alberta I had already walked across. Pretty impressive—that is until I looked at the distance between Calgary and St. John's, Newfoundland. The distance yet to be trekked was in the neighbourhood of 7,000 kilometres/4,350 miles! I was surprised. No... shocked! What had I gotten myself into?

Where was that excitement I experienced the first morning of this initial cross-country marathon walk? Gone were the chanting monks who had seen me off. Gone were the relatives who walked with me that first day. Gone was the anticipation I experienced lying in bed near the Pacific Ocean the night before the walk began. I was alone and lonely, with a commitment to bear.

It was the first time serious doubts had risen in my heart and mind concerning this walking project. I had become, at least for a moment, a Doubting Thomas. Where had my determination, enthusiasm, and desire gone? It seemed to have been replaced by insomnia and its demon friend, apprehension. A pair of rascals—that's what they were—and they were causing me great anguish.

Just then, my plight struck a familiar chord, leading me to recall the ancient dialogue between Krishna and his warrior friend, Arjuna. It seemed almost inappropriate to draw a comparison between my puny ordeal and that of the heroic Arjuna. How dare I think my unnerving glance at the map of Canada even remotely compared to Arjuna's glance at an army of colossal proportions; an army that was threatening to dispel his much smaller military divisions in an epic fratricidal war.

Arjuna observed his opponents on that ancient battlefield at Kurukshetra, in northern India, with trepidation. He saw family, elders, and teachers on the opposing side. Many of them he greatly revered. At the critical moment of taking up bow and arrows, and hearing the sound of conches and battle cries, he was struck deeply with indecision, confusion, and apprehension. Standing by him was his dear friend and chariot driver, Krishna.

READING ABOUT MY GURU ALWAYS LIFTS MY SPIRITS.

"Seeing my acquaintances present before me in such a fighting spirit, I feel the limbs of my body quivering and my mouth drying up," lamented Arjuna in chapter one of the *Bhagavad-gita As It Is*, translated and explained by my *guru*, A.C. Bhaktivedanta Swami Prabhupada.

Unable to take the stance of a brave warrior, Arjuna suffered a bout of low self-esteem, telling his companion, "I shall not fight!" and begged Krishna to award him with advice.

"You must have strength and confidence in order to rise up to the principle of dharma, your ultimate obligation!" was Krishna's response.

Krishna's advice to Arjuna became an inspiration to him, and today that same wisdom can truly inspire each and every one of us.

So, I lay back in my bed, face-up, staring at the ceiling, contemplating Krishna's words of encouragement, and translating them in my own mind. *Just do it. Sleep or no sleep, just do what you need to do and get on with the walk in the morning.*

I felt reassured, and the next day, despite having had little sleep the night before, I went ahead with a warrior's spirit. I even went so far as to compile an abbreviated poetic rendition of the *Bhagavad-gita* in an attempt to capture some of the essential points outlined in this most famous dialogue.

THE BHAGAVAD-GITA (SONG OF THE DIVINE)
(To be sung, narrated and/or danced.)

ARJUNA:
Seeing those before me causes me to shiver.
To lift my bow is as though I had never.
Hairs stand on end, mind is reeling.
I'm confused; it's new, this kind of feeling.
Sri Krishna, I just cannot fight.
There's something here that is not right.

KRISHNA:
Arjuna, you've lost your sense of duty.
A man of defense renounced a warrior's beauty?
For the wise there's a different point of view.
Of eternity, no birth, no death, known by few.
Consider the world, which is full of duality.
Good and bad is its only reality.
The major point is not to lament.
The soul is forever, that is my comment.
Moving through bodies from young to old.
From old to young, this circle does unfold.

ARJUNA:
Krishna, what is the force that compels one to do wrong?
If you could, please include this in your song?

KRISHNA:
It is desire, born of passion, then wrath.
That keeps us covered and obscures the path.
Perform your yoga, and your sacrifice,
For the Creator, and then all will be nice.

ARJUNA:
Krishna, yoga can be tried for calming the mind.
But the mind is an instrument of a different kind.
I'm fine if asked to harness the wind.
But the mind cannot be anchored or pinned.

KRISHNA:
Begin the process; take it easy and slow.
In the end, there's freedom; the soul will then glow.

ARJUNA:
You are my teacher, mentor and guide.
It was no mistake to have you on my side.
I have come to consider about you there is more.
It's your cosmic form that I wish to explore.

KRISHNA:
The form is manifest when we have the eyes.
Otherwise there's the tendency to despise.
I reveal it to those whose devotion is clear.
When friendship is firm, to them I am dear.
It is surrender through service that is so sweet.
It is surrender that is illusion's defeat.

ARJUNA:
Oh Krishna, my doubt is now gone.
I believe the fight should definitely go on.

KRISHNA:
Arjuna, my song is old but alive.
You have your free will, but now let me drive.

We all have trials, tribulations, and second thoughts. The mind plays games on us, but when we humble ourselves and invite wisdom into our lives we no longer have to sit on the fence. That sleepless night in Calgary was a wake-up call, an opportunity to realize that I am not in control of myself. I'm not God, but I am duty-bound. I have a purpose, I am busy, and I am happy.

CHAPTER 10

A SLICE OF ALBERTA AND FREAKS OF NATURE

"Mountains are not stadiums where I satisfy my ambition to achieve, they are cathedrals where I practice my religion."

–Anatoli Boukreev

I meet all kinds of people on my marathon walks, some for just a few moments, others for longer periods of time. Many folks just want to say 'hello' and offer encouragement or wish me well, while others are really interested in the reasons why I go on these walking pilgrimages. Some even join me for a kilometre or two, a few hours, or on rare occasions, for several days.

One of the most interesting fellows I have ever met on my travels is Michael Oesch. Michael is a man who hit a crossroads in life and decided to change paths and become a major walker. Later, he decided to make a documentary called, *Walking: The Wisdom of the Road*. And why not! He's certainly got stories to tell.

From his home in The Beaches, just east of Toronto, Michael backpacked all the way to Newfoundland and back. In terms of distance, this loop can easily be considered the same as walking across Canada. With that trek complete, Michael decided to conquer the western frontier, so five years later he hiked again from the sandy shores near his Toronto home, all the way to Vancouver. By my calculations, his total walking efforts add up to one-and-a-half times across Canada.

Michael found out about me on the internet, and after making contact, we met at Govinda's, a vegetarian dining facility hosted in our *ashram* in Toronto. He told me about the motivation behind his walk.

"The Twin Towers in New York collapsed," he said. "My marriage was falling apart, and alcohol was becoming an addiction."

So, Michael decided he needed to make big changes in his life, a breath of fresh air or perhaps a new beginning. After some contemplation about

49

what to do, he embarked on his walking excursions.

Michael was kind enough to help me as a support person for the last leg of my fourth trek across Canada, and at the same time, he took valuable film footage for his documentary. This time there was quite a gang of us on the road: Michael, Daruka, from Winnipeg, Karuna Sindhu, a fellow monk from Toronto, and I. I almost forgot Billie Jean, Daruka's life-partner, who is a blue-fronted Amazon parrot.

One particular morning, Michael drove me to the spot where I left off the day before—approaching Pincher Creek in Alberta. He knows my routine. I start early, hitting the asphalt or dirt trail by around 4:30 a.m., which allows me to complete my day's walking quota by early to mid-afternoon, with some short breaks along the way. He admired the schedule. Of course, I had the advantage of having a vehicle and a driver to back me up.

Michael's an avid listener and maker of music. On the way that morning he played Eric Clapton's "Further on Up the Road" from his stash of favourites in his car.

I thought it was a nice piece, but when I get to my starting point for any day, I sing my ancient Sanskrit songs to *guru* and God. It's an important part of my daily routine. Michael dropped me off and caught a little extra rest in the car before starting to film when the sun came up. Those Prairie sunrises are unmatched as far as natural beauty is concerned.

Meanwhile, I was having my own 'Prairie experience'. In the absence of hills and mountains, wind gusts seem to gain speed as they swept unobstructed across the landscape. This time, walking east to west, I was aware of approaching the earthly giant, the vast Rocky Mountains, as I could see them in the distance. Wind from the nearby mountains funneled through their peaks, swooping down at a fair speed through the valleys where I was making my way.

The forces of nature often cause me to reflect on life. Three little questions always come to mind: Who am I? How did I get here? And what happens when I die?

On this day, I realized I was nothing but a tiny soul doing a solo trek near the outskirts of Pincher Creek. The soul is so small that it is incomprehensible to mere mortals such as myself. The Vedas say the soul is $1/10,000^{th}$ the size of the tip of a hair! That makes it a tiny something embedded in our material bodies.

My 200-pound frame is substantial, but on this day, it was feeling the pressure of *Vayu*, the wind god. He is a mighty forceful powerhouse. That force, combined with mega-trucks whipping by, almost knocked me off my feet, making progress slower than usual and causing my body to tire more quickly. Now, when I say 'wind god' I am not referring to the supreme being, of whom there is only one. Just as Christianity and other traditions make reference to the presence of various archangels, the Vedas teach us that these etheric beings have influence over different aspects of the natural world.

The wind also has another fine purpose. I believe a strong breeze, or as a sailor might say, 'a topsail gale' can be a true friend. That's because it beats your pride and bashes your ego. It forces you to accept its might and to realize how insignificant you are as you attempt to fight it. This forceful feature of nature humbles this soul and reminds me I'm just a small speck in this vast terrain. That's okay, because I'm not alone—never alone. I always have my guardian angel with me. It's my witness, a kind of supervisor, or 'super-soul' stationed in my heart. From the wisdom of the *Bhagavad-gita*, this phenomenon is referred to as *paramatma*, a superior soul. I might

MADE A FRIEND IN ALBERTA-A RETIREE CYCLING ACROSS CANADA.

be bold to merge the cultural notions of Christianity and Vedic thought—the guardian angel and the watchful supersoul—but I firmly believe that divine guidance exists within each of us.

I wasn't the only one out there fighting the wind. Once, while tramping along on the shoulder of the road, I met Clara Hughes, a famous Canadian Olympic champion cyclist and speed-skater. She was supported by two people in a van. When Clara saw me, she raised her hand for a high five while giving an enthusiastic, "Hey!" She was all smiles, and after a short break, proceeded to pedal on.

I found out later that this six-time Olympic winner had completed, for mental health, a 12,000-kilometre cycling trip throughout Canada that summer of 2014.

"I can't think of a better way to meet people from the cities, to the coasts, to Canada's North, than getting on my bike and taking to the roads," Clara once said.

Now back to Michael. He had been filming himself on foot, a

reenactment of his previous walk. He'd also been in contact with Dana Meise of British Columbia, who was going to be featured in Michael's documentary about walking and the wisdom that comes with it.

Dana is now credited with trekking a full 21,000 kilometres on foot by way of the Great Trail, which takes you across Canada, including the northern and southern routes. Michael handed me his phone. Dana was on the line.

"I can't believe I'm talking to you," said Dana with some admiration in his voice.

Apparently, he had heard about 'The Walking Monk'. He shared some of his challenges—many to do with nature—of the wind and the mind. These two words are interesting. They are similar in nature. Just flip the first letter upside-down and a point is made.

Dana and I have had a series of calls since then. I remember once telling him about the stress of warrior, Arjuna, in the *Bhagavad-gita*. In the dialogue with mentor, Krishna, Arjuna likens the mind to the wind and says it would be easier to harness the wind than to harness the mind. Krishna advises us to focus on the task at hand and neglect the wandering mind. This way we can achieve what needs to be done without having to endure the mental anguish sometimes accompanying a flickering mind.

It appears that middle-aged Dana is steadfast in his determination and dedication. Like me, he's also had encounters with bears. Unlike me, he has suffered from *giardiasis* (popularly known as 'beaver fever') and has been hospitalized as a result.

Back on the road, just west of Lethbridge, I trekked through a string of towns and hamlets such as Coalhurst, Fort MacLeod, Lundbreck (where I met Clara), and Pincher Creek. My support team stayed close to me, especially during the afternoons. Karuna, who soldiered along much of the way on foot, was there when I finally got to the Rocky Mountains. In a place called Frank, we were emotionally moved after reading an historic plaque about the great loss of lives and sacrifice: "In the early morning hours of April 29th, 1903, most of the 600 residents were still fast asleep. At 4:10 a.m. a crashing and thunderous roar filled the dark, sleeping town and spilled out into the Crowsnest Pass. A wedge of limestone over one kilometre wide, 425 metres long and 150 metres deep broke free from the crest of Turtle Mountain."In about ninety seconds, it was all over. Homes, barns, and other buildings were destroyed. Worse still, seventy people lost their lives. It was the biggest natural disaster ever to hit Alberta. Stories are told of the brave man who fought his way through the fallen rock to flag down an approaching train. And there was a baby in the aftermath of the rockslide, who somehow ended up perched upon a boulder unharmed.

Karuna and I also learned that similar tragedies in the coal mining industry have also taken place in the last century along this stretch of territory. You can't help but feel for what these poor souls went through, and we said prayers and *mantras* for them as we walked through their town. Prayers and *mantras* are major components of my walks. I guess that makes these treks pilgrimages.

The people we met along the way were well-informed about our walk. The local media was always interested and published stories to let locals know I was in the area. The Rotary Club at Pincher Creek invited me to their luncheon meeting to talk about adventures on the road. Daruka, Karuna, and I were all invited to attend. The smorgasbord buffet was a welcome sight, and we had plenty of vegetarian options to choose from.

I began by telling the Rotarians about my windswept experience of walking across the open plains. I also explained the reasons for my extreme walking, the primary one being to honour God and my *guru*. A secondary reason was to take a break from life in the *ashram*, which had become a bit tedious for me. I was particularly annoyed with the gossip that seemed to plague the place. A long meditative walk was just the ticket. Sure, it was a challenge, but it was also an opportunity to meet Canadians from coast-to-coast. I longed to listen to their stories, and would occasionally share some of the lessons my *guru* had taught me.

"Gossip penetrates every community, right?" I asked the Rotary Club members. "After all, we're all human."

That remark resonated with everyone in attendance and after my talk, entitled "Tales from Trails," a gentleman told me a fictitious story about Mildred, the town gossip. Apparently, she started a rumour about a local man, telling everyone that Mitch had a drinking problem. As is often the case, the subject of the rumour was the last person to hear about it. It took him some time to discover the source, but eventually he found the culprit. He went to Mildred and asked her why she made up a story that wasn't true.

"I saw your car parked in front of the pub several nights ago," she replied.

Mitch left disappointed but soon came up with a plan. He came back that night and parked his car in front of Mildred's house and left it there overnight. That stopped the gossip.

Yes, gossip is like a forceful wind that knocks you down. When you are declared guilty of something not done, you can feel the storm, and it's a raging one, very unpleasant. I'd rather walk through a physical storm any day than deal with the mental turbulence of the lethal weapon of gossip.

You never know who you are going to meet when you are on the road. Each day is a new opportunity to meet folks, listen to what they have to say, and determine whether or not to share a *Bhagavad-gita* message—or just be a friend.

The power of the wind, the forces of rain and snow, the height of the mountains, the flatness and infinity of the Prairies, all serve to make man and monk meek.

CHAPTER 11

THE SILKY WAY

"Why should I feel lonely? Is not our planet in the Milky Way?"

–Henry David Thoreau

Going to bed well before midnight and rising before the sun comes up has many benefits. It's always quiet, and that mystical pre-dawn hour offers a time of sensitivity and an occasion to connect with the Divine. My fellow devotees and I wake up early every day and begin our traditional morning chanting and other rituals at 4:30 a.m. (local time) at ISKCON temples all over the world.

When I'm on the road I also get up early, partly out of habit, but mostly because I like to get an early start and complete some kilometres before the rest of the human world awakens. Amazing sights and sounds abound when you are out there on the road, alone, facing another new day.

Such was the case one brilliant morning on that great expanse of flatness called the Canadian Prairie. Billions of stars, said to be older than the sun, were grouped together to form a massive band of light in the darkened sky. They resembled a heavenly trail, an upper pathway, and oh, it was so inviting. I had experienced it before, but never had such a strong desire to levitate up from my earthly home and take a stroll along that wondrous thoroughfare. Had my desire been possible, it would have redefined walking—at least as we know it.

This wasn't a dream because I could still clearly feel my feet pressing into the ground. I tilted my head back as far as it would go and looked up, way up. A total surprise took my breath away and filled my eyes with wonder. I hadn't anticipated a crystal-clear view of what the Romans called the *Via Lactea*, which means 'road of milk'. Today we call this part of our glamorous galaxy the Milky Way.

What made this particular sighting even more spectacular was the fact that the awesome arched strip of light overhead lined up perfectly with the road beneath my feet. I was trekking along the Red Coat Trail in the heart of the Prairies, in the province of Saskatchewan. It's a 1,300-kilometre highway which goes along the same route taken by the North-West Mounted Police in 1874 on an expedition to bring law and order to the Canadian west. Out here the magnificent sky dominates.

Sometimes people ask me if I find the Prairies boring because of what they perceive to be a flat, monotonous landscape. The view-scape is often mind-boggling, and the depth of perception is something we are not used to; but the real joy of the Prairies is the expansive sky.

There I was, in the pre-dawn, at the time which monks of our order call the *brahma muhurta*, believing I had been placed in some sort of space fantasy. Perhaps the Milky Way was something I could experience or consume as a calming sedative beverage. After pinching myself, I came to the realization that this rich milky substance was most likely reserved for the pleasure of the gods. But I'm only mortal, a human, and not worthy of such a privilege.

Another pinch, another glance, and I was overcome with awe at the sight of that aesthetic band of lustrous softness. Right then and there, I renamed this fantastic phenomenon 'The Silky Way', and immediately felt like a reverent spirit in a state of universal mindfulness. Overcome by a humble state of mind, I realized I was just an insignificant being in that most foundational mellow of all moods—a tiny spirit in an amazing, expansive universe, or as the *Vedas* teach us, just one of an unlimited number of universes.

I was alone, more alone than ever before in my life. My support person, Daruka, was fast asleep along with his parrot companion, Billie, back at the motel room someone had generously sponsored for us. Motivated by a sense of duty, I quietly walked out of the motel for the solitude of the expansive Prairie. I was compelled to walk, and if I was to get those daily kilometres in, I had to hit the road early.

WALKING IN SKY COUNTRY.

The sight of this aerial vista made me yearn to share it, but I was alone wandering along a quiet highway without a soul in sight. Perhaps a motorist would come along on the way to or from work; but who knows, seeing the Milky Way might be a common occurrence for them. Then someone did drive up and stop. It was a woman, and I'm not sure which one of us was more surprised—me to see someone out here so early, or her when the headlights of her vehicle came across a ghost-like being in flowing saffron robes. She was, however, oblivious to the Milky Way, and had simply stopped to offer me a ride to the next town.

I declined, letting her know I was a pilgrim walking across Canada for the fourth time, just trying to encourage people to live the simple life. She wished me good luck, and then off she went. At that moment, to her, the awesome *avatar* of light was of no consequence. When the sun finally peeked up over the horizon, the quiet and subtle Milky Way incrementally dissolved. Daybreak had arrived on the Prairie, and an entire other world began to be revealed.

I soon spotted a pack of coyotes in the distance moving quickly across the flat landscape. Their appearance reminded me that I had not heard their chorus before dawn. During the *brahma muhurta*, these canine creatures often execute their high-pitched howling sessions. It coincides with the time monks in our temples sing their songs of devotion. It's debatable who sounds musically better, the monks or the coyotes, though both have their morning routines and rituals. Monks have their sacred chanting, and coyotes, their yips, yaps, and barks.

The wily coyote has quite the repertoire of songs reaching a high-pitched *staccato*. Suddenly, they stop, take a break, and stay silent. But a moment later, another colony starts up with their howls on the other side of the road. They then pause, and the first group takes up the song. I've experienced canine communication in stereo. Most times I can't see them because of the pre-morning darkness, but I can sure hear them, and know they aren't far away, maybe 200 metres off the infamous Red Coat Trail. The coyotes' presence is justified as they have a role to play in the Prairies' eco-system. Coyotes control the rodent population, particularly the prairie dog, a type of marmot or ground squirrel which is the farmers' pet peeve. When these predators start their yapping and howling it causes goose bumps to emerge and hair on one's arms to stand on end. But coyotes really don't scare me. Quite frankly, there's little to worry about. However, recent reports from Cape Breton's beautiful Cabot Trail revealed a woman had been killed by two coyotes. Although details of the attack were limited, it was reported that this was an unprecedented event. I do give some credit to the coyotes, though, as my chanting intensifies every time I hear them howl in the early morning hours. These 'prowling prairie howlers' certainly add to the dynamics of the land.

The Prairies are considered the heartland of Canada, and this flat terrain is sometimes also called 'Big Sky Country'. Saskatchewan is often called 'The Land of the Living Skies', 'The Bread Basket of Canada', 'The Wheat Province', or 'The Land of Seed and Honey'.

About a week after that exciting encounter with the Milky, I mean 'Silky' Way, I was trekking through what appeared to be more barren land. I must admit, the splendour of the golden wheat waving at me in endless fields, was both bountiful and beautiful. In the distance, a light, rolling, rumbling thunder resounded across the sky. This was a bit bewildering because there was barely a trace of cloud, and the summer sun was in full force.

TAKING A BREAK FROM THE LONELY PRAIRIE ROAD.

While I wondered what the rumble was, a herd of antelope came charging across the field, heading straight for the road I was trekking on. About a dozen of North America's speediest creatures were the cause of the thunder. They moved with grace and displayed a regal countenance with hides a shade or two darker than the wheat. I stood frozen, captivated by the sight. They leaped easily over the ditch, avoiding the orange-clad *swami*, galloping or bouncing across the road, and then with one last leap, cleared the second ditch. Off they went into the wild blue yonder, with heads focused forward, displaying beautiful horns that I wouldn't want to mess with.

Days later, as I neared the Alberta-Saskatchewan border, my next encounter with wildlife occurred just after a refreshing rainfall. It was between the peaceful community of Assiniboia and the town of Eastend, in the 'Valley of Hidden Secrets'.

I was armed with my sturdy umbrella, ready to shield my body from rain promised by the weather forecast. My travels have revealed the stunning truth that the Earth is replete with entities everywhere. They are all pervasive and most of them are not perceivable by our blunt senses. Many are minute in size, or in places we sometimes don't expect. For example, the inconspicuous migration of the tiger salamanders. Many have their lives cut short by the wheels of automobiles. Thousands emerged from nearby ponds, and although the pavement was covered with their squished bodies, some survived.

Inquisitive, but ignorant of the biological make-up of these fellows, I took the tip of my umbrella and just let it grace the back of one moving salamander. I decided not to actually touch him with my fingers, not knowing if his skin was slimy or perhaps even poisonous. Not knowing what to expect, I was literally surprised when he coiled and squealed. Until that precise moment I had no idea salamanders could make a sound. Lightly touching him again after he uncoiled, this time on the belly, he again responded negatively with a squeal, a twist and a roll.

"I didn't mean to hurt you, my little friend, and I won't do it again," I told him, feeling a sense of guilt. He was safe, I figured, being at the edge of the pavement, on the shoulder of the road. But my heart was heavy, and I regretted frightening him.

"So long, spirit soul! Hare Krishna!" I consoled over my shoulder, as I trudged down the road.

When I was a kid (my primary school teacher said 'kids' refer to goats and demanded we say, 'child')…rather, when I was a *child* walking the Tecumseh Road to school on a fresh rainy morning, I would do something nasty. The moisture in the clay soil would draw out earthworms who would begin to crawl across the pavement. For some reason, I carried a prejudice toward them. My demented bodily conception of life passed judgment on these fine creatures who do valuable service for Mother Earth. I would mercilessly go out of my way to stomp the life out of them. I was highly insensitive to their well-being and had no idea that they, like us, have a soul. I figured they were ugly, slithery creatures, and squishing them would do no harm. At the time, I was not aware of *karmic* reaction and only thought humans had souls.

In the third quarter of my life, I have discovered that walking heightens your sensitivity level because you are constantly sharing the environment with all kinds of creatures. Thinking about my salamander friend whom I had left behind, my conscience told me I owed him something.

Two days later, I came across another mighty migration of salamanders. This presented a unique opportunity to give back, reconcile, or pay up some of my *karmic* dues. On that same quiet road, the Red Coat Trail, I decided to take a moment and meet one of these fellows and come down to his modest level. I performed *dandavat*s, getting down on my stomach in prostration. While in that humble position, I could see that this meek and quite adorable amphibian had amazing eyes. I stretched out my right arm, looking him straight in the eye, before mildly stroking his body from head to tail with my index finger.

I hoped a benign, gentle approach would work, and was pleased to observe that while touching his head, his eye lids closed. He became motionless and appeared to wait for the next massage, then the next, and the next. This went on for some time until finally I could hear a vehicle approaching, and felt it was time to rise. I helped him the rest of the distance across the road and got out of the way for fear both of us would become road pizzas.

"*Au revoir*, you cool, silky dude. Hare Krishna!" I said, feeling much better than the previous encounter with his brother.

Just west of the town of Eastend, Daruka and I drove to the exact spot where I ended my walk the day before. It was the *brahma muhurta* hour, and our vision was poor in such low light. Little did we know, a herd of deer was standing across the entire width of the two-lane rural road. Spotting them at the very last moment, Daruka slammed on the brakes, but he was too slow to react, and they were too slow to move. BAM! We hit one of them. A hard hit. A member of the deer family fell to the asphalt. We quickly got out of the car, only to realize the poor thing was panting heavily from the shock of the collision.

We both offered some *mantras* for the soul's inevitable passing. After Daruka dropped me off to resume my walk, he returned quickly to the scene of the accident. Understanding that chanting helps the soul in the course of its departure, Daruka squatted by the deer's side and continued chanting until the deer breathed no more. Daruka is a sensitive man and killing the deer bothered him for days.

Waking up early in the morning and getting a fresh start on your day has its benefits. The quiet, chilly stillness of the morning can awaken your sensitivities. I have experienced many Saskatchewan sensitivities in this Land of the Living Skies.

CHAPTER 12

CLOSE CALLS AND THE LOG MAN

"I stop and look at traffic accidents. I won't hang around, but when I hear something terrible, as bad as it is, I've gotta look at it."

–Norman Lear

When you spend roughly eight hours on the road every day like I do, you are sooner or later bound to witness an accident. And if you are out there long enough, you might even be involved in one yourself. With most people rushing around at breakneck speeds, the odds are pretty high that it's only a matter of time before you witness or become part of something nasty. Well, truth be known, I've seen or been part of a few motor vehicle mishaps during my extensive travels.

Road rage seems to be the world's passion these days. Otherwise sane people, who might even describe themselves as pacifists, think nothing of using their car as a lethal weapon. Sometimes it looks like a demolition derby out there on our public highways. Mix fanatical drivers with inclement weather and you've got a deadly combination. Nature doesn't help matters with her blinding sun, slippery snow, sleet, ice, and fog.

Nature may play a role or be a contributing factor in some accidents, but we humans are clearly to blame most of the time. I never heard the term 'distracted drivers' until recently, but I've certainly seen my fair share of them. I've seen people with a cell phone in one hand and a steering wheel in the other. Many have a cup of coffee on the go, a cigarette to puff, and a wheel in hand all at the same time. People think they can drive and apply make-up simultaneously, too. It's like a dangerous high-wire circus act featuring an ample supply of multitasking and a dash of road rage for good measure. It reminds me of some of those four-armed deities in temples in India which display Vishnu's masterful wielding of multiple divine items simultaneously.

Some motorists succumb to fatigue, being physically drained and mentally stressed, yet continue pushing themselves to disastrous results, and in some cases, early graves. "Sleepy drivers rest in pieces!" is a bumper sticker sometimes tagged on the back end of massive semi-trucks. It's meant to be a wake-up call for dozy drivers.

One day I heard what I thought was a devastating crash—BOOM! BOOM! BOOM! As the shock wore off, I realized it was just a fellow with a more expensive sound system than the car he was driving—a mobile disc jockey bringing his groove to a neighbourhood near you. Nowadays, it happens all the time: noon, midnight, anytime at all. You're peacefully walking down the street, enjoying the fresh air, and listening to birds sing their sweet songs, when out of nowhere some guy invades the pastoral scene with cranked-up bass beats that shatter the soul in your heart, and shake the sidewalk under the soles of your feet!

We live in a materialistic world where most people are preoccupied with satisfying their senses and are inattentive to what they should be doing when driving. I believe the pedestrian is safer than the driver, at least in most cases, but everyone is a potential statistic. My advice is that 100 percent attentiveness should be given to the job of operating a motor vehicle. Otherwise, you are just an accident waiting to happen.

Yes, I've heard that driverless cars are in testing and could soon be the latest gadget to hit the market. The auto will be operated by computer and sensors. That should solve everything, right? Not likely! I'm that orange-clad skeptic who will always believe walking is the best way of getting around. I know walking might not always be the most practical application in this modern world, especially for those who want to see more of it, but if you must drive, be responsible, and if you walk, be responsible, too!

I have taken my fair share of buses, planes, trains, and automobiles to get where I need to be. I personally believe I'm a responsible walker when I'm sharing the road with others, at least most of the time. I prefer to take biking and hiking trails, or even an old countryside, dirt road. Busy highways are always a last resort for this walker. When I have to hit the highway, I stay on the shoulder of the road.

I know I've been pointing the finger at distracted drivers, but must admit, there was one instance where I was pretty much guilty of causing an accident. Actually, it's a shared guilt. I was walking with another Hare Krishna devotee who goes by the name of Vedavyasa. We were both dressed in traditional garb: the kurta (upper cloth) and the dhoti (lower cloth). He was in white, the colour for a novice or a family man. I had my usual saffron shade reserved for renunciants. We were on a sidewalk on the north shore of the mighty St. Lawrence River in the city of Trois-Rivières, in *la belle province*, Quebec. It was early morning rush hour and the road was under construction.

Veda and I were walking and chanting our *japa* (*mantra* meditation), when a motorist turned his head to gawk at the two peculiar-looking tourists. At the very same moment, the vehicle in front of him suddenly stopped. The gawker plowed into the rear end of the car in front of him. Not surprisingly, the car behind him rammed into his rear end. CRUNCH! This domino-effect continued with several more cars bumping into the one in front of it. Veda and I lost count of the actual number.

"I think we caused the accident because everyone is looking at us. We must have distracted them," Veda said.

"Are you serious? We're just vulnerable pedestrians," I replied.

Veda politely encouraged me to move with haste. He figured we would be better off leaving the scene before someone accused us of causing the whole mess. We picked up the pace and moved on.

Upon further reflection, I came to the hopeful conclusion that Veda and I couldn't be held responsible for distracting a motorist just because we were wearing alien-looking garb. However, can a man be held responsible for an accident if he takes a second look at a beautiful woman crossing the street? Most likely, yes! My *guru* would compare distractions to a razor's edge. A small and single moment of carelessness, and you cut yourself and the blood starts flowing.

Veda and I were spared any physical harm, but there were all these people around us who were involved in the accident. I don't think anyone was seriously hurt, but a lot of cars were damaged.

There have been at least four incidents during my treks across Canada when I felt like a victim of events on the road.

Walking along the highway near the exit to Ashcroft, British Columbia, with three companions (all of us in traditional attire), we became a target for a genuine hooligan in a sports car. Travelling at high speed, he veered over three lanes and made a mad dash for us. We were minding our own business when a loud roar of an engine came from behind. He sped by, missing us by less than a foot, scaring the daylights out of each of us and causing us to lose our balance and topple into the ditch. It was a deliberate cheap thrill. Fortunately, for the band of four pedestrians, we were of the pioneer stock of Hare Krishna monks from the 1970s. We had been forced for years to overcome this type of harassment, but this incident occurred in 1996!

A second near accident involved a resident of Windsor, Ontario, who was backing out of the driveway of her riverfront property. I'm quite obvious with my saffron robes and was walking on the sidewalk by her driveway. She was so focused on traffic coming either way that I guess she forgot to look directly behind. I wrongly assumed she would yield the right of way to a pedestrian.

Her bumper jabbed into my shins leaving me frozen in my tracks, momentarily paralyzed. Had she not hit the brakes when she did, I would have easily been run over and possibly dragged down the street under her massive machine. The odd thing about the incident was that the driver did not apologize. The face is often the index of the mind, and in this case, there was not a shred of guilt or remorse on this lady's face. As a matter of fact, her expression told me she was in a hurry and I was in her way.

We went on our separate ways without a word being spoken and I came to the conclusion it must have been a stressful day for her. So, I carried on, but that incident did trigger a thought about an expert driver in the form of Krishna. You see, Krishna is renowned for His philosophical presentation to his warrior friend, Arjuna. He is known as the Prince of Dwarka, the subduer of ruffians, the heartthrob of young women, and the childhood charmer of His village, Vrindavan. We might also take note that Krishna is credited for being an expert chariot driver. At the battle of Kurukshetra, He manoeuvred His chariot and team of horses in such a skillful fashion that He could put any modern-day race car racer to shame.

There were two more incidents where my life could have been cut short by careless, inattentive drivers. The first occurred in Thunder Bay, an industrial city in northern Ontario. I was making a legitimate crossing of the street when a car making a left-hand turn suddenly lurched toward me. I'm sure he just wasn't paying attention and didn't see me. He stopped in the nick of time just as his bumper tapped the back of my knees. It was a natural place at which to bend and fall forward. This time the driver felt guilty and politely apologized.

After that close call I made my way out of the city, but on the outskirts of Thunder Bay, I experienced another, more grave, close call. It was an incident involving a man I call The Log Man. It was the summer of 1996. I thought the day was going to be a bright one judging by the clearness of the early morning sky. The sun had just started to rise over the horizon while I was walking along the Trans-Canada Highway, near the village of Kakabeka Falls.

I came upon coniferous trees, tall and straight, which partially blocked the sun's glare, causing a strobe-like effect as I ambled along. A little later during rush hour, traffic was moving along at a fine pace. Animate and inanimate objects, man-made or nature-made, appeared to be in sync. All was well in my little corner of the world, or so I thought.

Chanting on my beads, with feet in steady stride, a sudden crash jolted the earth and exploded into the air behind me. It was a clash of sounds of epic proportion that shook my insides. I was immediately overcome with fear and anxiety. Turning around, I saw a tractor-trailer and its cargo of lumber strewn all over the two-lane highway. The cab of the eighteen-wheeler was on its side. I ran with speed not seen since I was a relay race champion in elementary school. The fate of the driver was my primary concern.

As I dashed toward the wreck, the driver struggled, finally managing to climb out of the rig before jumping down onto the shoulder of the road. He was concerned about his wrecked truck and trailer, unaware that blood was streaming from the side of his forehead.

Looking around, assessing the damage, he spotted me and seemed startled to see a guy in robes. By the look on his face, he might have thought, "Maybe I'm in heaven and this guy is an angel."

"Are you okay?" I asked.

"Yeah, but our family business is finished."

He looked devastated peering at the damaged machine and his load of lumber blocking the road. Motorists were now arriving and coming to his aid, just as I had done. Traffic came to a halt.

"Are you alright?" people kept asking the trucker.

He used the f-word quite a bit until one elderly lady nudged him, protesting the use of profanity.

"Now you stop saying that!" she scolded.

It flashed through my mind that perhaps I was the cause of the accident. The trucker saw me on the road near a sharp curve. Maybe I was a distraction and caused him to lose control. But as I was thinking this, he resumed his cursing and another trucker came to my side confirming I was not the cause, as if he had telepathy.

"This guy passed me down the road and he was going at an incredible speed. No wonder he toppled over." said trucker number two.

Almost everyone who stopped got out and helped each other remove the logs, one by one. I even helped out in the task. The police arrived, interviewed the distressed log man, and jotted down notes. The ambulance sirens were now in the air, rapidly coming our way.

I took that as my cue to move on, feeling grateful, *completely grateful*, that I had not been crushed by truck or logs. Had I been walking a mere fraction slower, I'd have been just 100 metres behind at the bend of the road—it would have been a case for quick reincarnation. I would not have completed the walk, and that would have been too bad.

Feeling happy to be able to continue my trek down the road, I couldn't help but wonder about the fate of the log man, his family, and his business. Perhaps, they too, would end up feeling grateful, because things could have been worse. There's nothing like the attitude of gratitude.

CHAPTER 13
HIGHWAY BULLIES

"Be sure you put your feet in the right place. Then stand firm."

–Abraham Lincoln

I'm sometimes asked if people ever give me a hard time while I'm out on the trail. In short, yes, but I could count the instances of highway bullying, redneck dynamics, and displays of ignorance on the fingers of both hands. The gestures of kindness far outweigh demonstrations of bullying.

Before I describe a few of those rare occurrences of road terrorism, I would like to explain my disapproval of the term 'bullying'. I used it here because it is a common term in mainstream vocabulary. However, it is a phrase that reeks of insensitivity toward one of the most benevolent creatures on Earth. I would like to see us replace that word with something else. How about the term 'aggressors'? By using the word 'bully' as in, 'bullying in the schoolyard', we are marginalizing a docile animal.

My adopted Vedic tradition reveres the bull and the cow as sacred. Cows are regarded as one of our seven mothers. The complete list goes like this:

1. Biological mother
2. Nurse/midwife
3. The wife of a *brahmin* (priest)
4. The wife of the king
5. The wife of the *guru*
6. Mother Earth
7. Mother cow

Cows are on the list because of the contribution of their great food source, the rich calcium in their milk. Think of all the dairy products that have satisfied the human palate for generations, and the wholesome sedative power they yield. Of course, we are assuming that the milk is of a protected *ahimsa* (non-violent) quality. Historically, people of my community known as *Gaudiya Vaishnavas* are vegetarians. There are also many vegans among us, but tradition holds that we are lacto-vegetarians using milk from animals who are never slaughtered. We drink the milk and make ghee, yogurt, and cheese. At farms operated by ISKCON, cows and bulls are allowed to live out their lives in peace, even after their productive years are over.

The cow's male counterpart is the bull. He, of course, doesn't give us milk, but we respect and admire his immense strength and value his major contribution to our domestic situation. It is through ox or bull power that the earth is massaged. The fields are tilled and prepared for seeds to yield grain, vegetables, and fruit. For centuries farm life has been enhanced by the presence of the bull as a provider, earning him the title of 'father'. Give him a lot of love and he'll reciprocate like anything. He should be allowed to live out his days in peace until his natural death.

It puzzles me why cows and bulls are still given a bad rap by mainstream society, even after being forced to give up their bodies to provide steak and hamburgers. Scientifically, cow and bull dung possess miraculous medicinal properties, and it is also good fertilizer for our gardens. The derogatory acronym 'BS' singles out the male excrement from that of the female, yet the properties are the same. The term 'BS' is a sexist remark at best, and I pray for a re-examination of its use. Henceforward, I will use the word 'aggressor' instead of 'bully'.

One aggressor I encountered out on the road was actually a female. I was approaching the end of a long day's walk near Dublin, Ireland, when a young woman, quite out of control, hurled a full bottle of beer at me. Despite being intoxicated, she displayed a remarkable volley of strength, and although she threw the bottle from across the street, she missed me by just a whisker.

Good thing she missed, because I was stunned and shocked, frozen in time. After she launched the projectile, she was engulfed in a bout of hysterical laughter. The bottle landed softly on a patch of grass, remaining intact. I didn't bother to read the label, but I presumed it was a Guinness because the old brewery was just a few blocks away. The Guinness brewery is one of the biggest tourist attractions in all of Ireland.

After the near miss I recovered my senses, and instinct told me to keep moving. I'm too much of an easy target and feared a second throw would be right on the money, but it never came. Perhaps her supply of intoxicating beverages had run out.

Back in Canada, in a town called Salmon Arm, in British Columbia, I was pacing along when a young fellow in a red convertible slowed down to give me an order.

"Get outta town!" he yelled. Then, in a rather cowardly fashion, he raced away. That brief encounter got me to thinking. I began to process not only his remark, but the tone and attitude. I was upset, angry, and hurt. There are times when I display an occasional spurt of fury and must remind myself that as a monk and a *swami*, I'm supposed to persevere. Perhaps turn the other cheek? Let things slide? Make myself meek? Or snap back with vengeful sarcasm, should I see him again at the other end of town?

"Listen, I'm taking your advice, I'm getting outta town, I'm going through it and your little town is not worth staying in!" I could say. But that wouldn't be fair, because Salmon Arm is a nice little town of about 20,000 human souls. There are lots of nice folks there, but I just happened to run across one yahoo in a red convertible.

Such were my thoughts as I pondered the incident, and I soon realized his statement was born out of insecurity and ignorance. My heart softened and became more compassionate. I really hankered to see him again in order to initiate a more positive encounter. Perhaps we could become friends and maybe he just might be receptive to my message about higher consciousness.

In 2003 on my second excursion across Canada, I was trekking through New Brunswick when I came across a fellow who didn't vocalize but used sign language to express his feelings. In India, there is a beautiful expression of language with the use of hands called *mudra*. In Canada, I'm sorry to say, the use of hands and fingers to convey messages is less developed and not very divine.

I was strolling along near Moncton when a fellow in a red pickup truck drove by slowly, rolled down his window, and stuck out his left hand with raised middle finger in the air. He regained speed neither waiting for nor giving me any opportunity to respond. My initial reaction was one of resentment, but again I concluded this unfortunate guy was most likely uncomfortable with himself and felt threatened or challenged in the presence of someone different.

Like Salmon Arm, Moncton is a nice place. I've met some good folks there who have been receptive to my message and who have supported my walks. The city is a microcosm of Canada, one of the few truly bilingual communities in the land. French and English have existed peacefully side-by-side for many years in Moncton and have welcomed newcomers from around the world. This one guy in a pickup truck certainly doesn't represent the majority of people there.

After a few similar instances in other nice towns, I felt the need to establish a strategy to employ for similar encounters in the future. I rehearsed mentally what I would do when meeting aggressors while I was walking. I would

1. Come to a halt
2. Raise my right arm
3. Wave the person to come back
4. Point my index finger to the ground for a one-on-one talk or tussle

I felt confident this technique would yield instant positive results, and I was right. The opportunity came while I was trekking along the Trans-Canada Highway near Sault Ste. Marie, Ontario. A couple of young men clad in greasy overalls were returning from a day's work at a local garage. They spotted me, and the guy in the passenger's seat boisterously hollered out some remark that I couldn't quite hear. So, I put my technique to the test. In the rear-view mirror they saw my response—the halt, the raising of my arm, the waving the aggressor back and pointing down for a heart-to-heart.

The driver hit the brakes, spun the vehicle around making an illegal U-turn, and with tires howling, roared back toward me. *What have I gotten myself into?* But by then the hecklers arrived to where I had taken a firm stand on the ground.

"Hey! What's up?" the passenger asked curiously.

"Well, you guys were yelling something at me," I responded.

"We were just saying hello."

Slightly embarrassed at having misjudged them, I continued, "If you want to be heard, you have to speak loud, right?"

I then told them about my pilgrimage, and they wished me a pleasant journey. It was a false alarm because these guys were actually nice, certainly not aggressors.

The last encounter with hecklers that I will tell you about is like a scene out of the movie *Rebel Without a Cause*. Near Cranbrook, British Columbia, two male motorists actually pulled over, got out of their vehicle, and approached me, making some of the nastiest remarks I've ever heard. Foul words continued to spew from their mouths as they got back in their vehicle, spinning their tires and sending a flurry of gravel, sand, and dust toward my head, torso, and legs. I quickly turned my back toward them to keep from getting a face full of gravel.

However, once again, I harbour no malice toward the fine folks from Cranbrook. Yet, I was bewildered as to why these tall, lanky kids, who were young enough to be my sons, could be so mean-spirited. Obviously, they were either brought up that way, or something happened during their lives to make them act the way they did. After my initial shock, I felt sorry for them and prayed that at some point in the future they might find a more peaceful way of life.

In the ancient *Bhagavad-gita* (1.36), Prabhupada's purport explains there are six types of serious aggressors:

1. A poison giver
2. One who sets fire to the house
3. One who attacks with deadly weapons
4. One who plunders riches
5. One who occupies another's land
6. One who kidnaps another's wife

Certainly, none of the above would describe the irritable people I've met, and therefore, my tough guys can't hold a candle to those mentioned in the *Bhagavad-gita*.

In life, aggressors are few, and blessers are plenty. The first group expose human weakness. The second explore human strength.

CHAPTER 14

YOU CAN'T JUDGE A BIKER BY HIS COLOURS

"I like life on the road. It's a lot easier than civilian life. You kind of feel like you're in a motorcycle gang."

–Leonard Cohen

They don't always have the best reputation, and the sight of them often scares the daylights out of some people, but over the years, I've managed to get along with them quite fabulously. So how would you describe a biker? I'm talking motorcyclist here, not some spandex-clad dude on a pedal bike!

Ninety-nine percent of bikers and the clubs they belong to are, for the most part, law-abiding. The other one percent belong to gangs who use force, violence, and intimidation, with firearms and even explosives as their weapons of choice. A typical one-percenter is more than likely rough and tough, and crass and cold. These rebels most often ride noisy piston-popping iron horses and lead a lifestyle of drug taking, drug dealing, womanizing, wife beating, and police brutality. They wear their colours proudly and belong to gangs.

I was born in the early 1950s, right around the time Marlon Brando starred in *The Wild One*, a movie about outlaw bikers which was actually banned in the UK until 1968. Growing up in the 1960s, I bought into the myth that bikers were born to raise hell. The poster for *Easy Rider* propagated the myth, with Peter Fonda and Dennis Hopper riding those huge, mean-looking machines.

The film was supposed to have defined a generation. I never saw *Easy Rider*, but if we viewed it now, Fonda and Hopper would probably come across as tame pussycats by today's standards. Over the years, bikers have increased in number, many of them cultivating that ruffian demeanour. But not all bikers are outlaws, even though many of them look the part. Trekking along as a monk and meeting members of those burly bunches,

I feel qualified to boldly declare that not everyone blazing a trail on a Harley fits a villainous profile.

For example, one fine morning while walking through Alberta's Crowsnest Pass, I heard a distant rumble of motorcycle engines merged in sound as if they were one machine. The roar was muffled behind the walls of the mountainside until over 100 road warriors blasted around the corner with maximum amplification. The sound was uproarious as the convoy of men with grand biceps and big bellies vibrated their way past. There likely were women, too, but it's hard to tell gender under their brain buckets.

They sure got my attention, and I probably spooked a few of them, as well. A pedestrian working their way through the mountainous landscape is a rare sight, but a walking ascetic is even rarer. It's not out of the ordinary to see a monk on foot in India or Thailand, but there aren't many of us who venture into the Rocky Mountains.

The army of bikers rode on by, mostly two by two, and sometimes one by one. I occasionally bowed or gave a random salute trying to communicate by gesture to the wearisome and weird. Their response was indifference.

As the tremendous deafening assault began to fade away, one final rider lagged behind to actually communicate. He tooted his horn to get my attention, then let go of his handlebars and raised his arms up above his head, palms together to form the reverential *pranam*s, as if to say, "*Namaste* (my respects to you)."

My jaw dropped and I gazed ahead as he cracked open the throttle and his huge Harley roared to catch up with his comrades.

During the same trek across Canada, but much farther east through a boreal forest on a two-lane road, I was walking with Jovany, a Cuban monk. He was like an assistant and kept me company by walking a stretch of highway with me every day. Canada Customs officials stapled a letter on his passport stating his visa was valid only as long as he supported my walking venture. He had not yet received his Sanskrit name, an honour given only after displaying dedication to the mission for a period of time. So, Jovany was a novice—the new kid on the block.

This Cuban boy was as new to snow as he was to Canada. He found his first fistful of the white stuff at the inner southern edge of a ditch, deprived of the melting May sun. He packed the snow, with its cold embrace, into a ball, and flung it straight up into the air, only to watch it come down and go poof on the road! The snowball ceased to exist, and Jovany was in ecstasy.

Everything was new for him, including meeting his first Canadian biker. We were heading eastward on Highway 11 near the town of Hearst, in Ontario, when a burly boy in black leather with a scruffy beard and dark shades veered his Hog over to the shoulder of the road. He looked pretty tough to me, and in a threatening tone he said, "I'm warning you guys!"

We were silent and listened intently.

"I'm warning you guys…" he said again before pausing. Pointing east where he had just come from, he continued, "There's a black bear back there and he came right at me. I sped up and he continued to chase me right down the road, so I'm warning you to be careful."

I thanked the biker for the precautionary message, all the while being relieved that he was being very kind and cool with us. Jovany was breathing heavily, and a long sigh escaped his lips as the biker fired up his machine and rode away.

We watched him ride down the road until he became just a spec, and then not even that. This episode reminded me how sometimes dogs look tough, deliver a threatening bark and show their teeth, only to turn into little puppies. The exterior doesn't always convey the interior when it comes to dogs and people.

Jovany not only met his first motorcyclist, but also his first black bear that day. We walked cautiously down the road, and sure enough, came across the bear who was preoccupied in the ditch munching wild strawberries. He acknowledged our presence by rearing up on his hind legs, dropping back down on all fours and lunging a few steps toward us with a threatening growl. We hastily moved on keeping an eye over our shoulders, but the bear stayed put in the strawberry patch. We determined that our encounters with the last two living organisms were different. The bear was a beast, and the biker was a teddy bear.

In Saskatchewan, I was putting one foot in front of the other on the Red Coat Trail (Highway 13) near the town of Eastend. It's located close to the American border. On that particularly sunny Prairie day, I heard the thunderous sound of an approaching gang of bikers. I offered various greetings, thumbs up, peace sign, traditional wave, and even a salute as they went by.

I received no response to any of those techniques, but I did see two of the guys looking at each other in disbelief as they sped toward town.

Oh well, they're gone. Potential pals—I won't be seeing them again.

An hour or so went by and the roar from before came from behind, and then passed me by. Indeed, it was the same fellows on their intimidating bikes. Suddenly, they pulled over to the side of the road. There were seven of them—a magnificent seven, as I recall. Each one shut off his engine, dismounted, and removed helmet and gloves. One or two unzipped their jackets as they proudly strode toward me. The biker who appeared to be the head honcho led the procession with a confident wide stride. His look was grave, and when he got about a metre away from me, he planted his feet in a firm stance.

"Me and the boys went into town for a few beers, and we saw a story about you in the local rag. I guess we're here to get some blessings." He stretched out his right hand and I reciprocated with a firm handshake. "We think it's great what y'er doin' out here on the road, kinda like a 'lone wolf' biker."

These rough and tumble guys made me feel good. We talked for a while, and I was thrilled they took the time to offer a little kindness. I was comfortable in

BIKERS ARE NICE.

their presence, but not enough to change clothes and straddle a Harley. After all these years, I'm still very happy with my vocation.

This cool exchange underscores my attitude toward bikers. These guys were respectful and friendly. My encounters with their ilk have been positive; they have been very kind to me. After all, monks are a minority and so are bikers. Perhaps we could actually be allies against 'the matrix' (or '*maya*'), the big, fat, materialistic world of illusion.

I've learned a lot as a walking, talking, Hare Krishna monk:

1. Bikers can be real sweetie pies.
2. You're never alone. If you're without a physical companion, you'll still always have three different types of company: your prayer or *mantra*, the trail itself, and the cool dude in your heart (God). No matter where you go, there will always be three *amigos*.

In 2014, I became an honourary member of the Hare Krishna Motorcycle Club in Gainesville, Florida. There's a shady-looking picture of me on their website, sitting on one of those iron horses. Their motto is, "Ride, chant, and be happy!" I'm still a committed walker and monk who has learned that even the toughest looking biker can have a kind heart. And remember, you can't judge a biker by his colours.

CHAPTER 15

JAZZ ON THE ROAD

"Some people try to get very philosophical and cerebral about what they are trying to say with jazz. You don't need any prologues, you just play."

–Oscar Peterson

Canada is a huge country. Believe me, I know because I've walked across this great land four times. It's almost 8,000 kilometres coast to coast, from Newfoundland to British Columbia. I've met a lot of great people, got really close to nature, and had to invent ways to overcome boredom and loneliness in some of the more remote areas of the country.

During walk number three, a certain eerie pessimism set in one dreary day up near Thunder Bay when the weather couldn't decide if it would rain or be a cloud-covered affair. It was just one of those days with low grey clouds and intermittent precipitation. With the exception of the whistler of the north—the white-throated sparrow—all else appeared rather dismal. His clear, pure whistles seemed aimed at this weary walker.

If you walk a lot, you know that rain often encourages an increase in urinary flow. After addressing my need behind a tree along Highway 11, I wiped my palms against wet weeds, and then completed the process of hand washing with my own brand of soap. The needles I tore off a nearby pine tree and rubbed between my hands, left an effervescent aroma.

I continued trekking along the road with not a soul in sight until a member of the local constabulary pulled up. He invited me into his car. We shook hands and he obviously noticed the piney smell.

"So, you're a Hare Krishna monk? Do you guys still make incense? I can tell you use it by the smell," he said.

I explained my method of natural handwashing and we shared a chuckle and a congenial chat before his tone became more serious. He was working on a case and looking for clues because the day before a man had gone missing in the area. The previous cordial conversation changed to a series of questions and answers. He wanted to know where I was going, where I was coming from, and my whereabouts and activities on the day the man disappeared. At that point, I recalled wondering earlier on why helicopters had been flying overhead for most of the day. Perhaps they were some kind of search party.

Anyway, here I was in a police car, possibly being considered a suspect. These parts of northern Ontario are sparsely populated by humans and I was near the scene of the crime. I was new and a stranger.

The officer was satisfied with my responses and pretty much accepted my intents and purposes. Here I was in the Canadian Shield, Earth's oldest rock formations, doing the genuine monk thing—taking a break from the monastery and going on a pilgrimage. I also informed the officer that Daruka, my trusty assistant, was somewhere nearby in a support vehicle.

The policeman went on his way while I contemplated that he had done a nice service by giving me some attention. The road can be an awfully lonely trail at times, and I can miss human interaction, especially hearing the sound of another human voice. But I do love the tune of the white-throated sparrow. They rank right up there with the hauntingly mystical call of the loon.

On this day, I actually missed hearing music, the kind that humans make. I really was craving the association of fellow devotees and singing together in Sanskrit or Bengali. Those songs offer gratitude to the *guru* and praise the magnanimous qualities of the Supreme. I missed being in a temple and *ashram* and relishing the excitement there.

I trudged along, immersed in solitude and feeling lonely on a barren, desolate stretch of asphalt. It had been some time since my encounter with the police. With the persistent greyness of weather overshadowing a monotonous road, I struggled along and eventually hit a low point. I had an overwhelming feeling of separation from my fellow man. Motorists weren't stopping to chat like they often do, so I figured it was just one of those days.

Even Daruka, with his blue-fronted Amazon parrot, Billie, hadn't come to check on me for quite some time. I just couldn't seem to find peace and contentment anywhere, and besides that, everything was wet and mosquitoes had converged in a conspiracy to make me their number one blood donor. I mentally channelled 'perseverance' to come to my aid, and believe it or not, that seemed to help a little.

Just then, in that doldrum of a day, a familiar upbeat sound reverberated behind me. The strumming and twanging of guitar strings and pleasant vocals grew in intensity as the sound approached.

"My Sweet Lord, hmm, I really want to see you…"

It was George Harrison, my favourite former Beatle, singing his classic anthem. Of course, George wasn't there in person, but I knew Daruka had snuck up behind me playing the CD in his vehicle in an effort to give me a boost. I didn't bother to turn around right away. No need to. The song caused me to pick up my walking pace and even break into a little jig right there on the open highway. I had no choice! George Harrison's masterpiece, "My Sweet Lord," makes the heart happy, and I was in bliss for the full four minutes and thirty-nine seconds. My spirits lifted.

Something intuitively compelled Daruka to come to me at that time, and as he rolled up beside me, he flashed a friendly smile through the open window of his vehicle.

"Okay Daruka, you made my day!" I applauded. "What else have you got?"

"How about Mahalia Jackson, the gospel singer, doing 'Didn't it Rain Children?'" he asked.

I knew that song and encouraged him to play it. I was not going to turn down a gospel song that stirs the heart. It was great.

Still, I longed to hear some *bhajans* (devotional songs) or lectures by our *guru*, Prabhupada, but Daruka wasn't able to respond to that request. Whenever I hear songs or instructive words from Prabhupada it sends me into another level of contentment. I've always loved spiritual offerings and before joining the ranks of monks I often filled my travel solitude with song. My favourite was Buffy Sainte-Marie's recording of Patrick Sky's "Many a Mile." Back then, I filled my hitchhiking days (which also included hopping trains) with the projection of song and other sounds. "Many a Mile" is a heart-wrenching song that haunted me for years when I was on the road because I yearned for a deeper dimension in life. The epiphany of these experiences is that travel and song go together like a horse and carriage, or soup and a sandwich—totally compatible.

Since evolving and taking up monastic life, I've learned those beautiful melodic songs authored by saints like Bhaktivinoda, Narottama, Lochana, and Visvanatha. Their songs, with penetrating heart-grabbing tunes, are indeed captivating and joyous. I simply have to remember to sing these songs under any condition.

As Bhaktivinoda expresses in a *bhajan*, "*sukhe dukhe bolo nako vandane harinam koro re*"—whether you are in a stressful situation or a chipper one, just fill your lips with chanting. As a wanderer in the wilderness or a roamer on the road, traversing an open valley or a tranquil forest, why not project the sound of liberty and optimism? If yodellers can produce their sounds in the Alps, then why can't a monk make noise in the boreal forest? I encourage you to do the same. Rain or shine, sleet or hail, sun or cloud, just sing as an offering, as a sacrifice, and for the joy of it.

I recall how back in 1996, when venturing on the first of my extreme walks across Canada, I regularly spent eight hours a day chanting on my *japa mala* (chanting beads). This ongoing process of repetitious utterance of sacred sound offered solace to my mind, but I also longed for accompaniment and thought a rhythmic background would be nice.

One early spring day it dawned on me while trekking through the mountains along Highway 1 out in British Columbia that I was already making music with nature. By some sort of divine empowerment, I realized the sound of crunching gravel made by my feet was providing the beat for my chanting. There is a timing which occurs when walking. It comes from the flow of blood creating your pulse and the beat of your breath inhaling and exhaling. It's like the soft pattern of movement you hear when waves roll onto a quiet beach. It's called rhythm, and it comes from nature. It's the constant ebb and flow of the movement of air and fluid within and without our bodies. It is the heartbeat of nature, and it's important to recognize it.

THE STEPS YOU MAKE CREATE RHYTHM AS THE TRAIN CREATES A JAZZY DRONE.

With acknowledgement of the beat of my feet, I felt I was creating a form of percussion. Simultaneously with the May thaw, nature was contributing to the jazz of it all. Snow that had been cradled in the arms of coniferous trees—the likes of fir and spruce—was now melting and sliding off a branch here and a branch there. Each slide of snow would land on the ground with a soft thud. Then, a raven mystically appeared, soaring high above, making its contribution with the flapping of wings, stirring up a woodwind beat. The raven also punctuated the atmosphere with an occasional 'caw'. All that was missing was the trumpeter swan. Oh, had he been present, we would have had a brass component to the band.

With the current ensemble whipping up some hot licks, I was feeling good, like James Brown, perhaps. I was being entertained by a purely instrumental experience. It was a discovery of the grace of nature. The only thing left was to insert a *mantra*, and that's exactly what I did. A *mantra*, accompanied by the sounds of nature, stirred the wolves and bears to dance, or so I fantasized. Music does that. It transports us to a welcomed fantasy, and when it becomes spiritual, it becomes otherworldly, a zone beyond time and space. You forget about the strain of the trek. The pain is gone. Your spirit is lifted.

And so it was. A dreary, rainy day brightened by creative music. You see, Canada is a huge country, and sometimes when you are out clumping along alone you have to invent ways to overcome loneliness and boredom. Those are the times when you look for nature's accompaniment and just play your own version of "Jazz on the Road"!

CHAPTER 16

REINCARNATION: WALKING FROM BODY TO BODY

"I could well imagine that I might have lived in former centuries and there encountered questions that I was not yet able to answer; that I had to be born again because I had not fulfilled the task that was given to me."

—Carl Jung

Four walks across Canada and several treks in other countries have allowed me to meet hundreds, if not, thousands of people. Most of them are very friendly and just want to find out what I'm up to and wish me luck in my travels. But occasionally, when people meet a monk, they want a private chat about spirituality and reincarnation.

People have been intrigued with the topic of the afterlife since the dawn of time. The concept of visiting this world in a particular body, which is just one of many such visits, continues to arouse, tantalize, stimulate, and even plague our thoughts. For some folks, the idea of coming back means completing an unfinished assignment, something begun in a previous life. If returning to this world permits us the opportunity to get closer to taming anger, greed, or lust, it demonstrates an amazing level of compassion on the part of the Creator. It's a divine policy that clearly states, "I'll give you another chance."

Back in the early 1970s a few very important questions in my own spiritual journey led me to my current vocation as a monk. Why is it that certain people are 'born with a silver spoon in their mouth' and have it all—affluence, money, and power? And why are others born into abject poverty? Why is such unfair treatment imposed upon them at birth? Could there be something about past behaviour that determines our present condition of life?

If *karma* is an undeniable invisible trigger or response to actions of a negative or positive nature linked to the law of physics which states, "for every action there is an equal and opposite reaction," then we can appreciate responsibility plays a major role in our destiny. I refer to this simply as the policy of the Creator, and it works its ways through reincarnation.

During my many walks I've had several encounters with people who just wanted to initiate a discussion on the topic of reincarnation or successive lives. In 2003 when I began a second Trans-Canada trek, I started from the east coast. I met a middle-aged couple near the Canso Causeway, the entrance to beautiful Cape Breton Island in Canada's Ocean Playground. This cheerful Nova Scotian couple pulled their vehicle over to the side of the road just to say hello and have a little chat. They encouraged me and wished me well on my cross-country walk, but they also expressed an inquisitiveness about reincarnation, the business of coming back to deal with unfinished business.

"You know, it's Mother's Day, so naturally I've been thinking of my mother who's deceased, and I believe she's going to come back to finish what she could not previously do. Do you believe in that?" the lady asked.

THE BODY CHANGES, THE SOUL DOES NOT.

I definitely concurred, which brought a nice smile to her face.

While trekking across Canada on my third walk which began on the west coast, I had another encounter concerning a past life recurrence. I was making my way slowly through the mountains in the Crowsnest Pass. During the early morning rush-hour traffic, a motorist suddenly pulled over. He had an eager and restless demeanour. There was something he wanted to know.

"I thought maybe you could help me with something," he said in a thick Russian accent.

"I'll try," I replied.

He told me of a recurring dream, with him being a monk during the Russian Revolution. He finds himself sitting down reading in a monastery library. Everyone in the library is struck with fear when a military man bursts through the door, holds up a gun and aims at him. The next thing he remembers is that everything goes blank.

"I'm quite convinced I was a monk," he stated. "Do you believe it to be true?"

"I have no reason to doubt it," I replied. "We are here now, we were here before, and I believe we will continue to be here again. In fact, we keep coming back to learn."

I gave the man my assurance that we visit the world in different bodies on multiple occasions. He was in a hurry to get to work, but obviously thought it important to talk to me about his recurring dream. Like the lady in Cape Breton, he was pleased to hear my response to his query.

One of my favourite verses from the ancient teachings of the *Bhagavad-gita* (2.27) goes like this: "One who has taken birth is sure to die, and after death one is sure to take birth again." This message of returning to this world underscores the concept of the soul's transmigration.

Later, during that third Canadian walk, I crossed the vast Prairies and was making my way through Thunder Bay, a modest city with a population of 110,000. A Buddhist leader heard I was in the area and wanted to interview me for his weekly show on the Lakehead University radio station. He actually came out to meet me on the highway and arranged for me to go on the air to speak about my pilgrimage in addition to Vedic teachings and lifestyle. After the interview, we continued our discussion about *samsara* (reincarnation). Off the air, he confessed that Buddhist teachings were very dear to him, and he believed in reincarnation. However, he had a few doubts because Buddhist philosophy gives no credence to the existence of the soul, yet at the same time, accepts the principle of reincarnation. The question then arises, *what* reincarnates, or changes bodies, if there is no *atma*, or soul?

"I have been grappling with that one for some time," my Buddhist friend confessed, before acknowledging the merits of the Vedic/Hindu belief which explains reincarnation more completely.

Garuda, my support person for the 2007 walk, and I had the good fortune to divert a bit from the main road, the Yellowhead Highway in Saskatchewan. We made our way to Little Manitou Lake, a unique natural treasure near the little town of Watrous. I was in pursuit of relaxation after a hard day's walk.

"A swim in Little Manitou Lake would be just fine," I suggested to Garuda. It has the reputation to be Canada's Dead Sea. This beautiful body of water possesses rich minerals and is three times saltier than the ocean, which allows you to float like nobody's business.

It was highly recommended by the locals whom I had met earlier in the day. "You can just read the newspaper while lying on your back. You won't sink," they said.

It was irresistible, and so I relished the swim. I came out refreshed but covered in the white healing minerals that make Little Manitou Lake famous. Fresh out of the water, I met Cynthia who was walking her dog. Being out in the country there is a common courtesy to greet everyone you meet. So, we exchanged greetings. Since it wasn't obvious that I was a monastic person, having replaced my saffron robes with swimming trunks, I introduced myself as a *swami*, a Canadian monk.

"Oh!" said Cynthia, who described herself as a young grandmother. "Maybe you could answer a question I have been harbouring for years." She must have assumed that monks have extra-sensory perception, can prophesize, do mystical things, and so forth.

"I'll see what I can do," I replied.

"I have several children, but my fourth child posed some difficulties during labour, and I needed a Caesarean. During the whole time of the surgery, I was able to see myself on the operating table." Cynthia claimed she was not in her body, and that her actual being was situated in the corner of the ceiling. She chuckled when she told me she was looking down at her body as the medical staff did their work.

"The surgeon gave me anesthetics that put me to sleep, but I could see and hear everything," she said. "After the surgery I came back into my body and I'm wondering if you can explain what happened to me?"

I made an attempt with the following scenario:

"Let's say you get into your car, put the key in the ignition, and start the engine. You back out of the garage into the driveway and suddenly it dawns on you that you forgot your purse. So, you put the car in park and go into the house to fetch it, while leaving the engine running. Then you return to the car and continue on your way.

"During your child labour you left your body, which is like the car in my story, and temporarily projected yourself to the ceiling," I told her. "Your soul was totally out of your body until it decided to re-unite with it. Your soul traveled, not far, but it did travel."

Cynthia seemed to relate to the story about her soul's brief journey. Due to its transcendent nature, that spark of life we call the soul, or *atma* in Sanskrit, is able to be mobile, and once a body is shed, as in death, it will then seek refuge with a new set of parents and enter into a new being and a new beginning.

Moving through this world, going from town to town on foot, is much like reincarnation. Each one of us travels from one body to another, and another, making observations, gaining wisdom and experience. Most assuredly one should, over many lifetimes, become a better person.

The soul's transmigration is verified in many places in the *Bhagavad-gita*, including 2.22: "As a person puts on new garments, giving up old ones, the soul similarly accepts new material bodies, giving up the old and useless ones."

The joy of meeting people is one of the major reasons I take to the road for these long-distance walking expeditions. The vast majority of folks are friendly well-wishers, but occasionally, I encounter someone who wants to discuss spirituality or reincarnation. Those are some of the most unique and rewarding conversations.

CHAPTER 17
GETTING NOTICED AS A MOVING TRAFFIC CONE!

"A great whispering noise began to rise in the woods on either side of the tracks, as if the forest had just noticed we were there and was commenting on it."

–Stephen King

I have done a lot of walking in my time and gotten a fair amount of coverage from the media. Small town media is more interested in my marathon walking excursions than their big city cousins. I was on my third trek across Canada making my way through the nation's capital. During my previous two walks, the Ottawa media didn't pay much attention to this humble monk crossing his homeland on foot, but this third trip found me in Ottawa on Labour Day Monday, and I guess it must have been a slow news day. Newspapers, radio stations, and television news crews had space and time to fill, and since there must not have been any 'hard news' happening, they looked for a good human-interest story.

Someone must have noticed The Walking Monk in saffron robes, because a TV news crew tracked me down and was anxious to start rolling their camera to capture my story. I thought this to be a great opportunity to let folks know what I was doing, so I agreed to be interviewed. Not only did I get interviewed, but the crew talked to many other pedestrians on the trail which ran through a suburban shopping and residential area.

"What do you think about this monk going across the land on foot, trying to encourage more walking?"

Everyone they talked to gave a positive response.

The TV crew, comprised of a reporter and cameraman, kept on my trail for some time. They set up tripod and camera, zooming in and out at several locations while I ambled along. After they got enough footage, they thanked me for my time, wished me luck, and returned to the TV station to edit their story. As they were packing up and leaving, another reporter and photographer from the *Ottawa Citizen*, one of Canada's most prominent newspapers, arrived on the scene. They took a couple of photos and conducted an interview before heading back to their office. I was surprised at this unforeseen media attention, especially in Ottawa. Reporters there are usually pre-occupied covering the goings-on at Parliament Hill and the affairs of the nation. But it was Labour Day and the politicians left town to return to their ridings all across Canada. Not much was happening except this orange/saffron-robed monk walking through the city.

As I continued, I began to wonder what would become of this media coverage in one of Canada's major markets. The next morning was very interesting. Motorists honked. Motorists stopped. Motorists got out of their cars to shake hands. One motorist even stopped to share a joke.

"Hey, I saw you on TV. Do you monks like jokes?" he asked.

"Sure. My *guru* was quite the humorist at times," I responded.

"I've got a monk joke for you," he continued.

ONE OF MY FIRST TELEVISION APPEARANCES.

The gist of the joke was that there was this young man who wanted to join a monastery, and in this particular order of cloistered monks they honoured a vow of silence. They were only permitted to say one word each year. The abbot of the monastery let the boy give it a go.

After one year of devout services to the monastery, the young recruit did well, kept his vow of silence, and when given the opportunity to express the one word for the year, he said, "Cold!"

The abbot arranged to get him a blanket. The second year ended, and his vow of silence was faithfully kept. His word for the year was, "Food!" As a result, he was given more oatmeal. When the third year wrapped up, the one word that came out of the young monk's mouth was "Quit!"

"Good," responded the abbot abruptly, "because you've been complaining ever since you got here!"

The punch line caused the joke teller and I to share a great laugh right there on the side of the road.

The early morning laughter was a wonderful way to start the day, and I moved on in good spirits. By the time I reached the town of Russell, people started coming out of their homes and stores to offer encouragement and congratulations. The media coverage was working! At one point, it was even difficult to keep walking with all the attention, but I enjoyed meeting and talking with everyone.

The story caught the interest of one special soul in particular. I received a message from a dear friend of mine who had joined the Hare Krishna movement three and a half decades earlier. Her father wrote her saying that he had seen my photo and story in the *Ottawa Citizen*. He had been very antagonistic toward the Hare Krishnas, especially after his daughter joined, but the photo and story changed his opinion. He was quite excited about it and told his daughter he had a change of heart—he now had a new appreciation for who we are and what we do. It made me feel good and confirmed that God does indeed work in mysterious ways. You can't underestimate the power of presence, nor the power of the press.

When I'm out on the trail, I'm not exactly incognito. My long, flowing saffron-coloured robes and bald head make me stand out. It's the kind of image not often seen in most Canadian towns and villages. When driving down a road, a motorist may be intrigued when spotting a brightly visible orangish object in the distance. They may blink their eyes and take a closer look because this strange object resembles a traffic cone which, by the way, seems to be moving. It's not a mirage the confused driver sees. Any doubts about unidentified orange objects may now be dispelled. Seriously, I've been told quite bluntly on more than one occasion that from a distance I resemble a moving traffic cone.

I've been called other things, too, but never anything too nasty. At least I've never taken comments I've received on the road or trail that way. Usually, light-hearted words are cast my way, often names with a spiritual theme such as 'Buddha Boy', 'Jesus', 'Gandhi', or

"DID I SEE THAT TRAFFIC CONE MOVE?" ASKS THE MOTORIST.

variations on the Dalai Lama. This last one gets confusing for some people to say. Is it 'Dalai Rama' or 'Hare Lama' or something else? Sometimes

89

I only hear a shouting voice from a moving vehicle, expressing greater accuracy like, "Hey Monk!" I always smile and feel honoured when hearing these kinds of terms because of the spiritual connotation.

There have been occasions when I've even been put into the warrior category. I reminded one traveller of Grasshopper, a student of Kung Fu Master Po from an old television series. I guess the shaven head and the robes are familiar to many people. I've also been addressed as 'Airbender', referring to a martial arts character who has an arrow mark going down his forehead.

This is all very flattering, and it would be nice to have the agility and flexibility of these martial arts fellows. I've always considered myself more of a peacemaker than a fighter though, but I appreciate being noticed and greeted by people on the road.

To be honest, I never knew these characters, Grasshopper or Airbender, until I looked them up online. You see, I just don't watch TV, and I guess I may never know what I'm missing. I've got my meditation and walking to occupy my time. Even though I may not know the origins of many of the names people call me, for the most part, I consider them to be compliments.

On my first walk across the land of the maple leaf, I had just arrived in Calgary when a cab driver of Indian descent pulled over. He was curious and reverential at the same time. He politely introduced himself as Bala, and said he noticed me on the road wearing God's clothes.

At least he didn't call me God, heaven forbid, because there's nothing further from the truth. A key part of the training in our monastic order is to identify ourselves as being part and parcel of the Creator. I've met some people who actually thought they were God Almighty, and believe it or not, some eastern philosophies strongly suggest something that preposterous.

Another new identity came into play when one of my support people, frustrated at trying to keep up with my walking pace, called me a machine.

"You're a machine!" was exactly what he said.

That remark made me pause. *Why a machine?*

After looking at my perplexed expression, he respectfully clarified his choice of words. He told me that I just keep going, hour after hour, day after day, week after week, just moving onward without ever taking a break.

A machine? Imagine that! Did he think I was a motor, an engine, or a generator? All along I felt like I was showing him enough appreciation and compassion, but he obviously just needed a little more down time, so I gave it to him.

The Telegram, a major newspaper in Newfoundland, kindly labeled me the "Forrest Gump of the Hare Krishnas!" And in Sault Ste. Marie, a city in northern Ontario, the local newspaper referred to me as "a two-toned orange Popsicle," because rain had darkened my lower robes while an umbrella kept the upper portion dry. That was a cool, sweet, and delicious remark.

But the term 'machine' lingered and became imprinted in my mind leaving a humble kind of feeling. Humility, after all, is very much a virtue and something not averse to the lifestyle of a monk. It's very conducive.

GETTING NOTICED BY MEDIA.

"Humility is not something that comes naturally. But it is a cardinal outlet that should be pursued more than any other," author Joyce Meyers once wrote.

The great master of the *bhakti* (devotional) tradition, Sri Chaitanya, whose line of discipline I follow, once summed up humility as thinking, "You are humbler than a blade of grass." It's a rather unique analogy because even if you are trampled upon, you won't protest. You just spring back up and do what needs doing with a humble frame of mind.

Sri Chaitanya, in fact, was quite the walker, roaming extensively throughout the subcontinent of India in the early sixteenth century. He was also quite the scholar. Like Aristotle, who said that the essence of life is "to serve others and to do good," Chaitanya reduced philosophy to thinking and acting as a menial helper to others and to the Divine. The Sanskrit word for helper is '*das*'. He saw himself as *dasanudas*, which translates as 'helper of the helper', or acting as a servant to someone else who is serving.

The attitude behind service is humility and it is from this platform that understanding flows. I once heard a preacher who played with the word 'understand' say, "Stand under and things will be seen from a better perspective." Another way to put it would be that realization of the self begins when the ego is subdued.

Since we're on the topic of identity, this is a good opportunity to dig a little deeper because we are living in a time when identity crisis seems to be the order of the day. There is much confusion in these times. I see it constantly during my walks. People are trying to find themselves and asking the big questions: Who am I? How did I get here? And what happens to me when I die?

Simple logic would conclude that if you are unaware of your true identity then you can't have a sense of direction. Confusion usually arises from an erroneous premise which leads to a false conclusion. The media, particularly advertising, has led us to believe we are simply our bodies, and the body is the only self. Ancient writings, such as the *Bhagavad-gita*, tell us that the body is actually a machine. But wait a minute, am I really a machine? If not, then what am I? Perhaps, the *operator* of the machine?

Most of us identify with a label that designates the body as black or white, doctor or lawyer, man or woman, Buddhist or Christian, French or English, and so on. These designations, however, are subject to change. Some of us actually believe the skin pigment of our body, or our vocation, is who we are. Yet, does that express who we really are *deep down inside*? I think not. What I do think is that all of these designations are temporary. Even our faith may change because some of us have been known to convert to a different religion or new spiritual way of life.

Okay then, is there anything that doesn't change? The answer is yes, the *real* you <u>does not</u> change! That's because you are the soul—a spirit which is constant. Your body will perish, but your individual soul will not. The ancient *Vedas* of India put it more directly: *aham brahmasmi*. I am spirit. And the spirit has three qualities. It is constant, it is cognizant, and it is content. The three Cs. The Sanskrit words are *sat*, *chit*, and *ananda*—constant, cognizant and content.

These concepts are ours to ponder. It's interesting to analyze the difference between the body and the self because it increases our understanding of the meaning of life.

Sometimes names or remarks are directed my way when I'm out there walking. I receive them all with delight, because people are just trying to reach out—to communicate. Even if somebody takes notice that my body is the shape of a traffic cone, I can simply satisfy myself by remembering that's not the real me they are pointing at. That's just the latest body I have borrowed to house my soul.

I am spirit and so are you!

CHAPTER 18

BEWARE OF DOG

"The dogs with the loudest barks are the ones that are most afraid."

–Norman Reedus

You've got to admire people who deliver the mail on foot, especially when they see a "Beware of Dog" sign. Postal service employees know some dogs can be pretty mean. I feel a special bond with many postmen and postwomen because we walk similar paths. We both travel on foot (well, at least they used to) and we both have a message to deliver. We also have brief encounters with lots of people, and sometimes brief, or not so brief, interactions with dogs.

'Dog is man's best friend' is a phrase that goes all the way back to an eighteenth-century publication which expressed the loyalty of dogs to their masters. That saying stuck and is still widely used three centuries later. However, if you are not a particular dog's best friend, you could be perceived by one as an intruder.

It's a common occurrence to hear a dog barking before ever seeing one, especially when walking along a country road. As soon as they see or hear any kind of movement, they'll growl or bark first and ask questions later. When one dog takes to barking, its next-door canine neighbour usually chimes in. It's a domino effect, and it doesn't seem to matter whether the dog next door is inside or out. Once a dog strikes up the chorus, it doesn't take long before every Fido in the area joins in. The resulting tumultuous uproar can include bass, tenor, alto, and soprano, and they keep it up until the perceived intruder has walked clear through their neck of the woods.

While some dogs are aggressive, some are downright friendly. I was trekking along one day when two massive unleashed German shepherds came at me after bounding across a rather large front yard. Their intimidating barks and aggressive behaviour made my hair stand on end as I prepared to be attacked. But as soon as they got close, I spontaneously extended my hand as if to say, "Leave me alone!"

Their interpretation was, "Oh thanks; you wanna pet me!"

I've had friendly fellows run toward me from their masters' homes and cling to my trail for long stretches. I initially thought that a dog's range was small, but some have more wolf-like instincts, claiming vast territories as their own. One owner cursed me after coming along in his pickup truck in search of his missing pet.

This episode occurred over in Ireland while walking from Belfast to Cork. A male mutt, who was at least part Labrador retriever, spotted me and decided to chum along. He was friendly enough, but had a rather interesting habit. Being territorial, he would urinate small installments, every minute or so, on both sides of the road. I kept walking and he kept trailing right along, frequently lifting a leg to mark his spot.

"Go back home!" I urged. No way. He wanted to hang out with his new best friend. A little later his real owner arrived, not with a shotgun, but with an irate expression and colourful language for me and the dog. It wasn't my intention to agitate anyone, so I raised my arms toward the heavens to indicate I was sorry. The man barked out a command and his loyal pet jumped into the truck and they tore off down the road.

Then there was the time in Trinidad when a pack of stray dogs lined up across the road. Their chorus of barks was vicious. They were not about to let my friend, Kartamasha, and myself proceed. It was a dark and early pre-dawn encounter, and the dogs figured they owned the road. Morning traffic had not yet dominated the world, but Kartamasha, who was trained by the military to be fearless, took charge. Following his lead, we torpedoed dead ahead, penetrating their perceived invincible wall, and left them knowing we were not easily intimidated.

Have you ever met a Saint Bernard? These fellows can be three feet tall and weigh over 250 pounds. It's the sheer size of these animals that can cause goose bumps of fear to run up your spine. Most of the time, Saint Bernards come slobbering along, wagging their tails in friendship, but that's not what I encountered out in Manitoba on the Canadian Prairie.

I was walking on the side of the road minding my own business when this humongous hulk of a dog came springing down across his farmer's homestead. He obviously saw, heard, or smelled me because he made a deep, resounding growl and darted out from behind a barn. With me in his sights, he quickly zeroed in on his human target. I shifted to the opposite side of the road hoping it would deter him. Traffic was rather busy with automobiles, trucks, and farm machinery moving along the road.

Surely, this will discourage him! I was wrong.

After crossing the front yard, he leaped down through the ditch, came up onto the shoulder of the road before his massive paws hit the pavement. I wasn't sure if I should fear for me, or fear for him, what with the onslaught of traffic. But his bark was real and his body enormous. He swiftly ran across the two-lane road straight for me.

I braced myself and prepared for the worst, but he brushed right past me and dashed into the second ditch. He kept barking, pursuing his quarry, which thankfully, was apparently not me. He was after something else. What was he in such a huff about? Just metres away I saw an animal even larger than the St. Bernard crossing a fallow field. It was a bear. I didn't stick around to see how this episode played out. I picked up the pace and quickly moved on down the road.

DOGS. ON THE ROAD, SOME ARE NICE AND SOME ARE NOT.

The valuable lesson I learned that day is that fear is often misdirected. Talking about his students, our *guru* once said (paraphrased), "We don't fear *maya* (temptation), but we fear, perhaps, a purging of ourselves."

I've had lots of encounters with dogs during my many years of long-distance walking. These encounters, for the most part, have been friendly and brief. Once in a while, our best friend can scare the living daylights out of you, because not all dogs are Lassie or Rin-Tin-Tin.

I was walking through the Appalachian Mountains in Pennsylvania, when from the front veranda of this guy's house, dashed a young, energetic, seemingly vicious barking dog—a young pit bull who made a beeline for me. Luckily, the owner was right on her heels, trying his best to catch up with his dog.

"Maya!" he yelled at the top of his lungs. Maya came right at me, but fortunately, loyalty to her owner kicked in. She stopped and would only come so close, but 'so close' was too close, as far as I was concerned. Maya's master really struggled to control her. She would lunge forward, and then retreat at his scolding.

"Maya, you stop that! Maya, you get back here! Maya! No! No!"

I took the liberty of asking the owner, a young dark-haired, fairly casually dressed fellow, "Do you know what the word *maya* means?"

"No, I don't" he explained while still keeping his attention on her. "It's a Sanskrit word, and it means 'illusion'."

His immediate response was, "Well, she's in illusion alright. Maya, stop that barking. Stop it!"

Just then, the owner's wife, having heard all the commotion, stepped out onto the veranda, and with a raspy voice like Janis Joplin, screamed in terror, "Maya, you get back here!"

It was comforting to know Maya had two bodyguards to come to my rescue. After the tension subsided, I went on my way, thankful their security system was functioning.

Having lived in an *ashram* environment, the word *maya* has become a much-used part of our vocabulary. If one of the monks shows some sign of spiritual weakness, comrades in the *ashram* might use the phrase, 'He's in *maya*!' to make an observation out of concern, of course.

In any event, I tip my hat to the masters of Maya, the dog. I think they did a good job of keeping her in check. A lesson from this episode is that while you lovingly keep your pet, make sure to keep *maya*, or illusion, out of your consciousness. The phrase 'Beware of dog' has more than one meaning. A dog can be threatening, can bite and terrorize, but it usually depends upon the relationship the owner has established with it.

One of my all-time favourite verses from the *Bhagavad-gita* (5.18) addresses how a transcendentalist sees a dog: "The true visionary sees with equanimity the wise person, a cow, an elephant, a dog, and the man who eats a dog, since he/she sees the soul within them."

CHAPTER 19
THE TIMES I LAUGHED ON THE ROAD

"I love people who make me laugh. I honestly think it's the thing I like most, to laugh. It cures a multitude of ills. It's probably the most important thing in a person."

–Audrey Hepburn

There are occasions where outbursts of joy just explode out of nowhere and take you to a different realm, perhaps even into a timeless zone. These outbursts of laughter help release pent-up pressures and can take the pain or monotony out of your day.

I wouldn't say walking is monotonous, because you never know who or what you are going to encounter, and there seems to be a new adventure waiting around every corner. Experience has taught me that a good laugh along the way will put a little life into your step and make the walk more joyful.

It was walk number two, back in 2003. I was on the Trans-Canada Highway in British Columbia, where nature abounds in splendorous mountainous wonder. I was trudging along by myself with little human interaction and rarely a house to be seen, let alone a town. It was fall; the tourists had gone home and the road was eerily quiet. I was fingering my meditation beads, chanting softly. That function alone—chanting—does tend to create a feeling of having company.

Traffic signs warned motorists not to pass other moving vehicles in certain treacherous spots. The signs clearly stated in bold black letters over a white background, "DO NOT PASS."

Someone, sometime, probably not too long before, had taken a brush with white paint and blocked out the 'DO', 'T' and 'P', leaving it to read, "NO ASS." Reading that just had me in stitches, as the saying goes. My laughter, if I recall, echoed throughout the valley. Despite the quiet hours and lack of company, I felt that someone was communicating with me. It wasn't a witty remark by any stretch of the imagination, but that touch of toilet humour helped break the ice of silence.

My support person at the time, Tim Hitchner, arrived several minutes later. "Did you read the sign?" I asked Tim, who's often tickled by such remarks, but he didn't think too much of this one. I found that kind of funny because I often relied on Tim for comic relief. At speaking engagements along the way I would introduce him to the crowd and he would do impersonations of Elvis Presley and Jean Chretien (who at the time was the Canadian Prime Minister). Mr. Chretien was from Quebec and had a thick French-Canadian accent.

On the road it becomes a necessary ingredient for a lively journey—to laugh, to smile, and to simply say, "Ha ha!" Now that word, 'Ha!' repeated twice strikes a familiar chord. There's this little place in Quebec, in eastern Canada, with a population of less than 2,000, called Saint-Louis-du-Ha! Ha! The origins of the town's name vary, depending on who you talk to, but it's the only town in the world with two exclamation points in its name.

One explanation which may hold some truth, claims 'Ha Ha' is an old French word for something that blocks your way. Perhaps it refers to Lake Témiscouata, located nearby, which was not passable near the present-day town, and required early paddlers to portage, carrying their canoes and supplies through the woods to the next section of open water.

LIFE IS COLOURFUL, FULL OF SMILES AND LAUGHTER.

Ice and snow were on the ground when I reached the border of Saint-Louis-du-Ha! Ha! It was November and winter starts early there. My friend from Toronto, Brian Gonsalves, and I were trekking along the slippery Trans-Canada Highway, being careful every step of the way.

Brian was familiar with some of the devotional songs I sing every day. In the song "*Guru Vandanam*" (honouring the *guru*), there is a phrase in the Bengali lyrics that translates as, 'Alas! Alas!' In Bengali it reads as, 'Ha Ha!' I was leading the song we call a *bhajan*, with Brian responding by repeating each line of the song. At the moment the phrase 'Ha Ha' was sung, Brian lost his footing on the icy road and landed squarely on the seat of his pants. The timing for 'Ha Ha' could not have been better. After the fall, I deliberately repeated the words for emphasis. The laughter that came forth from the fallen victim and the one left standing was uproarious, and we continued singing after the jovial interruption. By the way, Brian wasn't hurt, saying he was saved by his 'cheeks'.

Another interesting event involved Brian and Madhai, our principal driver. We were in Quebec, Canada's largest province. Madhai was doing most of the driving, but unbeknownst to Brian and I, he had neglected to renew his driver's license!

It happened early one morning while darkness still dominated the sky. The three of us were driving to the place where I needed to be dropped off, the spot where I had stopped walking the day before. We drove through a little town and noticed the police had set up a spot check station. It was Sunday morning, and some Saturday late night partygoers were still out and about. It was obvious the police were looking for impaired drivers.

Brian was sound asleep in the back of the van, and I was getting mentally prepared, as usual, to commence walking. Madhai's foot was a little heavy on the gas pedal and he was driving slightly over the speed limit. It was right about then we came across two police officers, one in a patrol car, and the other standing on the street, waving a massive flashlight trying to get us to stop.

Madhai didn't stop, at least not immediately. He forged forward for some distance, perhaps an additional street block. While the suspicious police quickly came after us, Madhai hollered at Brian to wake up and get to the front of the vehicle immediately. A confused Brian, trying to reach a conscious state, rolled out of his sleeping bag and crawled to the front. Madhai jumped out of the driver's seat and practically pushed poor Brian behind the wheel.

Brian, who had a valid license, managed to get in position, and just before the police arrived Madhai plunked his hat on Brian's head. No sooner had this taken place than the officer's bright flashlight glared straight into Brian's eyes. The police recognized that we had an out-of-province license plate and began questioning Brian in English instead of French.

"Why didn't you stop when I waved my flashlight?" the officer demanded. A surprised Brian exclaimed, "I didn't see it," which was actually the truth.

"What do you mean you didn't see it? I was practically standing in the middle of the street! And why were you speeding?"

Poor Brian was dazed and confused, so I took this as my cue to speak up.

"Actually officer, the three of us are on a special mission. I'm doing a walk across Canada and these two men are my assistants. I'm a Krishna monk and the purpose of the walk is to help unify Canada."

The year before, Quebecers had gone to the polls to vote 'yes' or 'no'—for or against separation from the Canadian Confederation. The voting results were in favour of Quebec staying in the country.

"I'm walking for the harmony and healing of the nation; encouraging our fellow men to get more in touch with their spiritual side," I continued.

I could see the police officers were becoming receptive. I even threw in a few French words in an effort to get them to rally behind our cause. They ended up letting us go and didn't even ask for identification papers, let alone a driver's license.

Pulling away, we had a good laugh, especially over the bewildered Brian and the swift manoeuvre of Madhai. We also felt a kind of special protection had come our way, one that perhaps bumps up your faith a notch or two. The other lesson learned was to not let your license expire.

I THOUGHT I SAW A MONKY MONK!

Laughter is a device that can relieve tension. It assists in bearing a burden and becomes an easy avenue toward tolerance. It's so powerful that it helps sustain us. Author Robert Frost once said, "If we couldn't laugh, we would all go insane."

Remember, outbursts of laughter help release pent-up pressure, and take the pain or monotony out of your day. I think you have to be fairly mature to be able to laugh at yourself. It is very healthy, and my laughter seems to be the most genuine and robust when I'm on the road.

CHAPTER 20
TO SERVE & PROTECT

"Honor bespeaks worth. Confidence begets trust. Service brings satisfaction. Cooperation proves the quality of leadership."

–James Cash Penney

Recalling Dave's encounter with the police at Rogers Pass (back in chapter seven) got me to thinking about other times I've come across the 'Boys in Blue' during my many marathon walking adventures. For the most part these meetings with policemen and policewomen have been cordial and pleasant. Often the officers have heard about my excursions through the local media and stopped by to greet me when they see me walking down the road. Occasionally there's been an awkward situation, and once in a blue moon, I've had little run-ins with the police.

Undoubtedly, one of my favourite spots on planet Earth is tucked away on Lake Superior's north shore. It was near Pancake Bay that one of those blue moon situations arose, and although I generally try to keep as cool as a cucumber, this time I lost my cool.

I was walking westward, minding my own business, as usual, near the town of Wawa, notoriously known as a nightmare for hitchhikers. Wawa has become part of Canada's hitchhiking folklore because if you get dropped off there, you could be standing with your thumb out for days before getting another ride.

Rumour has it that back in the 1960s during hitchhiking's heyday, one poor lad got stuck there for so long that he got discouraged and walked into town, found a woman, got married, had children, and settled down.

Before I became a monk, I hitchhiked around Ontario and feared getting dropped off in Wawa. However, down the road a mere ninety kilometres (fifty miles) away, there was a more favourable place for hitching a ride. White River was a modest town and became famous when Harry Colburn bought a bear cub from a trapper for twenty bucks. He named the cub Winnie and soon after, author A.A. Milne created an animal cartoon character called Winnie the Pooh.

So, back then at White River, some hippies turned me on to hitching a ride on the big steel rail. They suggested I hop the Iron Horse freight train when it rolled through town. It was commonly done, and like many hobos before me, I jumped aboard as the train crawled out of town. The conductor was very nice and showed me where to sit amongst the cargo. It took me all the way to Hogtown (Toronto), about a thousand kilometres away.

But that was many years ago. The next time I was in the area I was walking across Canada, and an Ontario Provincial Police officer pulled over.

"What are you up to?" he asked.

"I'm walking across Canada," I replied.

I'm not really sure which one of us got irritated first, but it wasn't long before things turned sour. I pulled out a brochure that described the intent of the walk and handed it to him. The officer looked it over, read the details and continued questioning me.

"A walk for the spiritual healing of the nation…has anyone checked you out?" he demanded in an aggressive manner.

"You mean ID?" I smartly replied.

"Yeah," he said, staring at me intently.

"Look, I'm walking across the country," I sternly said. "I'm a Canadian citizen and I'm walking on Canadian soil, and so far, no one has checked me out."

He still wanted to see my identification papers, but I didn't have them with me and informed him my passport was with my support person, Tim Hitchner, back at the campsite at Pancake Bay. I gave him the license plate number of the van and told him what campsite we had stayed in the night before.

"I'm innocently walking, doing what our body is meant to do!" I protested.

"Okay, maybe I'll stop over at the campsite" he replied. "Are you sure no one has checked you during your trip?"

"No officer, no one has CHECKED ME OUT because I'm not doing anything wrong!" I responded in a rather loud voice.

With that he went on his way. We had no cells phones back in those days, so I wasn't able to warn Tim that this rather obnoxious OPP officer might be headed his way. I trekked on for another twenty minutes before I noticed the police car pull up behind me again. *What now.*

"So, you're sure no police officer has checked you out?" he repeated, picking up exactly where he had left off before.

At this point, I was really starting to lose it, and what's more, I was starting to question the officer's mental stability. As a monk, you are 'born to be mild' and trained to be a smoothie. You are taught to exercise patience and tolerance, but there are times, the *ksatriya* (warrior) in you, cannot be suppressed because the truth must be told with force.

"Look, officer, no one has checked me out. I'm doing nothing wrong. I'm peacefully walking in my own country," I began to rant. "But I'll tell you the people you should be checking out. It's those motorists who are killing the moose, killing the bears and porcupines. I see plenty of roadkill—sometimes three moose carcasses a day, and drivers are killing each other in head-on collisions; *plus*, they pollute the environment with their nasty exhaust fumes. They are spoiling the peacefulness of nature with their noise pollution! THEY are the criminals! THEY are the culprits! There are thousands of them out here on this highway, and it is THEM that you should be checking out!"

The officer was puzzled, but before he could reply I took off in a huff and stomped down Highway 17. I was angry. Mr. Sweetie Pie Swami, as I'm sometimes called, had turned into a monster. I was mad, but felt justified, like an activist who raises his voice to protest the inequities of society. I shouldn't admit this, but I felt good walking and talking with purpose.

After the incident in Wawa, I was a little leery about policemen even though the latest encounter caused no real harm. There was no real police brutality, albeit, in my books, he was a little aggressive and somewhat misdirected. I moved on and decided I shouldn't let that experience ruin my relationship with the police.

Looking back over the years, interactions between Krishna monks and policemen have been rather clumsy at times. During my first summer as a monk when I was a tall and lanky lad, I'd often be out on Yonge Street in Toronto approaching pedestrians with our literature. One day, two officers who were also rookies in their chosen profession, pulled their cruiser over to investigate me. In a jovial fashion, they asked if I had bird poop on my nose, referring to the light earth-coloured marking on my forehead. They had a good laugh trying to humiliate me, but I was on a mission for Krishna and just continued going about my business.

Another time, near Yonge and Bloor Streets, a patrol officer observed me talking with pedestrians, and it soon became obvious that he didn't like what I was doing. So, he got in my face and shoved me against the brick wall of the Stollerys Men's Wear store. He was physically harsh, and in a gruff voice said I should leave. But after moving a few steps away from him to regain my personal space, I stood my ground. I felt I had a right to continue communicating with the public, and that's exactly what I did. These two instances were rather mild compared to what some of my peers went through in other parts of Canada and the United States.

In time, our relationship with the constabulary in Toronto drastically improved, mainly after a meeting involving the police chief, a room full of constables, and some of our monks. It was a chance to get acquainted with each other. From then on, the police began to look at us as a harmless, pious, spiritual group, and our perception of them was as *ksatriyas*, or martial men and women, out to serve and protect. We gained mutual respect for each other and have had a good relationship ever since.

Now back to the Trans-Canada Highway in '96. Two or three days later, about a hundred kilometres down the highway, I occupied a rare telephone booth located in a tiny hamlet. I was talking with someone at my home base in the Toronto temple when I noticed a vehicle pulling up and parking right beside the phone booth. Turning my head, I saw the familiar logo of the Ontario Provincial Police.

I pretended not to notice and when my call was over, I flung open the telephone booth door and was about to continue my walk. Being still somewhat frazzled from my last encounter with the officer in Wawa, I decided to ignore this one. It's not my usual style, but I walked right past him as if he was an invisible man. With his window rolled down, the stocky man in an officer's uniform said something that rather surprised me.

"You don't have to ignore me," he said in a grave tone. He then broke into a genuine smile, almost as if to compensate for the last officer's behaviour. Perhaps they had a chat with each other over their two-way radios.

"I know what you're doing; it's a great mission. Please take my card and call me if I can be of any help to you," he kindly said. "By the way, how's the walking going?"

I smiled as I accepted his card, and we had a nice chat about my journey. That conversation broke the ice and more than made up for my previous encounter with the officer in Wawa. Still smiling, I walked away, thinking citizens and law enforcement officers can communicate congenially, as can a man of the cloth and a warrior.

I must admit, most officers I meet are impressed when they hear I am walking from one end of the country to the other. Usually, it eliminates any kind of suspicion, and talk then turns to appreciation and encouragement. I've often received moral support, and sometimes they have given me food, and even cash donations, to support my walk. Some think my walking is a heroic deed, and that I'm some sort of warrior spirit. They approve of my message about being strong, healthy, wholesome, and keeping out of trouble. They tend to like the hike.

Once in 2007, I was trekking with Garuda along the shoulder of the Yellowhead Highway just outside of Edmonton. It was almost rush hour and traffic was just starting to roar by us on the four-lane stretch as the sun came up on another pleasant spring morning. Suddenly, we heard sirens as a police car came up behind us at breakneck speed with emergency lights flashing. We then heard stereo sirens as a second police car came into view in front of us on the other side of the divided highway. The patrol car coming toward us lunged across the grassy median, sped across two lanes, and stopped in front of us on the shoulder of the road. What a scene: two middle-aged Caucasian males in Hindu holy men's robes walking along the highway with cop cars boxing us off from the front and rear.

"I don't know what all the fuss is about," I remarked to Garuda. "At least they can't nab us for speeding."

The officer in front opened his door, stepped out, and expressed what was on his mind.

"Don't worry about a thing; we heard about your walk and just want to get our picture taken with The Walking Monk."

The two policemen looking spiffy in their uniforms stood straight and formal with big grins on their faces as they posed for the photographs.

By now the Yellowhead was starting to get busier, but motorists slowed down considerably when they saw emergency vehicles huddled by the side of the road. It was no mishap, no crash, accident, or even ticketing. They saw two happy monks and two smiling policemen standing there having a pleasant conversation on the side of the road.

"In our adopted tradition with its roots from India," I explained, "you two officers would be considered *ksatriyas*, defenders of the law, and my friend, Garuda and I would be considered the *brahmins*, or teachers of morality. When citizens step beyond the principles of morality and breach the policies, the *ksatriyas* respond by giving warnings, pardoning the offenders, or dishing out penalties."

The two officers listened with great interest.

"When people ignore the standard laws, there is a reaction," I continued. "Teachers are known to be proactive, and the police are reactive, but these two groups work hand in hand and are on the same page."

"That sure sounds like a good way of doing things," responded one of the officers. "It was a real pleasure meeting you guys; please walk safely."

It was time to part because *dharma* (for us) and duty (for them) had to be executed. We parted with firm handshakes and they drove off as we walked on. Motorists who saw the lack of confrontation were a bit surprised—you could see it in their faces—as the officers left in a quieter manner than when they had arrived. I couldn't help but wonder if the world would ever see a time when men of the cloth and men of the uniform could work closely together for a peaceful, safer society.

THE COPS WERE TOPS ON THE ROAD.

And that brings me back to Dave's encounter with the police at Rogers Pass. He hit the nail on the head when he told the RCMP officer that I was walking for the spiritual healing of the nation. I really do appreciate the work our more upstanding police officers do and support their efforts 'to serve and protect'.

CHAPTER 21
MILD TO MEAN ATTACKS

> "The father mosquito asked his son, 'How's your first flight, son?' The son answered, 'Feels great, Dad, everyone was clapping for me.'"
>
> –Anonymous

Often when I am walking in remote, unpopulated areas, I get this feeling that I am not alone. Well, not exactly *not* alone, because Krishna is always with me and my *guru* is always by my side. Even in wilderness areas, I know there are other beings out there, some large and some small.

On one occasion, in Canada's most diminutive province, I was not alone in more ways than figuratively. Three *brahmachari* monks were with me walking along the Confederation Trail in Prince Edward Island, moving at a good clip, probably just shy of five kilometres an hour. It was a beautiful morning and the sun had slowly risen as we made our way from the west end of the province near Tignish, traveling on this very promising trail. As the four of us strolled along we soon realized we were definitely *not* alone.

The air was misty, as it often is in May, and before long we approached a swampy kind of wetland. This rails-to-trails path cuts across the middle of the island through all kinds of terrain. We were in the midst of the aforementioned wetland when one of the monks remarked, "This is such a quiet trail. It seems like we are the only ones out here."

That was only partly true, as we soon found out. There were no other human beings on this section of the trail, but we did have visitors. We noticed one, then two, now three, and then many more who made their presence known. We soon realized we were in the land of mosquitoes. Of course, Prince Edward Island isn't the only province where these tiny critters reside. I've encountered them everywhere across this massive country.

Scientists say mosquitoes have been around for about 100 million years, and I bet they'll be around many millions more. These pesky, aggressive, tiny little helicopters have a formidable sting and are hard to detect until they begin drinking your blood. I call them 'mystic-eatoes'. The bloodthirsty females require our red fluid to produce their eggs. The males are the true flowerchildren of the community, feeding exclusively on vegetarian nectar.

Mosquitoes are most abundant around lakes, rivers, creeks, swamps, and various other wetland areas. Their population explodes in May and early June as they take flight in anticipation of great prospects. They make no discrimination: moose, deer, bear, and monks are on their menu.

So, what is the best way to combat these voracious pests? Citronella is fairly effective in terms of repelling mosquitoes, but I haven't found a sure-fire way to stave off their distant relative—the black fly. Mosquitoes sting, while black flies bite. I consider both to be vampires.

We may wonder why God created these little devils. Well, I believe they are part of the food chain. On one of my walking sojourns, a young boy asked me, "What good are mosquitoes and black flies?"

My answer was, "They are food for birds, bats, frogs, snakes, and other critters."

He felt much better after hearing that.

The onslaught of swarming insects makes me think about chapter two of the *Bhagavad-gita*, which explains dualities. I have come to realize that mosquitoes and black flies are just part of nature. We all know that Mother Nature is gorgeous, but she also has her dark side. Ours is a world of opposites. The sights, smells, and sounds of nature are intoxicating, but she also harbours nastiness beyond words.

I've learned to accept 'mystic-eatoes' and their cousin, the black fly. When I encounter either of them, I try to keep calm and not be alarmed by their presence. They seem to respond more quickly to movement and the discharge of carbon dioxide. Out on the trails I can't stop walking when I encounter these little critters, so when one lands on me, I either brush it away or firmly press my hand against my body, instantly reincarnating her.

To lessen my carbon dioxide emissions, I keep my mouth closed as much as possible. On the day in question in PEI, my three companion monks and I had a hard time with that particular practice. We were trying to chant while keeping our mouths closed, but unfortunately, we realized we occasionally were breaking our vow of vegetarianism.

Wade Hemsworth wrote "The Black Fly Song." It is a cute explanation of the malicious attack by these irritators and is found in the Canadian

Songwriters Hall of Fame; it can be listened to on YouTube—check it out! Just thinking about the song lightens the burden, but out on the trail, I try not to open my mouth to sing the song in order to keep my vows.

The lesson from walking through either a cloud of 'skeeters' or black flies is tolerance, which is cherished by someone who's a monk. So, these pests are a bit of a nuisance, but we Canadians have learned to live with them. Mosquitoes and black flies are not the only things that 'bug' us; deer flies and horseflies are much worse. They go after humans, too, and instead of stinging or biting, they can tear small chunks of flesh right off our bodies.

Swimming in the refreshing waters of northern Ontario in the spring, summer, and fall seasons is always a treat. However, these two types of flies are

THESE GUYS ARE NASTY-HORSEFLIES.

unforgiving, especially when one gets out of the water. It's always better to stay submerged as much as you can, and once you get out, break off a small branch from a tree and use it as a swatter unless you brought the real deal with you.

Once, while trekking along the open road, I carried such a swatter. It was very effective, but I got to thinking that folks along the way might think I belonged to one of those orders of monks who engage in self-flagellation. Historically, some Christian monastics took to the practice of mortification of the flesh, which is supposedly a joyful form of self-torture to subdue temptation. This is not how I've been trained in the Hare Krishna tradition.

One good reason to be out on the open road is that these little flying gifts from nature are affected by gusts of wind. Mosquitoes, black flies, and the larger deer and horseflies have a hard time zeroing in on their targets when there is a breeze in the air. Trails in the forest are often sheltered, and without a breeze we become easy targets for these winged critters.

On one occasion in Saskatchewan, something larger than the aforementioned pests was intent on attacking me when I walked into its territory. It reminded me of a scene from Alfred Hitchcock's thriller, *The Birds*. While walking in the Prairies you come across sloughs (pronounced 'slews'), a kind of wetland, which provide habitat for many species of birds. Being extremely territorial, a flock of blackbirds were not enthusiastic about my trekking near their nests. As soon as one feverish bird noticed me, it sent out a distress signal to warn the others. A vicious assembly of 'flying aliens' then decided to dive-bomb me, taking serious aim at my head with incredible speed, missing my eyes and ears by mere centimetres. I call them aliens, but I'm sure at the time they saw *me* as an alien, too.

Their efforts were effective and had me working hard to protect myself and get away. At one point during the assault, I started running at breakneck speed until they left me alone. I ran for about half a kilometre. Later on, I had to confess to all of my supporters and well-wishers that I didn't walk all the way across Canada, I actually ran half a kilometre of it.

My final story about aggressors in flight was very real, and also involved physical contact. Slightly embarrassing, this tale has to do with an area of our bodies that we normally keep covered. My support person, Madhai, and I decided to take a break near beautiful Lake Huron, one of those massive bodies of fresh water known as the Great Lakes, which are located in central Canada. We were lucky to find access to a desirable beach because most of the prime locations are monopolized by private landowners.

Madhai and I found a spot near the water beside a public forest. Urgency arose and I was forced to deal with a call of nature. I took a short stroll and found a place remote enough to take care of matters. It was near a dark and very shady tall forest where I squatted to take care of my business. It was then that I was attacked by several serious stabs in my backside that felt like jack knives.

I screamed in terror, responding to the pain with Krishna's name resounding out of my mouth. I instinctively sprang into motion after spontaneously pulling up my wares, going as fast as my feet could carry me and daring not to look behind. I could hear buzzing and flying objects just over my shoulders. Hornets, yellow jackets, or wasps? I don't know, but their stings were very painful.

I returned to where Madhai was dozing. I guess I was panting and in mild shock because he woke up and asked with concern, "Is everything alright?"

At that point, I refrained from describing the traumatic occurrence, but I did say, "I don't feel like sitting down right now. I'll just continue walking, and you can meet me down the road after you finish your nap."

That afternoon, I chanted *mantras* with more fervour and sincerity than usual. Reclining and sitting down was hard to bear for about three days until the swelling from the bites subsided.

The above scenario may sound like some kind of *stand-up* comedy routine. I guess the hornets started a joke and I was the *butt* of it.

I hope this story kept you on the edge of your s*eat* because I just had to get to the *bottom* of the matter.

Om tat sat.

CHAPTER 22

BY GEORGE!

"You know the future's a huge gigantic place. I have no idea what's going on out there, I'm just going to walk into it and see what happens. I used to walk like a giant on the land. Now I feel like a leaf floating in a stream."

–Neil Young

The Canadian Shield, also known as the Laurentian Plateau or *Bouclier Canadien* (in Canada's other official language) is home to some of the oldest rock formations in the world. These Precambrian igneous and metamorphic rocks are the ancient geological core of North America. It was in this mother of all rock quarries that George found me.

Remember Garuda, my long-time friend? He was chasing fifty years of age, when he and his sixteen-year-old son, Tulsi, had joined me to walk through this unique part of Canada. We were working our way east along Route 17, a section of the Trans-Canada Highway. Covering a good forty kilometres a day didn't bother young Tulsi too much, but poor Garuda's arthritic ankles caused him some real pain.

This father and son duo were real troopers as we trudged through the towns along the north shore of Georgian Bay. This region is the traditional domain of the *Anishinabek* First Nations peoples. Samuel de Champlain was the first European to explore the area back in 1615, and named it *La Mer Douce*, the calm sea.

One hot Sunday afternoon, we noticed another walker behind us in the distance. It was rare to spot pedestrians in these parts, and we thought it might be a local Sunday stroller. We were curious and saw that this person was wearing a hat, but we couldn't determine a gender.

We soon arrived at the town of Iron Bridge, which was originally named Tally Ho for the call the lumberjacks would make back in the 1800s when they paddled into the trading post there. My companions and I decided to stop for a while on the bridge to watch the river flow by under our feet. This break allowed our mystery walker to catch up, and we decided to wait and greet this fellow foot-traveller.

As the walker got closer, we determined the gender to be male, because under a straw hat with its curved brim, there was a beard. Dressed in shirt and shorts, this guy could have passed for a yodeller from the Alps. He was at least six feet tall, and as he approached, I realized I knew him. It was George, and I was baffled to see him way out here in the middle of the Algoma wilderness.

I first met the very quiet and unassuming George years before at Toronto's Hare Krishna temple. He hung out with us back in the seventies, attending *Bhagavad-gita* classes. I remember how he loved the *prasadam* (blessed food) served at the weekly Sunday Feast.

The *Bhagavad-gita* made such an impact on George that he decided to translate the great book into the Czechoslovakian language. That surely was a noble task for a man who was born in the Czech Republic and wanted to share the wisdom of the *Gita* with his countrymen. He always struck me as a bit of a hippie and free spirit who liked to travel.

Traveller, indeed! Free spirit, for sure! A true-blue *yogi*, perhaps! There he was on the bridge with no backpack and carrying nothing at all. George had heard about my first walk across Canada and was intent on finding me. He kept hitchhiking and walking, seeking me out, and finally found me. He was dropped off by a motorist before following us. He could have waved his arms in the air signaling for us to wait up for him, or even yodelled, but he didn't.

Eccentric, maybe? I always accepted George as a kind of *vairagi*, a very aloof-from-the-world kind of person. We made space for him in our tent that night. Mosquitoes are also voracious in that neck of the woods, and it was good to get under cover.

George trekked along with us the next day, and eventually we came upon Serpent River, a winding flow of water which has a natural water slide and invigorating bathing place. It was a most refreshing discovery and George immediately stripped down to a loin cloth and immersed himself in the cool, clear water. He also picnicked with us as we indulged in the wild blueberries and raspberries we foraged. But then, he just went on his way alone after an inspirational conversation about Krishna. For several hours George had companions, and then went back to wandering solo in the wilderness.

Our paths crossed again in the summer of 2008, on my third Trans-Canada walk, when he showed up out of the blue, this time on Highway 11 in Ontario. I couldn't believe my eyes because there he was again, with nothing but the clothes on his back. He just depended on the provisions that came his way. He figured out where I might be and hitchhiked through that area until he found me.

This time he spent just a few hours walking with me before sticking out his thumb and heading off. During that brief encounter George told me about his excursion to James Bay, way up north, and how he slept in the forest in polar bear country. I wondered how he could hunker down for the night with no sleeping bag or blanket in that harsh wilderness. He had a content look on his face as he described this remarkable adventure. I was in awe and even a bit envious of this vagabond traveller!

Two years later during an annual retreat in India, someone squeezed my arm as I was just about to leave a temple. It was a devotee I recognized from Eastern Europe who asked if I knew George, the guy from the Czech Republic, who used to frequent the temple in Toronto.

"Of course I know George!"

He then told me the man who translated the *Gita* for our *guru* was no longer with us.

Somehow, George had gotten himself across the Atlantic and into Europe. It appears that he was walking, grew tired, went to sleep, and didn't wake up. Apparently, he was high-up in the mountains and froze to death. The devotee who told me this story is a credible person, so I have no reason to doubt his account. And as for George, I haven't seen him since, so it must have been true.

I moved with a heavy heart that day because I admired George, a man who came out to see me twice on my cross-Canada walks. He was a good man who had done some honourable things in his life.

I really miss that man, my friend George.

EVERYTIME I SEE THIS PICTURE OF GEORGE (BEHIND ME) I SHED A TEAR.

CHAPTER 23

I BELIEVE IN EVERYDAY MIRACLES

> "People usually consider walking on water or in thin air a miracle. But I think the real miracle is not to walk on either water or in thin air, but to walk on earth. Everyday we're engaged in a miracle which we don't even recognize: a blue sky, white clouds, green leaves, the black curious eyes of a child–our own two eyes. All is a miracle."
>
> –Thich Nhat Hanh

When the topic of miracles comes up, we almost always think about incredible events of biblical proportions. The parting of the Red Sea so the Israelites could escape the tyranny of the Egyptians, and Jesus walking on water are two miracles that come to mind. Of course, Krishna also was responsible for a large number of miracles which we discover by reading the *Bhagavad-gita As It Is* and the *Srimad Bhagavatam*.

If we keep our eyes open and pay attention, we can experience miracles. Every one of us experiences them in some way, shape, or form and sometimes several times a day. But do we even recognize them? Are we even aware of what is happening around us? Many of these events are challenging to explain and often perceived as mere coincidences, or maybe blessings. Sometimes it's easier to explain a miracle by believing in divine intervention. A miracle often brings a positive message and encourages us to take a leap of faith. I try to regularly take those leaps of faith, and encourage you to do that, as well.

I've experienced many over the years, but three in particular stand out in the course of my walking. While some of you might call these 'mini-miracles', they were certainly significant for me. Taking a good walk at least once a day increases clarity of mind and helps us retain life's little details. I believe walking allows a lot of good things to flow into our brains, from physical things like oxygen and blood, to things we can't see or touch like humility, fascination, and compassion. And if you can trek in an area away from the urban madness—where weapons of mass *distraction* abound—it's all the better. My advice is to pick a peaceful trail.

The first miracle occurred one fine morning in December of 2015. It's the time of year that winter grips my native Canada, but on this occasion, I was blessed with good *karma* and found myself in Hawaii. I was trekking along Highway 99, known as the Kamehameha Highway, on the island of Oahu, heading from the south shore at Pearl Harbour to the north shore, where the surfing waves are awesome.

When I walk like this, I'm almost never in a particular hurry to reach my destination because I'm content to fully experience the journey. I always observe what's around me and have a tendency to take it a step further and become an explorer. I'll look, maybe touch, then perhaps pick or pluck, smell, and maybe even consume. I'm like a big kid in a saffron robe out there, fascinated with the nature of the world and anxious to explore. If something is within arm's reach and up for grabs, I'll go for it (if I'm not imposing on private property).

MIRACULOUS HOW A SMALL CREATURE CARRIES A HUGE STING. HAWAII.

That day in Hawaii was no exception. Coming from the Great White North, my senses were aroused when I spotted a yellowish coloured guava fruit on the ground just lying there beneath its parent, the tree. *Here is something exotic, and a nice little miracle all by itself.* I had been trudging along for a while and figured I deserved and could use a nutritious piece of refreshment. However, I was somewhat reluctant to claim the one gravity had already taken. I figured ants probably had honed in on it and were enjoying a delectable lunch. I picked it up anyway and upon further examination, saw it was slightly bruised from its fall. Not caring for the damaged one, I wondered if there were others. Looking up, way up, the only fruit in sight were several delicious-looking specimens clinging to the uppermost branches of the tree.

I must admit I was overcome with desire and very much wanted one of them. At the exact moment I made that wish, *at that very second*, it happened! The tree released one of its beautiful guavas. It appeared to float down as if in slow motion. It landed softly in some thick grass and rolled gently to a stop at my feet. I bent over, picked it up, and took a moment to examine it. This guava was impeccable, and with its hefty weight, I considered it was about the size of a baseball. I felt the smooth texture of its skin and the fragrant smell of the ripe fruit before offering it to Krishna through the power of *mantra*. I sat down, enjoyed the moment, and indulged. It was succulent and contained multiple seeds. This was nature on demand. It came to me instantly.

Many folks will come up with a 'logical explanation' for what happened, but I'm inclined to say it was a little miracle—a work of divine agency.

Let me set the stage for the next miracle. Decades ago, even before I became a monk, I used to like to check out the *Reader's Digest*. It was often one of the only interesting things I could find to read in rural Ontario. One of those stories had a real impact on me. It was about the magnificent whooping crane and its being added to the official list of endangered species. I was fascinated by the article which stirred in me a sense of urgency. *We humans have to do something to save them!* I don't recall too many details about the content of the article, but I'll never forget the photo of a majestic bird flying in full freedom with its immense wingspan.

As the years and decades passed, occasionally I felt a little sorrow when, out of nowhere, the image of this beautiful creature would glide into my mind when on pilgrimage. I was walking the northern route of the Yellowhead Highway which stretches across Canada's four western-most provinces of Manitoba, Saskatchewan, Alberta, and British Columbia. Garuda, my support person, had just parked his vehicle to spend some time walking with me when I said, "Now that we're here in the Prairies, where the sky is ever before you, have you seen any whooping cranes?" I was flashing back to that old *Reader's Digest* article.

Out of habit, Garuda and I began singing a Sanskrit song in honour of our *guru*, "*Guru Vastakam*." We had no sooner finished the first of eight stanzas, when to my surprise, I peered up into the cloud-cast sky and saw a long, streamlined, whitish bird with wings that would rival an angel. It was soaring and swirling about, and when I pointed it out to Garuda, he was as awestruck as I was. Then, unbelievably, a second, third, and then a fourth mystically emerged out of the clouds above.

"It's the whooping crane!" I shouted, interrupting the song.

"By golly, it is! You just mentioned them a minute ago," said Garuda.

We watched in amazement and returned to our song, having an extraordinary feeling that we were indeed witnessing a miracle. It could not be a coincidence.

Those endangered feathered *magnificos* only stayed with us for a few seconds before disappearing back into the clouds, but they will remain in our hearts for the rest of our lives. Garuda and I both considered what we saw to be a confirmation that there are some things science cannot explain.

I'll leave you with one final miracle, but want to be clear that the word 'final' does not imply there is an end to the workings of the Great Spirit. Miracles, big and small, are continually coming our way in a sacred eternal reality. We just need to open our eyes to *see* them and open our hearts to *receive* them. Little blessings.

Garuda and I would often stay at campsites to take our evening rest. The Ojibwe Campground is located near Sault Ste. Marie in northern Ontario. The operators of this particular establishment must have thought its clients would enjoy listening to music on the local radio station twenty-four hours a day! I must admit, after a short time, I started to feel quite unsettled by the songs blaring over the speakers. They were your standard pop songs, something that was labelled 'bubble-gum music' back in the day.

An especially irritating song was just about over when I said to myself, "Why don't they play something a little more uplifting, like George Harrison?"

Unbelievably, the irritating little ditty faded into oblivion, and George's song, "Awaiting on You All," came over the speakers. The opening lines suggested we don't need a love-in, a bed pan, or microscope, but we need to open up our hearts. He finishes with recommending we chant and get free.

I'll never forget this mini-miracle which brought a smile to my face and a song to my lips.

So, there you have three of the many miracles that I have experienced. If I were to stack up all of the ones which have occurred over the years, I would have a mountain. I have no doubt that spiritual magnitude not only exists, but abounds in the world. Remember, miracles do not have to be of biblical proportions. I encourage you to keep your eyes open and pay attention to the daily miracles that are surely appearing in your life.

Formerly, I was a lost child floating in the universe. Today, I'm a monk with feet planted more firmly on the ground. That's a transformation. That's a miracle. A big one.

Miracles, *grands ou petits*—I love them all!

CHAPTER 24
ROADSPILL OR ROADKILL

"The greatness of a nation and its moral progress can be judged by the way its animals are treated. I hold that the more helpless a creature, the more entitled it is to protection by man from the cruelty of humankind."

–Mahatma Gandhi

Marathon walkers have lots of time to notice many of the details and realities which often escape motorists. The fact that walkers are clumping along at a snail's pace, allows them to see more, hear more, feel more, and experience more. Once you embark on your trekking journey, it doesn't take long to begin experiencing the good, the bad, and the ugly.

With every marathon walk, I am greeted by fresh stool samples, animal droppings, scat, whatever you like to call it. Every country road, main highway, four-lane road, and hiking trail is a toilet for wildlife. Perhaps animals are trying to tell us what they think of our highways and byways.

Canada is my homeland, so I've become familiar with what lurks, crawls, or flies there, as well as what drops there. It's quite common in bear country to see fresh piles of dung left by the furry fellows. You can learn a lot about bears by looking at their stool. After hibernation the colour of their feces is dark because they have been consuming the sweet, dark plant life that is first to shoot up out of the ground in the spring. Later in the summer bear dung is more reddish, a result of wild berry consumption. Seeds are also compacted in their stool samples, which are fairly odourless. I know this because I've scrunched down for a sniff on occasion. You get bored and a little inquisitive out on the road, so sometimes you check things out a little more closely than you normally would.

It may surprise you that coyotes have a similar diet. Like bears, they too are naturally herbivorous, going for young, sweet plants, fruits, and berries. During winter they are forced to hunt rodents in an effort to survive. Coyotes hunting in packs can also bring down a young, old, or weak deer. They have an extensive menu and their stool samples are plentiful on the trails I've trekked. Good stool indicates a healthy life, and from my observations, the creatures of the wild have better quality food than most humans. The quality of what they leave behind can be considered a measure of success.

There is life and there is death here on Earth, and the road discloses what lives and what dies. Our highways are an open canvas for smears, splats, and spills of all kinds. This free display of artistry is creative with a variety of textures and colours. Jackson Pollock, the expressionist artist, would be impressed with the drip paintings on the road.

Red is the most pronounced colour in the road's artistic renderings. The motorist is the artist, and what he leaves behind reveals much about the death circumstance. I walk, look, am disgusted, and then walk away. Viewing animal droppings is much more pleasant than peering at a strewn, smashed carcass. By glancing quickly at the mess, I can't help but wonder if this is the main ingredient of hamburgers and other meat. Intestines, blood, flesh, muscle, bone, and stool all mixed together; how could anyone? I mean, really. Sometimes the road exposes the alarming truth.

Early one morning before sunrise, a speeding truck veered over to avoid me as I walked along the shoulder of the road. He missed me, but hit an unfortunate deer, causing a bloody explosion. All sorts of deer parts went flying through the air, missing me, but creating a horrible mess on the guy's truck. I felt sorry that one of God's beautiful creatures had been destroyed, but was thankful the driver missed the monk.

I do not intend to gross-out the reader, but want to make a point that walkers don't kill animals with their feet. Tires, bumpers, hoods, grills, and speed do. Just how many creatures die from fatalities on our roadways globally each day? Can anyone guess? It's an astronomical figure for sure. In the continental United States, it is estimated that more than one million vertebrate animals are run down by motorists every day.

Do animals deserve this? Not likely. We humans might think we play a role as agents in the balance of eco-recycling, but we could be a little more sensitive. When our pets are struck by a car and our dog or cat becomes a statistic on the list of deceased critters, we lament. But many of us have a cavalier attitude when a creature of the wild, a pet of nature, gets smoked on the road.

We draw interesting lines of discrimination. In India, the thought of killing a cow for food is abhorrent, while in the west, we think nothing of it. In most western countries the thought of killing a dog and eating it is thoroughly disgusting, but in a dozen or more countries dog meat is a desired delicacy.

It really would be best if humans let the animals be, unless they attack us, and we have no choice but to defend ourselves. Animals are human-like, biologically and psychologically. These kindred spirits are our brothers and sisters. Knowing this, a growing number of human beings have taken up the more favourable vegetarian and vegan diets.

The list of roadkill species is lengthy. Racoons are blinded and confused by headlights and become a standard target. Possums, skunks, squirrels, muskrats, and porcupines are victims, too. Even moose and deer become hypnotized and freeze when headlights blind their eyes at dawn, dusk, and nighttime.

In some areas of Newfoundland and northern Ontario, moose frequently cross the road. During one of my forty-kilometre daily walks, I saw five moose carcasses. Unlike most other critters, one of these massive creatures might just take the motorist out with him. In many places, governments allow an open season on deer and moose, reducing the size of the herd and making hunters happy. It's a form of population control. Animals likely believe our population is too large and would probably call for a human cull, if they could.

Maybe there are just too many motor vehicles on planet Earth piloted by too many fast and senseless drivers.

Walking brings us closer to wildlife because we share the same turf. We observe them and they check us out, as well. It

THIS MOOSE MADE ITS DASH AND WAS STILL ALIVE.

might never go any deeper than that, but a kind of connection or relationship is made, even if the encounter creates fear in either, or both parties. I can't speak for the animals, but from our perspective, sensitivity is enhanced, compassion is increased, and getting close gives us a new appreciation for animals and our shared habitat.

I once cheered for a caterpillar to make it across the road unharmed as a massive truck headed his way. I did the same for a salamander I noticed on a road down in Pennsylvania as a truck pulling a travel trailer roared toward the poor creature. The truck missed him, but the RV wheels rolled right over the beautiful fellow who was prematurely reincarnated.

Another time a snapping turtle was slothing along as traffic rolled toward her both ways on a two-lane highway. The turtle was a good two feet long and prehistoric in appearance. I pointed at the turtle and waved down the driver of the first vehicle. The motorist stopped, and so did the turtle. She drew her head, legs, feet, and tail into her shell.

She was obviously intimidated by the metal monster in front of her. Another car came, and then another, and the queue of vehicles continued to grow in the eastbound and westbound lanes. I kept letting the drivers know that there was a vulnerable creature on the road, just in case they couldn't see the humble soul. Traffic stayed at a standstill, and so did the turtle.

What were the motorists to do, stay there forever? So, right there on the spot, I volunteered to become a wildlife crossing guard. What a sight—a monk in saffron robes, waving drivers onto the shoulder of the road to pass the frightened turtle. Traffic inched around like the rickshaws in India that roundabout the cows. Eventually, the traffic disappeared and almost immediately the turtle poked out a head, four legs, and a tail, before making her way to freedom, crossing the second half of the highway at an ever-so-slow pace. So long, happy camper!

THE ROAD IS A PLACE OF LIFE AND DEATH.

Humans cannot claim a true monopoly on the world. We must be fair and share the land and waterways with other creatures. Our highways are impositions and corridors of slaughter for millions of animals. We stake claims on the land, but why such big claims? Beijing has a highway, which in one area where the toll booths are, boasts fifty lanes. That's tragic! There likely won't be too many pandas crossing the road there.

Maybe there's a better way to travel and transport all the things we think we need. At the very least, we can slow down and cause fewer casualties. People are impervious to all of the insects who get smashed on the front of their windshields. When creatures increase in size, it tends to get our attention, especially if that creature is a moose. With new auto sales of more than eighty million each year, we can expect more wildlife and human deaths.

The World Health Organization reports 1.3 million people are killed in motor vehicle accidents every year. That's one human death every twenty-five seconds! Maybe we should all try to drive a little less and walk a little more. That way we'll see more, hear more, feel more, and experience more.

My fellow humans, I appeal to you, be smart and have a heart. Put your heart and feet together and remember, when you walk, you rock!

CHAPTER 25

MANY RETURNS TO A FAMILIAR DOOR

"So I say to you, ask and it will be given to you; search and you will find; knock and the door will be open for you."

–Jesus Christ

I've walked across Canada four times and gotten to know this country's geography pretty well. I've gone west to east and east to west, travelled highways, byways, portions of the Trans-Canada Trail (now referred to as the Great Trail), sideroads, backroads, short-cuts, and lots of other pathways in this great nation. I've visited many different towns and villages along the way and met some great folks. I've also met people who were indifferent to what I was doing, and still others who were borderline hostile.

I've learned that if you travel across Canada, no matter which route you take, you are bound to go through one specific small village in Ontario. It is quite uncanny that crossing Canada you have to funnel through Rosslyn, located just west of Thunder Bay. All roads, including Highways 11 and 17, seem to bottleneck through that town. It's a place you just can't avoid.

It was a hot day during the summer of '96, on my first marathon walking excursion, when I first dragged my feet into Rosslyn. I was tired, sore, exhausted, and extremely thirsty. I had been on the road for days in northern Ontario and must have been a sight.

"Hey!" shouted one of two lads relaxing on a deck. "Ya wanna beer?"

His timing was perfect. Perhaps he was a mind reader. More than likely, he saw how I was slagging along under the hot sun and felt sorry for me. It was hot enough sitting under the shade of their deck umbrella.

"No thanks, I'm a monk; I don't drink beer," I said. "But I sure would like to have a glass of cold water."

"Sure, come on up," the guy said.

I took a few strides from the shoulder of the road to the gravel driveway, to the grassy lawn, and then up the steps to the deck. I shook hands with these fellas, sat down, and told them about my walking mission. I didn't venture into deep spiritual subjects. I could tell they weren't really ready for that, but their spirit of kindness was well appreciated. My new friends got me some water and I was able to quench my thirst and take a little rest in the shade. I was relieved to know there were real people out there who were willing to help out a stranger walking through their town.

We chatted for a few minutes, with them sipping their beer and me downing a couple of glasses of water. Then I moved on, hoping this brief encounter might lead to some future contact involving spiritual conversation. With that in mind, I hit the road again.

Some days, people, especially motorists, don't seem to notice you when you are plodding along the side of the road. I often get the feeling they are so caught up in their own bubble that they just don't care about their fellow human beings, like that time when hitchhiking and feeling abandoned, I hit that major crossroads in life and decided to become a monk.

The calendar pages flipped through months and years until they reached 2003. I was on my second trek through Canada. This time around, I went the opposite direction and saw the country from a totally different perspective, going east to west.

My timing for the 2003 venture was synchronized with the airing of a documentary, *The Longest Road*, by the National Film Board of Canada, about the history of the Trans-Canada Highway. It was highly publicized, and I was featured as 'the thread', as the producers put it, to link the various stories of the good and the bad involving the construction of Canada's 'main drag'. The Trans-Canada Highway is the longest continuous ribbon of road in the world, and the documentary viewed it through the eyes of a monk.

I was well into the second walk, approaching Rosslyn once again, when it dawned on me that I knew someone there. I had fond memories of the kindness I received from the two guys on the deck. I remembered which side of the road the house was on, and kept an eye open for that one-storey, fifties type of humble home.

It wasn't long before I spotted it. I saw not two, but one fellow at the end of the driveway. He had a stocky build and was bigger than the boys I knew. In any event, I proceeded to try reconnecting. The fellow's back was to me. He had a chainsaw in his hands and was wearing industrial earmuffs to contend with the noise made while cutting up a birch tree.

I didn't want to tap him on the shoulder while he was running the chainsaw because he was absorbed in cutting wood; it was likely to be firewood to ward off the cold of the upcoming northern Ontario winter. I was less apt to startle him if I walked around and stood in front of him. I wanted to see if he even remembered me—that's if he was one of the same guys I met in 1996.

The chainsaw was working hard chewing its way through the birch, when the man noticed my feet, then *dhoti* (lower robe), and *kurta* (upper robe). He stood erect and immediately hit the kill switch to silence the chainsaw. He removed his earmuffs and stood staring at me.

"Hello, I'm the monk who came here in '96; I'm walking across the country for the second time," I explained. "Are you one of the two guys I met here then?"

"No, I'm Ken, and I bought this place from them," he replied. "Now, what did you say you are doing?"

"I'm walking across Canada for the second time," I said.

"Well, let me shake your hand," Ken replied.

We talked for a bit and I told him all the good reasons for my walking adventures. He was impressed and found it novel to meet a monk way out there in northern Ontario. I, in turn, found it special to have a meaningful chat with someone, who among other things, was a lumberjack. Perhaps our paths would cross again.

Time moved along swiftly, as it always does, and I soon contemplated a third walk. It wasn't hard to come up with reasons to strike out across Canada on foot again. I longed for the open road once more and wanted to have the time of my life seeing different trails, making new friends, physically challenging myself, and sharing Krishna consciousness and the philosophy of self-realization.

Health was a big factor that made me want to do it again. I'll never forget the day my dear humble monk friend, Bhakti Tirtha Swami, passed away from cancer at the age of fifty-five. Like other Hare Krishna monks who pioneered the cultural movement with roots from India, Bhakti Tirtha Swami, was determined to share Krishna consciousness with the world.

So, in 2008 I set out again, this time from Vancouver, British Columbia, to St. John's, Newfoundland. When I arrived in central Canada, and that long stretch of northern Ontario highway, I once again approached Rosslyn. It was bright and early when I came upon that same bungalow with the deck in front of it. I wondered how my friend Ken was making out.

Even though it was barely 7:00 a.m., I walked up the gravel driveway, across the grassy lawn, up the steps, across the deck, and knocked on the front door. No answer. Again, I knocked. No answer. And again. Silence.

Defeated at not having the opportunity of greeting my friend and perhaps planting a seed of *bhakti* (devotion), I turned to leave. I took a few strides down Ken's driveway and was ready to leave the home forever when I heard a door slam in the back. I turned around, and what looked like Ken's back was proceeding to the car. There was a female next to him and she had a baby in her arms.

"Hey Ken, isn't that your monk friend?" she asked.

"Yeah, it sure is!" replied Ken.

Ken had expanded his empire with a family since I had last seen him. Yes, it was good to see him again, although this encounter was briefer than our first meeting. Their little bambino was being taken to the hospital, and for this reason our exchange was short but sweet. Both Ken and I, and now Betty, anticipated meeting at the same crossroads again. But, for now it was, "So long!"

A pertinent comment to make in this juncture of the story is that although I've chosen celibacy as my way of life, I'm all for family values. I always hope in my heart that most people find a life partner and settle down in a way that's conducive for physical and spiritual wellbeing. These two components make a person whole. "Strive for a sweet balance," is what I say to travellers or nesters like Ken and Betty.

Since I am a monk and don't share life with a woman, occasionally people ask me how I get my physical thrills. My answer is: in devotional life there's plenty of stimulation. I've got music, dance, food, philosophy, and a chance to hug, which is sufficient for me. Fulfillment reached.

Flipping ahead to 2012 with my fourth cross-Canada trek, I came upon that modest place once again. Yes, the house was still standing. I really wondered how many more offspring Ken and Betty might have. That first toddler would be four or five by now. As I got close to that now familiar house, I could hear some commotion inside. I knocked on the door. Nothing. Did so again. Still nothing. With all the noise going on, people inside couldn't hear me. I became a little more aggressive with my knocking. Finally, a man with a rather large frame appeared.

I immediately got the feeling my timing was not very good.

"Yeah! Whad'ya want?" asked the irritable man shouting in an intimidating tone.

"I'm sorry to disturb you, but my friend Ken…" I started to say.

"He's not here anymore!" the man shouted.

"Oh, I see. I met him when I was walking…"

"He's moved! He doesn't live here anymore!"

"Where can I find him?"

My question was answered by the slam of the door in my face. I suppose I asked too many questions. Frankly, I thought he was going to fetch his moose-hunting gun if I didn't leave the property. That would have been the stereotypical hillbilly response.

My conclusion is that in making repeated visits to one home, I had born witness to various incarnations of sorts, of souls travelling from one physical domain to the next. In this case, I had focused on one house where I observed the occupants coming and going. I'm sure there's a verse in the *Vedas* which could be used to better explain this situation.

I was sorry I missed Ken, but my intuition tells me I'll meet him again. If I ever do a fifth trek across Canada, I'll likely stop at the bungalow with the deck once more, to see what new realities and adventures happen when the door opens.

THE FIRST OCCUPANTS OF THE HOUSE I VISITED ON ALL MY CANADIAN WALKS.

A door must be like the Creator. It sees many people passing through, coming and going.

CHAPTER 26

INDIGENOUS GOODNESS

"When I fought to protect my land and my home, I was called a savage. When I neither understood nor welcomed his way of life, I was called lazy. When I tried to rule my people, I was stripped of any authority."

–Chief Dan George

I was freshening up in the men's washroom at the Ojibwe Campsite when he walked in.

"Why are you walkin' across Canada?" he sternly asked.

"For the spiritual healing of the nation," I responded.

"Spiritual healin'?"

By the slur of his words and the way he staggered in, I could tell he was under the influence of some kind of intoxicating liquor.

"Only us Indians know how to do spiritual healing," he replied.

"Many years ago, I adopted a culture that has its origins in India, and spiritual healing has been a big part of that culture. It's called *Ayurveda*. It's a culture that's been around for a long time," I explained.

"You're white and you don't do no spiritual healin'!" he said, while continuing to stagger about.

I could see that our conversation wasn't going to be overly productive, so I resisted saying anything more and proceeded to brush my teeth.

"You white men do no healin'," were his closing words as he went out the door.

I could have tried to reason with him, debate the issue, or get into an argument, but that didn't seem like a reasonable thing to do. I wanted to tell him I was sorry for the unforgivable things my European ancestors had done to his people. As the door closed behind him, any thought of a two-way dialogue seemed like a dream and could only remain a dream unless we both tried again.

I wanted to tell him I admired his people and sympathized with what they've endured over centuries of abuse. Before becoming a monk, I was interested in a career in social work focused on the Indigenous people of Canada. Fine arts and a desire to assist Native people of the north were the two vocational options I had considered so many years ago.

We should be sensitive to the reality of history and understand that there remains confusion among those noble and big-hearted people because there are too many unresolved matters to be settled, including disputed land claims.

On September 6th 1996, I literally stepped into one of those confusing situations while walking along the shores of the gorgeous coastal waters of Lake Huron in Ontario. I was near Ipperwash when a local First Nations man pulled his car over to offer me a ride.

"No thanks," I said delivering a well-rehearsed line. "I'm doing a walk for the spiritual healing of the nation."

"Do you know that today is the first anniversary of the death of Dudley George?" he asked.

"I'm sorry," I replied. "I don't know Dudley George."

He was surprised, but then told me how Dudley led a peaceful protest over the misappropriated sacred burial land of his people. The Crown had confiscated the land to use for a military training base during World War II, but after the war was over the land was never returned. Dudley George was shot by a policeman, angering the Ipperwash people who were also upset about the unfair land dealings.

There was a huge sign posted at Ipperwash informing people that genocide had taken place there. I could feel tension in the air. Apparently, a delegation from Ottawa, the Canadian capital, was to arrive that very day to open communication and begin to negotiate with the distraught Native people.

I told my motorist friend that I was happy to be informed, and recently while trekking along, I met a Native woman, Janet Cloud. She, like many others, was living in tight quarters in the old Second World War era army barracks. We chatted through a tall, formidable fence, and I told her what I was doing as a pilgrim. I wanted to know more about her ways, her people, and her culture. She invited me inside, but I would have to enter through the main gate. I made my way to the entrance of the compound where I was met by an informal security person. I told him Janet Cloud had invited me to come in for a visit.

He knew her and was informed I was walking across Canada, but didn't know if he could let me in. I was referred to another person, and soon more men came out of nearby buildings out of curiosity, perhaps even thinking I was some kind of security threat. I don't believe they had ever seen a monk before, and my presence ignited a commotion of uncertainty. Within seconds at least fifty people surrounded me and no one could decide whether to let me in. Finally, a voice from afar yelled out, "Hey! Remember me?" All heads turned to the source. A forty-something man, of stout build, with a happy face, and a single braid down his back, continued, "Yeah, the peace walk we did on the west coast!"

That remark alone seemed to relax the crowd. I admit to not being on that walk, but I more or less went along with it. It seemed like a good icebreaker, and being recognized by a respected member of the community seemed to calm the crowd.

The tense situation was resolved and I was finally allowed to visit Janet Cloud, who introduced me to some of the elders. They were all very kind in sharing their views on life. What really struck me were the parallels between the beliefs of the Chippewa nation and my own traditional, and what theologians call 'Vaishnava' beliefs, which in India is well established.

In fact, this reminds me of my Hindu friends, some of the first immigrants of Indian origin in Nova Scotia. Soon after arriving in Canada's Ocean Playground, they decided to have a celebration for Diwali, the Hindu New Year. They did a big promotion inviting *all* the Indians to the event and guess what? The Punjabis, Gujaratis, and other new Indian immigrants came, and so did the Indigenous peoples with their feathers and drums.

My encounters with Indigenous peoples have taught me a lot about their way of life. I've participated in the beating of drums in Alberta, husking harvested wild rice in Ontario, and worked alongside folks who were tanning deer hides among the jack pine forests of British Columbia. We also shared sounds, *mantras*, knowledge, and wisdom. Their teachings come from their elders, and mine from the ancient *Vedas*. We've sat happily together sharing our spiritual traditions, but I must admit I declined the opportunity to smoke the peace pipe.

Our Indigenous peoples love to sing, dance, eat, and walk. But they have been treated atrociously by European settlers who came to conquer them and violently convert them to Christian religions, stripping them of their dignity and noble values. The last of Canada's nightmarish residential schools closed for good in the 1990s. The time has come for reconciliation.

I've walked across Canada four times and have visited many villages, towns, and cities. But I can honestly say that one particular First Nations town is Canada's most friendly community.

Back in 2003 when I was trekking across Nova Scotia, I took the road off the beaten path through Eskasoni. It's a small First Nations village with just a few hundred people, yet considered to be the largest Mi'kmaq community in the world. Early that morning, as I approached the town it was starting to sprinkle and there was a threat of more serious rain to come. A woman who had attended my talk in Sydney, a city in Cape Breton, pulled her car over and generously offered me an expensive red Gore-Tex coat to shield me from the rain. That was a true act of kindness.

That day in the *Cape Breton Post*, a small picture with a modest caption about my walk, appeared on the obituary page. I was confused and wondered why the newspaper put my story there.

"Relax, Swami," a local man told me. "In Cape Breton, everyone reads the obituary page!"

As I ambled along and passed by a Mi'kmaq daycare centre, two teachers anxiously ran out to greet me. They carried the clipping of the article from the *Cape Breton Post* and asked for an autograph. We talked a bit and I explained Krishna was the name I used for God. They replied that their name for the Creator in the Mi'kmaq language is *Kisulkw*. They, then, returned to tend to the beautiful children in their care.

Soon after, an Indigenous man came along in a pickup truck, rolled down his window, and offered a golfer's umbrella, saying, "I think you could use this."

Another motorist pulled over just as I started to move on. He opened his wallet and whipped out a bill, offering a generous donation to support my walk. Word had obviously gotten out that a monk was in town, and it seemed everyone wanted to meet me. The next thing I knew, a school bus had stopped right in the middle of the road and a dozen or more First Nations students poured out. The rain was a little heavier now and they automatically gravitated to my humongous new umbrella. Seeing my robes, they looked up curiously and asked what I was doing.

"I'm walking across Canada."

"What for?" several of them asked in unison.

"To encourage people to be more spiritual, get back to the basics, and back to the land."

They seemed to understand and looked up at me through their wondrous, delightful eyes. Then they got back in their bus to be delivered to their respective homes. The rains came pouring down with much more gusto, so I decided to retreat to the general store, the only shop in town. I stepped inside and was greeted by perhaps the only Caucasian person in the village. She was an older woman who resembled Granny from the old *Beverly Hillbillies* television show.

"Oh, you're the monk who's doing the walking!" she exclaimed. "Well, you can take anything off any of the shelves that you like or need."

I was overcome by the warmth of the people of Eskasoni, and even somewhat stunned. I didn't grab anything off the shelves, but felt overwhelmed by the generosity of the residents of this tiny place.

When the rain let up a bit and I dared to brave the road again, I had one final encounter with those good folks. Just on the edge of town, a very animated fellow greeted me warmly.

"You came to our town," he said in a somewhat befuddled way. "No one ever comes to our town."

He paused for a moment, and in an explosion of joy, blurted out, "Thanks! Thanks for coming!"

The response from the residents of Eskasoni was so heartwarming, I will never ever forget the way they greeted and treated me. It was a real lesson in just how sweet humans can really be. It's time we all work together to right the injustices and heal the wounds suffered by Indigenous peoples all around the world.

CANADA'S FIRST NATIONS/INDIGENOUS ARE A TRULY GENTLE PEOPLE.

I really empathize with the earliest guardians of North America. I offer my *dandavats*, with my body outstretched on the ground in respect to them and *Kisulkw*.

CHAPTER 27

LESSONS IN LUST AND LOVE

"Humans like to think of themselves as a faithful species, but when it comes to true fidelity, many other animals offer better examples of how to keep a relationship together."

–Bryan Nelson

Strange things seem to happen to me in the early morning hours, right around the time the sun rises in the eastern sky. I always like to get an early start and am often out on the road before the sun comes up.

There I was, minding my own business, heading westbound on Highway 2 in southern Ontario. I have a tendency to wave at people when traffic is light and with Sunday morning unveiling herself, I felt optimistic that folks would be a little more laid back and friendly, than they would on a workday morning. With this in mind, I was especially enthusiastic in giving those few passing motorists a joyful wave-of-the-hand.

As the next vehicle approached, I smiled and issued my best wave of the day. The middle-aged, bespectacled woman drove on by, but suddenly for some reason unknown to me, slowed down, made an abrupt U-turn, and then drove right up beside me. The next thing I know she pops out of the car, followed by a Labrador Retriever. With the car door wide open, I could hear Johnny Cash singing on the radio. It was his iconic "I Walk the Line," a song written and recorded in 1956, which sold over two million records, and became Johnny's first number one hit. As this bizarre scene played out in front of me, Cash crooned his song.

With the man in black singing away, the woman came staggering toward me, so I figured she may have been coming from an all-night party. She said in a seductive voice, "What are you doing?"

"I'm a monk on my fourth walk across Canada, and I'm trying to promote pilgrimage," I quickly replied.

"Well, I know a beautiful spot down in the valley where the sun is coming up over the river; we can go there," she said with a wink and a grin.

Even I could see that this was a clear proposition! I nervously expressed that I had a commitment to stay on the road so my support person could catch up to me. With that comment her enthusiasm began to wane.

But she wasn't eager to give up so easily and again issued an invitation to go down to the river with her.

"Ma'am, I'm a celibate monk and I have my mission," I interjected somewhat coldly.

Johnny Cash wasn't helping matters and I cringed every time he sang, "because you're mine." But I focused on "walking the line" as I was determined to stay the course and continue on my chosen mission.

Finally, the woman gave up, and the dog barked goodbye as they sped off down the road. What a way to start the day! I hope she eventually finds her true love, the Creator.

There have been a few other occasions when motorists, both women and men, have attempted those kinds of persuasions. Each time I took the opportunity to let the pursuant of the flesh know I wasn't interested, and that there's a greater love out there, more profound, deep, and endearing than we can ever imagine.

All of this talk about lust reminds me of an incident of real love which I encountered along a lonely highway. Back in the summer of 1996, during my first Trans-Canada walk, I was going eastbound on Highway 11 in Ontario, when I saw a creature in the distance moving around on the shoulder of the road. The animal became unsettled as I approached, and then began to expand itself, and abruptly, with an incredible wingspan, ascended into the air. It was the glorious great blue heron.

Up, up and away it ascended in graceful flight, but there was something left behind on the side of the

WITH LUST WE ARE LOST. WITH LOVE WE ARE ABOVE.

road. I knew the heron is carnivorous, but almost always feeds in the water, so what could it be? Soon my steady stride revealed the object was not prey but the dead mate of the beautiful heron now in flight. He must have been struck by a vehicle and killed instantly right there on the road. Sprawled out with gorgeous wings in a motionless state, his head, beak, and body were lifeless. It was a fresh kill; there was no deterioration of the body and the crows and raccoons had yet to discover their latest roadside meal.

Instantly my soul felt gripped by fate's ugly side. I resented that the culprit, a car or truck, had done this deadly deed, killing a beautiful bird and bringing pain and despair to its mate. Had this happened to a pair of crows, I might have been less sentimental, because, like most people, I have preferences or partialities toward some species over others.

The slender great blue heron is the largest heron in North America. It has a certain poise and dignity about it, and I've enjoyed watching this amazing creature fly across the sky and land in shallow waters. It is one of nature's gifts to the universe.

It's dedication, loyalty, and commitment is admirable. That's true love beyond romance. For the rest of that day the image of those two lovers, one in flight, and one dead along the side of the road, plagued my mind. The great blue heron offers us a lesson, and on that day, these two birds provided a stunning example of what it really means for two earthly creatures to be in love. They were true *gurus*!

"Here (in this world) lust is going on in the name of love. And because it is not love, it doesn't continue very long - it breaks." Words from my *guru*, Srila Prabhupada.

CHAPTER 28

HELPFUL HUGS

"They lower blood pressure, alleviate fears and relieve stress and that's just the tip of the beneficial iceberg that can come from a good, hearty hug."

–Huffington Post

A hug is an international act of affection that transcends language and culture. The word 'hug' probably originated somewhere in Scandinavia and may have been borrowed from the Norse word *hugga*, which means 'to comfort'. It may also be related to the word *hugr* which loosely translated means 'courage'.

No one seems to know when the activity of hugging actually began, but we do know it is a universal gesture that expresses our need to be physically connected in a way that transcends words. I believe hugging has existed since the earliest days of humans.

I admit, I'm a hugger, and sometimes I even hug trees. Sometimes folks just need some love or encouragement, and a hug is a handy way to let them know you care. Sometimes, in certain situations, it's the only thing I can think of to do, and oftentimes it works better than words.

On one of my four walks across Canada, I came across a guy who was staggering along old Highway 1 near Calgary, Alberta. I could tell by his stride and unkempt appearance that he was perhaps a little tipsy. But I was happy to see him, especially since it had been several hours since I had any social interaction with a fellow human being.

As we met, I stopped and immediately gave him a warm hug. I'll bet it was the first time that a white man ever gave a hug to this particular Indigenous fellow. The embrace was a spontaneous reaction. I felt it was the easiest and most genuine way to express my gratitude for him being there. He seemed stunned, right there on the shoulder of the road, when I put my arms around him and said, "Hare Krishna." The encounter was brief, but he accepted the gesture, and I could tell after his initial surprise, he was okay with it, it showed on his face.

"The face is the index of the mind," my *guru* used to say.

We are not these bodies, we are spirit souls. That's something I try to remember every time I meet someone. In this case, the man and I met as total strangers, and the next second we became friends. The conversation was short, but the meaningful hug said more than words could convey.

HUGS ON THE TRAIL PUSH YOU ALONG.

While continuing my way on Alberta's Highway 1, my thoughts turned to another occasion where a hug came in handy. I was in Jagannath Puri, one of the most holy places in India, when my old pal, insomnia, came to visit while I was trying to get some rest.

Puri is a city on the Bay of Bengal, and residents and visitors alike are blessed by the constant sights and sounds of ocean waves lapping onto its beach. So, unable to sleep, I went out, hoping a stroll on the beach would help me become peacefully tired. It was 1:30 a.m., and there I was walking and chanting with my *japa* (meditation) beads in my hand, when two young local men approached me.

"Where are you from?" they sternly asked.

"Canada," I said.

"What are you doing?" they questioned.

"I always go for walks in the morning," I replied.

The two chaps misunderstood my accent. 'Morning' to them, sounded like 'money'.

I tried to explain, "No, not money, *morning*. Now! Before afternoon."

From there the conversation went nowhere intellectually or socially. They had too many empty questions, and I just wanted to terminate my interaction with them. I was uneasy, feeling their motives were leaning more toward the dark side.

Even though I genuinely love Indian folk, my strategy was to quickly end this particular encounter. So, I decided to give them a hug. Perhaps it would have a disarming effect. I went to each of them and offered a short but purposeful bold bear hug. The recipients became silent with the unexpected gesture and it seemed to stop, for the moment at least, any further discussion.

"Namaste. Hare Krishna!" I boldly proclaimed.

I ambled off, chanting *Hare Krishna*, and left them basically standing there confused. I couldn't help but think that these guys were thieves operating under the cover of darkness, so I was relieved to get away. While forging ahead and not looking back, I dodged the incoming ocean tide lapping up onto the beach.

With no one else about, I thought I would take extra precaution in case they came back. The watch on my wrist was concealed by my sleeve. I did recall them asking for the time, and without looking at my watch I had answered with the approximate hour and minute. I took the watch off and placed it in my bead bag.

I continued walking and chanting, but soon noticed two very elongated and distorted shadows stretched along the sand and quickly coming my way. I stopped, turned and looked to see the source. It was the same guys who I had just met. They quickly approached me with cold glaring stares, foregoing the superficial smiles they had exhibited earlier.

"We want money!" they demanded.

"I'm a monk and don't have any money," I declared.

Then one fellow reached out and started to frisk me. What could I do? I let him do his search and as he did so, the second guy placed his right hand to the back of his jean pocket as if to pull out a knife. The frisker searched me from top to bottom, and then grabbed the bead bag that was dangling from my neck. He felt the beads and on top of them discovered something else—the watch. He pulled it out of the bag and with a victorious gesture let his friend know he had hit the jackpot. Little did he know, the watch was only worth about five dollars. He immediately dashed off with the prize while the second fellow stepped toward me and formed the traditional *pranams* with his hands.

"Sorry!" he said with his head slightly waggling, before turning to quickly follow his buddy, struggling while running through the soft sand.

Maybe there was some guilt for stealing from a *swami*? Despite this encounter with petty thieves, I still love India. Even small-time criminals have a little bit of culture.

Two years later, I came back to Puri on a pilgrimage with a group of devotee associates. It was broad daylight when we trudged through the sand on the same beach. I was talking to my companions about Jagannath, the prominent deity of Krishna, who draws hundreds of thousands of pilgrims to the city each year. Many come for the big *Ratha Yatra* festival.

Just then, I saw the watch thief flogging some trinkets.

"Hey, you don't remember me, do you?" I challenged with a disdained look.

Apparently, he did not, because I'm sure he has many clients. At least he looked as if he now was working hard, earning his keep by selling stuff. Or perhaps he steals by night and sells by day, still not making him the best of men.

But who am I to judge? We all are on our own paths. Decisions we make in this lifetime will determine what kind of existence we'll have in the next.

Hugs really are an international act of affection transcending language and culture. I still am a hugger, although there are times and places where I am somewhat reluctant to go out walking after midnight.

CHAPTER 29

MY LONGEST DAY

"You have competition every day because you set such high standards for yourself that you have got to go out every day and live up to that."

–Michael Jordan

I'm a really disciplined and competitive monk. Growing up in the 1950s and '60s on a small rural Ontario farm, instilled a work ethic that still drives me onward today. My competitiveness is more with myself than my fellow monks or other people. As I grow older, this self-competitive nature has waned a little, but is still ingrained in my mind and body.

Back when I was forty-three, my competitive nature was in full bloom. That was 1996, the year I did the first of four cross-Canada walks. I knew if I were to complete this almost 8,000-kilometre marathon before winter set in, I would have to start early in April, set a torrid pace, and keep it up all the way from British Columbia to Newfoundland.

I felt justified hustling along the highways and trails because I anticipated disagreeable weather by the time I reached the finish line in St. John's. This epic endeavour would cover ten provinces and take the better part of eight months. That included an extra month for dipping down into the central part of the country, where the bulk of the population resides. My desire to walk through southern Ontario would not only add additional time, but extra distance as well.

So, there I was in Canada's western-most province, about to begin the walk on April 12th, 1996. I had smartly figured out the average distance I would have to walk every day in order to complete my journey. I had to get used to kilometres instead of miles, which was a bit of a challenge. I grew up with inches, pounds, feet, and miles, but Canada went metric in 1971. During this gradual transition, I became a monk, and although not completely reclusive, I was somewhat removed from the workings of the world and missed out on Canada's metric conversion education.

It turned out I could reach my walking goal by averaging forty-two kilometres, or twenty-six miles a day. I was pleasantly surprised to discover later that this is the distance for a marathon walking or running event. The first organized marathon was held in Athens in 1896 at the first Olympic Games of the modern era. The ancient games, which took place in Greece from around 776 B.C. to A.D. 393, never included such long-distance races.

The idea for the modern marathon was inspired by the legend of an ancient Greek messenger who raced from the town of Marathon to Athens with the news of an important Greek victory over an invading army of Persians in 490 B.C. After running the forty-kilometre route and making his announcement, the exhausted messenger collapsed and died.

For the next few Olympics, the length of the marathon remained roughly the same distance; but when the games came to London in 1908, the course was extended. Apparently, Queen Alexandra wanted the race to start on the lawn of Windsor Castle so the royal children could watch from the window of their nursery. The finish line was in front of the royal box at the Olympic stadium, a distance that just happened to be 26.2 miles. The boost in mileage stuck, and in 1921 the length for a marathon was formally standardized at 26.2 miles (42.195 kilometres).

For me it was a cinch, an easy task, in the beginning, to maintain a pace of a good forty kilometres per day. Some days were challenging because of time away from the road for speaking engagements, always on the topic of *bhakti* yoga. Reaching people with messages from the *Bhagavad-gita* and other Vedic texts, was part of the reason for the walk.

After working hard to cross several mountain ranges and their carved-out highways in British Columbia and Alberta, I easily moved through the cool windswept foothills. But it was in Saskatchewan that I really hit my stride. One fine day, I hit seventy-three kilometres, but by the time I reached southern Ontario, I was determined to beat my previous record. In September, I reached the Niagara River at Fort Erie, where Lake Erie funnels into the river, eventually ending up at the massive horseshoe-shaped Niagara Falls.

I decided this was a good time and place to set a new personal best. It was the celebratory day of Radharani, traditionally called *Radhastami*, known by many *bhakti* yoga practitioners as the day of the Goddess (God as female). Radharani is Krishna's counterpart, or His divine girlfriend. That gave me a huge incentive to go big, in terms of distance, whether my feet liked it or not. To accompany me and give me an extra boost, was the Niagara River—fast running with some serious rapids.

It's a big advantage when you walk beside a river, especially one whose current is flowing in the same direction you are heading. Over the years, rivers have become my *amigos*, my liquid friends, whereas roads and trails are my dry friends. On this day I even got intimate with my liquid friend by plunging into its waters to find relief from the heat, far enough away from the current not to be swept away.

Another dear friend joined me for part of the walk that day, a human friend, a colleague whom I shared time with at the Toronto monks' living quarters, or *ashram*. Mark Griffiths, aka Murali Krishna, was excited to join the walk and was accompanied by his buddy, Malcolm, and also by his young son, Tyler. It was encouraging to have their company and see their enthusiasm for this long-distance walk of mine.

By the time I reached the Falls, I was tired out, and my walking companions had departed. Nevertheless, I trudged along by the incredible gorge where Niagara's waters flow unceasingly. The night rolled in, and it wasn't particularly easy to see my *amigo* because there was a steep cliff that restricting me from viewing the waters. However, I could hear it, and

ONE OF MY BIGGEST DAYS WALKING ALONG THE NIAGARA RIVER.

that in itself was inspiration enough to keep me going.

My support guy, Madhai, was getting as exhausted as I was, even though he was in a vehicle. Everything was becoming rather quiet, except for the sound of the rushing waters. Madhai and I appeared to be the only ones around as all of the tourists had retired for the day, checking into accommodations for their travellers' sleep.

I trekked past the monstrous turbines that produce hydroelectricity, and my footsteps were slowly transformed into a shuffle. And then they came to a full stop. I decided this was my final step for the day. I could see a sign for the great Canadian landmark, Queenston Heights, a historic site to mark the battle between the United States and Canada, which was still a British colony back in 1812.

We were weary warriors as we examined our map and took note from the vehicle's odometer that I had done a whopping and glorious eighty-

143

one kilometres. Eighty-one! That's LXXXI in Roman numerals. All done for the pleasure of Radharani!

I had a great rest that night, one of the best during the entire trip. Insomnia was not an issue as Madhai took his slumber in the van, and I, in a tent in Murali Krishna's backyard. I guess I was snoring rather loudly because I aroused two of the neighbour's dogs who curiously came sniffing around. Their snouts pushed against the wall of the tent, but I figured they posed no danger. I was so tired that I wasn't bothered by their barking and nudging, and I was content with my new record.

But should it remain at eighty-one?

October 29th was my 178th day of walking. My support consisted of Madhai, Brian Gonsalvez, and a modest Ford Econoline minivan donated by a generous person, Prabhupada Das, of Markham, Ontario. The day before, I had walked through Montreal, and then the city of Trois Rivières, eastbound along Highway 138, accompanied by a spookily Halloween-ish wind.

We parked for the night near the mighty Rivière St. Laurent. Cool air currents tossed leaves about, and a barren tree with colourful branches was silhouetted against a grey sky with one outstretched limb constantly tapping against an old barn's tin roof. As the sombreness of the night became a reality, the only lit object that came into my view was the illumination from a one-eyed monster, someone's TV screen through a window.

The three of us slept well in the comfort of our van, which we parked at some business in the village of Sainte-Anne-de-la-Pérade. Yes, the slumber went well until the gnawing of self-competition woke me and scratched at my heart like a cat's claws digging at thick drapery. My watch read 3:50 a.m. There was no shower and no bathroom facility, so I grabbed my trusty *japa* meditation beads and left a note on the dashboard for my crew to read: "Dear Madhai and Brian, I'm going down the road, eastbound. Catch up to me. I'll be the only monk out there— easy to spot."

The sky was clear. Stars were lit. How auspicious. Also, I had with me my *amigo*, a river, the mighty St. Lawrence. It was my liquid friend, and a couple of hours later it began to glisten as the sun came up over the horizon.

"Let's go!" it seemed to say periodically, like a soft cheerleader. It would vanish at times, obscured by houses, factories, trees, and the like.

Eventually Madhai and Brian came along, and they, too, had 'mooched it up', a term we used meaning to get up and go in the clothes you had slept in. We couldn't waste time looking for a shower, but eventually would wash our faces in a gas station washroom.

"It's going to be a big day, I can feel it" I said. "Just letting you know because I'll need you both at my beck and call."

I trekked through many villages and towns on my longest day. I saw a woman hanging her wet laundry on the clothesline, and a man walking and carrying a garbage bag full of dried autumn leaves. He lost traction and rolled down the front yard slope into a ditch with the leaves now strewn all over. He laughed, and so did I. A good sport, in my books!

While this was happening, the kilometres were accumulating. Forty, fifty, sixty, and then seventy just as night began to creep in, early, as it does that time of year.

"Hey guys, you really gotta pitch in and take shifts to keep me going; one awake, one asleep," I said. "I might need one of those ninety-nine cent bags of peanuts just to keep my senses awake."

"Okay, no problem," the boys replied.

I eventually stopped, sat in the van and drifted off for a minute or two before leaping out the door, as if the enemy had come to attack our home base. Back on the road with renewed vigour, the eighty-kilometre mark was approaching, then eighty-one, and soon eighty-two, breaking my former record. The eighties dragged on slowly as I approached ninety kilometres, another milestone.

ON A SUPER-MARATHON DAY, A NAP IS VERY MUCH NEEDED.

I calculated that by 3:50 a.m. on October 30th, I could reach 100 kilometres. Luckily, by this time there were sidewalks and lampposts to light the way and give me hope during those wee early hours. I came to the precincts of historic Quebec City, then the old iron bridge between Sainte Foy and Levis. I crossed over my liquid friend. Traffic was practically nonexistent, and it was then I realized Madhai and Brian were also absent. I guessed they had both bit the dust or the pillow.

Please, Krishna, provide that inexhaustible energy that You, among many things, are known for, even if it be to satisfy my ego.

Confirmation of the mercy of the Divine did come with ninety-one, ninety-two, ninety-three, ninety-four, ninety-five, and ninety-six kilometres. It was now 3:00 a.m., and soon ninety-seven, and then

145

ninety-eight. There it was! I spotted our van at the Desjardins Enterprises expansive parking lot. Smoke was billowing out of the exhaust pipes, a sign that my comrades were inside trying to keep warm.

Twenty-four hours had expired since I began this day's marathon. My watch read exactly 3:50 a.m. when I completed kilometre number ninety-nine. As I approached the van, Madhai opened the door and both he and Brian expressed congratulations. My legs were sore, and as soon as I stopped, they became as stiff as a board. Lifting my right leg to step into the van was quite a strain. Then my left leg followed, and clutching onto a seat, I hoisted myself in before collapsing inside for a complete and deep sleep.

The next morning there was just one little problem as doubt began to creep in. Did we *really* do ninety-nine kilometres? We doubted the van's odometer and with some disbelief, we studied our map, confirming ninety-nine kilometres, or sixty-two miles. The road signs also confirmed the distance, and perhaps the strongest of all testimonies came from the pain in my legs.

Done! The record was broken.

That day we actually encountered a mini-ice storm, and I just didn't have the energy to slide across the countryside. After all, it was supposed to be a cross-Canada *walk*. After a few kilometres and much rest, I prepared to hit the road the next day.

I sometimes question the self-competitive spirit I've had since I was a child. But in this case, I do believe it paid off, driving me to reach a new milestone in my walking pursuits.

A small epiphany: you can never really declare anything done, because just like rebirth, a new project is always on the horizon.

CHAPTER 30

THE TIMES I CRIED ON THE ROAD

"Heaven knows we need never be ashamed of our tears, for they are rain upon the blinding dust of the earth, overlying our hard hearts. I was better after I cried than before–more sorry, more aware of my own ingratitude, more gentle."

–Charles Dickens

One thing I've learned over the years is that you can expect the unexpected during extended walking excursions. My road trips are usually lengthy and consist of putting one foot in front of the other over and over again. It's always an adventure, and sometimes I've been overcome with emotions by spectacular natural scenery. It can be very lonely out there, and at times, for no apparent reason, my mind gets flooded with memories from the past.

If I were to define the word 'adventure' without peeking at my trusty Oxford dictionary, just leaving it to my own whim and experience, it might look like this:

>   ***ad-ven-ture:*** *an exciting and stunning exploration of things; an entering into new, raw, and challenging territory.*

Adventure can also be an exploration of the self, travelling through a time of wonder, triggering memories fine and harsh. It can produce an adrenaline rush and easily push emotional buttons which are self-humbling. With adventure, you are dealing with nothing really predictable in terms of who or what you meet. It is one big, beautiful surprise that can make you wise, be serendipitous, or even cause tears to flood the eyes.

It was autumn of 2012, and I was trudging along in northwestern Ontario. Mist dominated the day, hanging thick in the air. I figured the sun had its work cut out for it if it wanted to make its presence felt. As powerful as it is, there are times when you doubt the sun's ability to penetrate and burn through a stubborn fog. On this day, I concluded it would take a miracle to experience the comfort of a warm sun.

Good luck, Sun; try to lift this foggy veil if you can!

Because it was fall, the days were getting shorter as time quickly marched toward winter. To make the most of each day and continue making steady progress on my walk, I had to start early, which meant contending with the darkness of the early morning and dealing with unfriendly fog and mist.

I was walking along the shoulder of Highway 11 feeling, and appearing, fairly invisible in the hour or so before dawn. The blinding glare of high-beam headlights from an occasional vehicle, and the sound of my footsteps grasping the gravel at the edge of the road were reality checks for this lonely walker.

Eventually, the darkness faded and traffic picked up as a few dedicated folks headed off to work. I doubted that it ever got terribly busy on this quiet stretch of road just east of the town of Fort Francis, in what's known as 'canoe country'.

Wouldn't it be nice if there were only canoes slowly plying their way along the wonderful waterways instead of nasty trucks and cars racing along the asphalt? What a world it must have been when the Ojibwe Aboriginal people dominated this area, silently being transported by lightweight birchbark canoes.

As morning crept in, it looked like the sun was starting to win the wrestling match with *Indra*, the god of moisture, and his low-lying misty clouds. The first morning light allowed me to see a strange and interesting name on a nearby highway sign. I was approaching Nigigoonsiminikaaning, a First Nations community culturally rich in the vast history of the Ojibwe. I tried saying 'Nigigoonsiminikaaning' out loud a few times, and even though I was likely mispronouncing it, it had a resounding ring of antiquity to it.

I might not be fortunate enough to see the village though, because it probably would be located off the main highway, nestled and tucked away in the boreal forest. Over the years, I've missed out on a lot of great communities that way.

The world of images and wonders were opening up as the fog lifted that morning. Autumn always brings a distinct aroma of freshness and amazing colours. The true pigments of the hardwoods displayed their yellows, oranges, burgundies, and reds. The softwood evergreens persisted in the background of nature's canvas, making for a magnificent mosaic. The Precambrian rocks, some of the oldest granite in the world, gently washed by the morning mist, revealed their glistening pinks and greys.

I was clearly visible to traffic now, with feet picking up the pace and right-hand fingers working the familiar *japa* beads to the sound of my voice uttering the great *mantra* of deliverance. Suddenly, Mother Nature took hold of me, and right then and there possessed me. Being stunned by nature's ambiance, I had no choice but to stop walking. I was awestruck, knowing that a great Master Artist had created the scenic splendour.

When I say 'awestruck', I mean it in a very literal sense. I was hit by something amazing and entered into a moment of paralysis. The awesome power that was on display was humbling. My eyes welled with tears of joy. Who knew beauty could be so impactful, that it could buckle your knees and pull you down to the ground?

Not wanting to leave that spot of captivation, I wanted to freeze the moment by making it not a moment. I wanted the colours and smells to be suspended and stilled forever. For some reason, I had been allowed to savour something solemn that will not, I beg, be forgotten, but be etched in my memory bank for the rest of my days.

Finally, gaining composure and wiping away tears, and continuing to be wrapped and overwhelmed in a feeling of gratitude, I plodded along, eventually coming to a scenic lookout at Rainy Lake. Adding to the beauty of that cliff's edge were five bald eagles perched upon the upper branches of a tall pine. They dispersed upon my arrival, displaying extensive wingspans over that great body of water, simply pronouncing their freedom. I was rather oblivious to the motorists and what they might be thinking about a monk in wonder. This particular morning was an unexpected adventure of exhilaration for me.

THERE WERE SOMETIMES SAD AND CONTEMPLATIVE MOMENTS.

In the spring of 1996, near the Ontario/Manitoba border, I was chanting as usual on my beads, and really needed to, because it was rather miserable with an excessive amount of rain in the air. A rainsuit kept most of the water out, but at forty-two kilometres (twenty-six miles) per day, you can't help but break into a sweat inside non-breathable plastic garments. Plastic rain gear was all Dave and I could afford. We were poor. We were living, but barely scraping by. Few donations were coming our way, and yet we were feeling prosperous because the air we were breathing was good, the water for drinking was clean, and the scenery was great.

I had recently renounced what little cash I was holding and surrendered it to Dave. Perhaps this was a case of artificial renunciation because there was hardly anything to turn over to him. I was determined, come hell or high water, to continue walking on and on and on.

At one point I grew tired, and Dave wasn't around, so I chose a small depression in a ditch along the side of the Trans-Canada Highway in which to take a much-needed nap. I coiled in that natural pit with raindrops pitter-pattering on the plastic rainsuit. The fetal position was most comfortable, and between my knees and nose, I noticed a thistle plant with its purple flower. I began to communicate with it merely through appreciation.

"You're making me so happy. You stand so free and in all your glory. The Creator put you here for a purpose."

My contemplation was a bit morose at first, because one purpose of this first particular walk was to find solitude after personally being unjustifiably accused of an ugly, fabricated incident. I thought I would never survive such maliciousness, but the colour and shape of the thistle flower lifted my spirit. At that moment, I had no worries, no cares.

I could just as well have let Dave run off with his old jalopy and whatever little cash and food we had. At that moment I felt detached from the world, regaining confidence, and even joy. I broke into a flood of warm tears that mixed with the cool rain running down my cheeks.

Traffic sped by. No one stopped. I guess no one assumed me dead.

During the fall of that same year, 1996, I was trekking along the Trans-Canada Highway near the Ottawa River. It was overcast and cool. I had been devotedly chanting and walking for more than eight hours every day. Then, seemingly out of nowhere, I was gripped with unbelievably clear images from the past and broke into a soliloquy of thoughts.

Oh Mom, no one can replace you. Poor Mom, diabetes took your life, and you also had challenges with mental health issues. You used to tell us people were talking about you. It made you insecure. Your depressions sent you to bed and your six children wept for you. You seemed to drown in sorrow, and even though you often had the blues, I will never forget what you did for us and the fun times we had.

We canned pears and peaches with you and enjoyed those delicious preserves during winter. One cold afternoon, you discovered the clean laundry that was hung outside to dry had turned into stiff, frozen boards. We shared a great laugh that day. I remember coming back from school and seeing you knitting socks and sweaters to keep us warm during the frigid Canadian winters.

You were often quiet and withdrawn. Sometimes we would horse around in the house and you would be so absorbed and lost in your thoughts that you wouldn't pay us any mind. We were curious about those thoughts and pleaded with you to tell us what you were thinking about. We would tug at you, disrupting your knitting, and you would smile and say to us, "Binnenpretje!" a Dutch word meaning 'secret amusement'.

You weren't pleased when I became a monk and felt I had done something too extreme. But you know Mom, both you and Dad always wanted us kids to be religious as Catholics. Years passed and you finally accepted my choice of religious paths as a Hare Krishna monk. Before you left us, I hugged you in the hospital, but you didn't have the strength to return the squeeze. And that's totally alright, because for all those years, you were a good Mom.

ON MARATHON WALKS IT'S INEVITABLE THAT YOU THINK ABOUT YOUR MOTHER AND FATHER.

Those precious memories brought torrential tears to my eyes, so much so that my face and jacket became drenched. I wasn't sure if the motorists speeding past me could see my display of emotion, but I really didn't care.

I'm a monk and I'm entitled to two things—emotions and adventure. After all, monks have feelings, too. We're humans, for God's sake. Unexpected adventures can cause extreme emotions in spectacular natural settings, or when our minds are flooded with thoughts from going down memory lane.

Om Tat Sat.

CHAPTER 31
TO DAD WITH LOVE

"When a father gives to his son, both laugh; when a son gives to his father, both cry."

–William Shakespeare

<u>ABOUT DAD</u>

Dear Creator,

You struck a good balance
When you linked the leaf and petal
Came a man of heart and muscle
Smooth as silk and hard as metal

With pride he told his pastimes
Of a place of windmills & dikes
Which fuelled life then and there
With feet on skates and feet on bikes

Folks then bore brutal war
Watched the stock market crash
Lost jobs but not nerve
Convictions could never be smashed

He left the land below sea level
For a promised place remote
Atlantic waters rippled by
On a real and wanderlust boat

He married a lady called Rose
Life was of both fragrance and thorn
They begot two guys n' two gals
Then twins were newly born

He walked us down the outdoor trails
But inside told of birds and bees
He gave us each those daily chores
And how to milk those cows with ease

He grew those plants with his green thumb
Toiled decades on the assembly line
With different strokes he cracked those jokes
He was just fun-loving all the time

Patience he learned in a very hard way
He gave us our choices in life
Our music was not to cope with
It gave him some stress and strife

His was a life full of colour
Sporting half beard and wooden shoes
He was extraordinary, yet ordinary
An upbeat dad you thought to never lose

His heart froze in the land of the petal
His body lies in the land of the leaves
Oh Creator, rest his soul in heaven
For he was born to give and to please

He really didn't like it when I decided to drop out of college and become a monk. I loved going to Cambrian College in northern Ontario and was doing great in my fine arts studies. But deep down inside of me there was this insatiable gnawing for something more spiritual. I really wasn't sure what I was looking for at the time, but had an overwhelming passion to find out what it was. And it couldn't wait; I had to find my path right then and there.

"But why do you want to leave a perfectly good religion?" Dad asked, referring to my choice to leave the family's traditional path of Christianity for some quasi-Indian thing that the Beatles were dabbling in.

"Well, I'm still Catholic. I haven't left the faith, but just want to give this a try," I said to my Dad.

Leaving school without getting my degree really pained my parents, especially my father, who believed when you made a commitment to do something you had to follow it through, no matter what. I didn't want to hurt him, and it was hard to explain that I wasn't switching Gods, because Krishna is the same Supreme being. In fact, *bhakti* yoga is very Christian, very Jewish, very Zen, very Native, very Celtic, very Islamic, very Buddhist, and so on and so forth. I believed then, and I still believe now, that *bhakti* yoga captures all spiritual approaches in so many ways.

I stated my case, but was not going to argue with Dad. You just didn't do that with him. His concerns had me defending my views and decision within my own head. He was a good dad, but he always had this leash that psychologically held onto us kids. However, the leash was long enough to allow me and my five younger siblings to make our own decisions and carve out our own lives. Somehow, he trusted us. He groomed us with a firm, but fine, moral and spiritual hand while laying down a strong foundation of self-reliance. Deep down, he was confident we weren't going to go too far astray.

"Do as you like!" were his final words on the subject.

Years later, twenty-three to be exact, Dad had come to terms with my chosen vocation and destiny. Perhaps he respected my self-determination—something I likely inherited from him. Many of my peers who chose the mainstream materialistic way of life lived out sorry tales of substance abuse and failed marriages. I hadn't chosen a normal vocation, but by now Dad saw I was happy with my spiritual calling. And after more than two decades, he could see this wasn't some sort of passing fad encouraged by the 'Fab Four'.

In 1996, at age seventy-seven, he came to check up on his 'different' son by joining me on a stretch of highway during my first walk across Canada. He came out to support me. He contacted the mayor of Blenheim, Ontario, the town near where I grew up from the age of ten years onward, to let him know about my marathon passion. He was there when I shook hands with the mayor, and it was he who shone with pride in the photo that appeared on the front page of the Blenheim News Tribune, our local weekly newspaper.

We shared several kilometres together, along that imperceptible slope of road called Highway 3. He had come to back me up. It was a 'feel good' situation for both of us.

In 2003, I tackled my second big walk. He made a deliberate effort to share more time together. My sister, Rose Ann, drove the two of them all the way north to Manitoulin Island, which was part of my walking route. We met at a motel, chatted, and arranged to stroll together the next morning. As usual, I took to the road early, but for some reason, we never did find each other.

I was left to wander and wonder, and in those moments of pondering the past, I began to think about his influences and contributions to my life. The flashbacks from the distant past were quite endearing. Yes, indeed, memories become clearer while walking.

Dad sat me down when I reached puberty to tell me about 'the birds and the bees'. He used a most serious, yet soft tone, as he explained what married women and men do together in the privacy of their own bedrooms. He read passages from a Christian book about the wholesome approach to sex. It was a series of maybe three or four sessions. I couldn't understand it all at the time, but when I saw the animals in our barnyard doing their special thing, I put two and two together.

Dad went beyond the call of duty, in my opinion, as a parent. He always gave us chores to do which began at 5:30 every morning. He would sing out in a chipper tone while I was still asleep, "John (my given name), let's go." It was as if to say, "Duty is upon us and so is the fun."

For the summer holidays, he sent Jerry, my younger brother, and me into the garden to pull weeds. That was pretty easy compared to sometimes spending hours pitching stenchy animal waste into the manure spreader. He also arranged summer jobs for us working in nearby orchards. At one point, all six of us kids were harvesting in the cherry orchards in the great out-of-doors to make some money.

Dad was clearly priming us for responsibility. He even took us to the bank and helped us open our own personal accounts. Even though he was a hard worker and expected us to work hard, too, he loved to have fun and enjoyed the simple things in life. For recreation we went swimming and beaching at one of Canada's Great Lakes. Our chosen destination was Lake Erie.

And then there were the nature trails. He loved the green canopied world and his passion made us fall in love with nature, too. The long vines, a feature of the Carolinian forest typical of southern Ontario, made it feel wild and free, just like Tarzan's jungle. Winter meant Sunday spins in the car over the frozen lake. He would make the car skid and slide a little, which only increased our adrenalin rush.

The work was hard, but the recreation was fun. It was free and very organic. And it was all in the family (with no stigma of Archie Bunker grumpiness intended). Sometimes Dad would take us for an hour's drive over the American border to spend a day at the Detroit Zoo. For us country bumpkins, the city folks were as interesting as the apes in the cages. Dad's second job as maintenance man at the Ford Family's duck hunting lodge would give us kids an occasional chance to go fishing. Sometimes we would help Dad clean up the place, which was odd to our innocent eyes because the walls were adorned with pictures of bare-naked ladies.

Dad had a green thumb and could grow anything. When his 'Dutchie' friends would come around, they inspected and admired what was growing in his garden. Looking back, I am reminded of the strong fragrances that emanated from that garden. A slight gust of wind would allow the nostrils to get a good whiff of the vegetables and herbs which were still in the ground, something generation X, Y, and Z kids may never experience.

There was one area of resistance, on my part, in dealing with Dad. Having grown up through Europe's depression, and then World War II, he was naturally a product of a harder way of life.

DAD'S WOODEN SHOES. YOU WOULDN'T WANT TO WALK ACROSS CANADA IN THOSE.

Comparatively speaking, in the 1960s, us kids had it fairly cushy. One day, he handed me the axe and a chicken and said, "Off with her head."

I declined.

Dad was good enough to accept that I could still 'be a man' after a compromise left me to pluck her feathers after he executed the poor hen.

It always caused confusion and turmoil in my mind that our friends, the farm animals, could eventually become dinner. Those entrées Mom whipped up and presented on our dinner table just didn't sit well with my psychological self. When I finally met Krishna monks at age twenty, they told me about the alternative culture of vegetarianism. This new way of eating, steeped in the tradition of India, liberated me, and I haven't consumed meat, eggs, or fish since.

Back to that first walk in 1996. Dad and I trekked along Highway 3, which in many places hugs the edge of Lake Erie. We walked by a pasture and checked out the livestock, especially the beautiful cows. We also saw orchards and an occasional mansion perched on a cliff to take advantage of the vista view. All of this country scenery appealed to us as we strolled along, savouring each other's company. The countryside and the farmland were for Dad, while the road was for me. As we walked, that comparison and difference became obvious to me.

The ties of emotion can be strong for all of us, and I find that even now, long after Dad (Jan Vis) departed from this world in 2007. Despite my appreciation, all of what he did for me cannot be repaid. Walking stirs up the sweet, and sometimes bitter past. Our relationship was sometimes difficult, and sometimes sweet. We were never super-close, but our relationship was good enough for me. His Christian values and principles are worth embracing, and that's what he left me.

I have visions of him sitting at the dining room table reading the newspaper after a hard day's work at International Harvester, a manufacturer of trucks and farm machinery. He often had a cigar in his mouth and was relaxed, except when we teens put Led Zeppelin on the stereo. He was a liberal, a father, and a dedicated husband who looked after Mom when her diabetic legs had to be amputated. He was also a worker, a friend, and a *guru*.

He was proud of his children: Connie, Jerry, Rose Ann, Paul, Pauline, and me. And when I visited him in the hospital during his final days, he used what little strength he had left to tell the nurses, "That's my son. He's the oldest. He walked across Canada several times. He's the strongest man in the world."

Thanks Dad; I am far from being the strongest man in the world, but I do appreciate my Father's pride.

CHAPTER 32
RANDOM ROADSIDE PRAYERS

"Prayer is not asking. Prayer is putting oneself in the hands of God, at His disposition, and listening to His voice in the depth of our hearts."

–Mother Teresa

Human beings always seem to crave, desire, wish, want, and yearn for anything we think will improve our lives. It seems as if our needs are a sign of life—proof that we are alive. Let's say we have a problem, real or perceived, and want to fix it. Perhaps it's beyond our capacity, so we seek help from family, friends, the universe, or the Creator. It's difficult to go solo, and sometimes surviving means leaning on someone and getting by with a little help from our friends.

All of which reminds me of a rainy day in Ireland (if I may jump to that), trudging along a country road, when I decided I really needed an umbrella. I wanted to stay dry, but after a short contemplation, I let that 'need' go. Instead of an umbrella, what I really wanted was some company, even if just for a moment. With that thought now occupying my mind, a young woman driving to work noticed me and pulled over.

Stopping along a winding road during the morning's heavy traffic is a daring thing to do, especially in Ireland. There's practically no shoulder on the roads over there, and just one narrow lane in each direction for cars. As for people like me, there might be two feet of walking space bordered by blackberry vines that love to cling to a monk's robes.

So, I was standing in a tight little space when this young motorist, with a worried look on her face, offered me a ride. It was a kind offer, so I thanked her and explained I was walking the whole of Ireland to encourage pilgrimage. She then expressed what was really on her troubled mind. She had an uncle in the hospital and wondered if I would pray for him. I said I would and was about to ask for his name and a few details concerning his predicament, but traffic had lined up behind her vehicle and the other motorists were most anxious to be on their way. Under pressure, she expressed a quick appreciation before revving up her engine and heading down the road. I never did get her uncle's name or info about his affliction, information which would have helped me make some kind of reference or specific appeal in my prayer.

I prayed all the same, just attempting to send good wishes and a positive vibration his way. This lady was thinking about the well-being of someone dear to her on the way to work, and when she saw my robes, acted quite impulsively in a call for help. I could feel her empathy.

On my third trek across Canada, I had just walked through Kapuskasing in northern Ontario, the birthplace of James Cameron, the famous movie maker. He wrote, directed, and produced the 1997 blockbuster, *Titanic*, as well as *Terminator* and *Avatar*—all cinema successes.

I FIND THE MOST POWERFUL SPOT FOR PRAYER IS ON A BRIDGE OVERLOOKING A RIVER.

On the outskirts of Kapuskasing, a family spotted me on the side of the road, stopped their car, got out, and made a request. They were very sincere and open-hearted, and wanted me to pray for them because they were having some family challenges and said they really needed my help.

Somehow, I surmised they were Catholic, but that didn't matter. They happened to see a man of the cloth, a clergyman, and felt I could render some service. Often when one is seen wearing vestments, people believe you might have special connections.

I felt obliged to offer assistance because they appeared desperate and were looking for hope and consolation. It didn't matter to me what church they belonged to, because even though I'm not a practising Christian, I do believe in the Christian God. After all, are we not all breathing the same air, drinking the same water, and taking in the pleasant rays from the same sun and moon? Thus, it has to be the same God we all approach. If the prayer asks for courage, strength to cope, and intelligence to deal with the tough spots in life, then it must be a universal plea not limited to one path or faith.

So, we stood together by the highway, heads lowered in reverence as I offered prayers and *mantras*. They were consoled, and this little bit of service for this troubled family made me feel good, too. It made me feel like all of this walking had a purpose and gave me one more reason to believe in the power of the Divine.

At Christina Lake in British Columbia, I was walking along the Crowsnest Highway (Highway 3) when a van pulled over. A woman hopped out and asked for my assistance. This episode was completely different than the previous two, but very interesting, nonetheless.

"Hello. My friends and I have just had a dragon boat built for our lake, and it's a tradition to have a monk do some rituals before the ceremonial launching," she said. "We heard you were in town and thought maybe you could help."

"I'm flattered, but I'm doing this walk across Canada and can't leave the road because my support person won't be able to find me," I said. "I would like to help, but I just can't leave the road right now."

"I understand," she replied, "but there must be something we can do, because you are the only monk around."

Further conversation revealed they wanted to conduct this blessing ceremony as soon as possible. So, I walked down to the nearby mountain stream and chanted some *mantras* with my right thumb in the water. It was kind of like being on the shores of the Ganges. I then took some water and sprinkled it on the lady and her friends before reciting more sacred sounds as everyone solemnly stood in a huddle formation. We finished it off with the great Hare Krishna *mantra*.

The proceedings were met with approval by the half-dozen dragon boat folks, and they made a generous offering in the form of *daksheen* (donations), something I did not anticipate. They liked the synergy, the auspiciousness of it all, so the mission was accomplished.

Approaching the Rocky Mountains in Alberta, I met Sanford and his two teenage boys. "We're Sanford and Sons," he said, in reference to the popular mid-seventies' TV sitcom. After that brief encounter, they drove off. Half an hour later, I saw Sanford standing at the end of his driveway. It was then that I realized he was an Indigenous person.

"I saw your pamphlet that says your name is *Bhakti*, which means 'lucky' in my language," he said. "I could use some of that luck, because the boy's mother left when they were young; now they're into drugs and I don't know what to do. So, can you talk to them?"

I agreed, and Sanford walked with me down his long driveway and called out to the boys. They came out from behind the house, and it was obvious they had just been smoking marijuana. All I could do was give hugs, blessings, and encouraging words. I left hoping for the best, but feeling very much concerned for Sanford and Sons.

Sometimes when I complete one of these long-distance walks, I fly back to my temple home in Toronto. Once when I was checking in at an airport, a lady ticket agent asked me to pray for her.

"Sure. Has something happened?"

"No, but just in case something does."

We all seem to crave, desire, wish, want, and yearn for the things we think will make our lives better. Out on the road I meet real people, and once in a while someone is moved by my presence and approaches to see if I can connect with the Creator on their behalf to seek His help or guidance. These opportunities to perform random roadside prayers mean as much to me as they do to the folks who request them.

You have a lot of time on your hands when you are out on the road alone—time to think, and time to create. Here is a little prayer that I wrote when out there trudging along. I call it "A Walking Prayer."

Dear Creator,

I express my gratitude for the privilege to walk.
To move about and make friends along the way.
To feel the texture of the land and the touch of a hand.
To smell the scents of sweet blossoms and grass.
To be awed by nature's vistas and views.
To marvel at creatures of land, water, and sky.
To see both life and death and the struggle between.
To go through the rigors of pain in the legs.
To learn from it the quality of detachment.
To gaze at the truth of duality in my face.
To feel the sun's warmth and the winter's embrace.
To step into the tall, to make me feel small.
To build physical strength, fortitude, character.
To help realize the world's fragility and whimsy.
To see the pillar of the Source behind the force.
To understand service as all that there be.
To share what I've learnt and to pass it on.

CHAPTER 33

THE MISUNDERSTOOD MONK

"I am not a teacher, a king, a merchant, or a worker; not a student, a proprietor, a hermit, or a monk. I am simply a servant of the servant of the master of the most devoted."

–Sri Chaitanya

There are a host of stereotypes which come to mind when encountering *yogis*, sages, *sadhus*, ascetics, and monks. It might not be justified or fair to lump everyone together, but generally these people often display extraordinary feats, and may even perform a miracle or two. Despite these traits and miraculous displays, they are human just like everyone else.

For an inside look at a quasi-holy man's world, just visit India's famous *Kumbha Mela* when twelve million people converge at the Ganges River. They all arrive with a goal to bathe in the holy river at an astrologically auspicious moment. A curious onlooker might consider the experience some kind of spiritual Disneyland. Buses cart the masses to the site, while the meek walk there.

It was at the foothills of Earth's highest mountains, the gateway to the abode of Hari (Vishnu), that I had the pleasure to be present at a *mela*. It was a long time ago, but I believe it might have been the spring of 1980 when I arrived at Haridwara, at the base of the Himalayas, to participate in the event.

It sure was an eye-opener, seeing some *yogis* walk on burning coals, while others lay on beds of nails, oblivious to physical pain. Still other ascetics stood on one leg, for God knows how long, to prove their might and mind over matter. I saw some saffron-clad fellow with matted hair demonstrating the art of dexterity with his right arm upraised. He apparently had demonstrated his endurance by holding that pose for weeks.

Another common form of *tapasya* (austerity) found a mystic sitting on a straw mat with fires burning on all four sides. Combine that with the fierce heat from the sun and it was literally an intense inferno. And just when you might think you've seen it all, some *yogis* submerged themselves in the Ganges for an awful long stretch of time, holding their breath by using *pranayam* (breathing meditation) techniques.

Then there were the *naga babas*, an interesting group who are clothed only by the elements. They believe their nakedness exemplifies detachment from the material world. Some even exhibit interesting displays with their private parts by doing tricks with sticks, while others purposely pinch a nerve to ensure total celibacy, the ultimate trademark of an ascetic.

I have never personally been interested in going to such extremes, but have found that walking is a practical and simple way to stay celibate. In other words, never stay in one place long enough for anything to happen. I didn't come to this conclusion by myself; I learned it from the sages of the past, like Sukadeva Goswami, who always kept moving for the same reason. Being a genuine *naga baba* who lived five millennia ago, he rarely stayed anywhere longer than the time it took to milk a cow. Though he did break his self-imposed rule once when he sat for a week to teach the *Bhagavat* philosophy to an entire assembly of sages, monarchs, and celestials.

Now, how do I, a simple walking monk, fit into this culture of the super extraordinary? I came to my first *mela* for spiritual awakening and to participate in communal public chanting. Chanting has a purging effect on the hearts of participants and listeners alike, and I could think of no better place to carry out this transcendental activity.

When I first joined the *ashram* in Toronto in 1973, I began reading the books of our *guru*, Prabhupada, and was amazed by his explanation of the eight mystic perfections known as *siddhis*. Here's what he describes:

1. *Anima siddhi* - becoming smaller than the smallest.
2. *Mahima siddhi* - becoming bigger than the biggest.
3. *Prapti siddhi* - the ability to reach out to anything, even the moon.
4. *Prakamya siddhi* - to enjoy anything you want
5. *Isita siddhi* - to control and manipulate illusion.
6. *Vashita siddhi* - to control minds.
7. *Kamavasayita siddhi* - to achieve powers of control and enjoyment.
8. *Autpatthikah siddhi* - being original, natural, and unexcelled.

Fascinating feats, aren't they? Naturally I wondered what these mystical perfections had to do with my life as a monk, because to master such *siddhis* one must be extremely disciplined. I was in awe while reading through the pages of *The Nectar of Devotion*, not so much by the extraordinary feats, but by the achievement of devotion, which is something much higher. A sincere seeker of the truth may discard the eight mystic perfections as show-bottle, meaning not genuine spirituality. True spirituality involves a change of heart, a transformation of consciousness.

Whether in India or elsewhere, people are always bedazzled by what holy men can do. It is a phenomenon or mystery for many. I don't claim to be in the same league as the *sadhus* I have described, but some people are astounded when they hear that I have walked across Canada four times.

"Really, you're walking the whole thing?" they ask. "Are you floating; are you sure you're not using a flying carpet?"

In Fort Francis, Ontario, which borders the United States, a young man whose family owned a rustic home overlooking Rainy Lake, hosted me for a talk.

"Talk?" asked his invited friends. "How is that possible? Because monks don't talk."

They assumed I had taken a vow of silence when I became a renunciate.

"Well, that's a mistaken notion," I responded. "In the Hare Krishna order, we make lots of noise chanting, beating drums, and shaking tambourines."

In Winnipeg, three young boys spotted me walking along the sidewalk near their homes. They were fascinated, perhaps believing I was a Kung Fu master who could break bricks with my mind, Bruce Lee style. These boys, who looked to be about seven or eight years old, were whispering to each other as they followed me. After three or four blocks, I stopped and turned toward them to see how I could be of service, and also to dispel any delusion they might have.

"Can you show us how to stick fight?" a tender young voice asked in anticipation.

They really wanted me to say yes, but I must have disappointed them when I explained the gentler art of *bhakti*, or devotion to the Divine.

"Huh?" uttered one of the boys with eyebrows raised as high as the sky.

There was a similar episode in New Waterford, Nova Scotia. I was on an early morning stroll near the shores of the Atlantic Ocean. It was a greyish sort of day, quite mystical, with the winds seeming to carry significant but quiet messages through the air. It was a rural area with dirt roads and very few homes dispersed here and there. My *dhoti* (lower garment) was being tossed about by the ocean breezes and I was chanting on my *japa* beads. It was before I started doing these marathon walks, but I was secretly training for that first Canadian adventure. While I was strolling along that Nova Scotia coastline, a group of five or six youngsters spotted me on their way to school. They started to follow me and I could sense they were intrigued. I stopped and the group also stopped, looking rather curious and timid.

"Excuse me," a small blond boy asked stepping forward as the spokesman for the group, "but can you walk on water?"

"Well, I haven't mastered that yet, but I'm concentrating on *bhakti*," I said. "That means I am trying to discover who is really behind this great creation that we live in."

"Thank you," was the shy response as he and his friends went on their way, still very much in wonder.

Another group followed me like a shadow near a First Nations community called Garden River on the shores of Lake Superior. They were young tweens and teens, some pushing bikes, and others walking, engaged in chatter. I assumed they were trying to figure out how to approach me and sure enough one of them finally caught up with me.

"We heard you were walking across Canada," he said.

"That's right," I responded.

"Can we talk to you?" he asked.

I agreed, and we stepped into a nearby doughnut shop to chat. The group easily exposed their inquisitive minds. I pulled a book out of my *kurta* (shirt) pocket which I keep for occasions like this, called, *Coming Back*. This opened up our dialogue onto reincarnation, changing bodies, and how we move forward in life, learning powerful lessons through each successive new experience.

"Each new life poses fresh challenges that push us to the limits of what we can understand," I explained. "Life is all about opportunity and taking that next chance to escalate our full potential, especially our spiritual potential."

We talked and covered much territory, almost everything under the sun. I was undeniably in my element as a monk, teaching and sharing what I know. Our current consumer capitalistic world tends to obscure information about the self. In many ways people are deprived of this inner wisdom that is actually innate and lying dormant in the recesses of the heart. Perhaps my all-time favourite line from my *guru* is the following when asked, "Swami-ji, why did you come to the west?"

He replied, "To tell you what you have forgotten." In my opinion, he was the most genuine of all holy men, a true *sadhu* who spent considerable time educating his students about the qualities of a genuine saint. He practiced what he preached. He walked his talk.

Incidentally, the Sanskrit word *sadhu* refers to 'one who cuts through matter', one who lives very much in the spirit.

My various treks have allowed me to become more of a *sadhu* than a rubber-stamped *swami* with some fancy, formal ordination. Being out there and exposed to the world automatically forces me to become a teacher *and* a student of life at the same time. I often become a counsellor, a humanist, an observer, and most of all—an assistant to humanity.

MONKS ARE OFTEN MISUNDERSTOOD, BUT WE'RE JUST ORDINARY PEOPLE.

I'm not better than anyone else, I'm just here to be a helper. It is the greatest privilege to be able to do these treks, and a most humbling experience. When I am walking in the great outdoors, I know I am an insignificant moving speck, a tiny part and parcel of the Great Source. I am a contributor to the Universe.

The public is mystified by the holy person who comes in different colours as exhibitionists, martial artists, hermits, nuns, or anyone else who carries a simple practice and outlook on life. A monk is seldom to be found, yet there is a piece of monk in all of us, I believe, aloof from the world, ready to serve.

CHAPTER 34

MONK FOR A MINUTE

"Life without love is useless and poor, they say. Appoint me in thy service, Oh Lord, with love as my pay."

–Bhaktisiddhanta Sarasvati

I was nearing the end of that first cross-Canada walk, a nearly 8,000-kilometre trek. I was on the east coast and would soon board a ferry to Newfoundland. The fall lobster season had begun in Nova Scotia, and a fresh snowfall contributed a softness to the land and a silence to the air.

Long-distance walking takes a toll on your body, mind, and clothing. When it comes to the latter, I take precautionary measures to keep my robes intact. Rain, snow, slush, wind, and road salt do major damage to the thin, delicate fabric.

So, on this day, I applied due diligence and decided to wear my 'civies' (civilian clothes), or what in the early days of our zealous missionary spirit we called '*karmis*'. This meant pants, shirt, socks, boots, winter coat, etc. I was now a monk incognito for a day at least, and I was fairly dry and warm, too. Adorned in that attire, I struck out for another forty kilometres on my journey. Each day was an adventure. You never knew what or who you were going to encounter, but you *did* know that each day would have its own character and unique circumstances.

I was thrilled to meet a journalist from *The Chronicle Herald*. I wasn't sure how she found me because I was just in regular clothes. She was a younger woman, and she had a tape recorder in her hand (remember those old relics?). In a rather formal manner, she asked all the usual questions, "When did you start this walk? Which day do you hope to finish now that you're this close to the end? Why are you walking? And how many pairs of shoes did it take you to get to this point?" Then she asked me something that rather stunned me. "So, now that you've almost completed the marathon, what is the greatest experience that you've had on this trek?" I just went blank. I rather froze. I just didn't know what to say. Just one second seemed like a few years passing. I didn't want to come across as a zombie, or a monk taking a sudden vow of silence. But then it struck me. I had the answer.

"The greatest moment I've had on this walk is here with you standing there asking me this question, and I'm standing in front of you trying to come up with an answer. *That's* the greatest thing that's happened!"

She kind of lit up, and said, "Oh, I get it, I know what you're saying. It's like living in the moment, being in the present." That pretty much sewed up the interview with the journalist.

Living for the moment is very profound.

I like the east coast because the people there are not only laid back, they are among Canada's friendliest folks. So, it would hardly be a surprise if some local 'fellar' stopped to offer me a ride. On this day, I blended right in and might even have passed for a local; however, a name like Bhaktimarga Swami is not the kind of handle given to your typical Scotsman or Irishman.

In the Maritimes, surnames often begin with the prefix Mc or Mac, which in Gaelic means 'son of'. So, it's not uncommon to meet a MacPherson or McDonald out on the east coast. Some of the Indigenous people in the Maritime region are members of Mi'kmaq First Nations, formerly called Micmac. So, out on the east coast, it's not hard to find a Mc, a Mac, or a 'Micmac'.

I was not surprised when a Mr. MacCallum pulled over to offer me a ride, somewhere in beautiful Cape Breton.

"Would you like a lift?" he politely asked.

"Thanks so much, but I'm walking across the country. I left British Columbia a few months ago and I'm headed to Newfoundland to finish," I explained.

"Really! Can we talk?

"Sure!"

"I'll treat you to a beer."

"No thanks, I don't drink."

"How about a coffee?"

"I don't drink coffee either. Sorry!"

"Maybe a soft drink?"

"Okay!"

"I'll meet you at the building up ahead on the right, by the bend."

"Fine!"

I arrived and realized the building was a hunter's lodge. I entered and there was Mr. MacCallum sitting with his friends. It was early in the day, so they were having their morning coffee. At this point, I was welcomed into a kitchen/dining room area where I was introduced to and shook hands with about a half a dozen guys.

"Tell us about your walk," requested MacCallum in a friendly way.

At that moment, I noticed a copy of *The Chronicle Herald* on the counter.

"That's me on the front cover. They interviewed me yesterday and published the story today."

I also dropped the hood of my jacket to reveal a shaven head and the typical Vaishnava tuft of hair at the back. MacCallum was next to me and leaning forward on the back of his chair like a cowboy. The other men, all deer hunters, also sat around the table. I pulled up my chair and began to speak.

"Actually, I may not look it today, but I'm a monk and I've been on pilgrimage."

The guys were obviously intrigued about the marathon walk, but their interest shifted slightly.

MacCallum asked, "What do you have to do to be a monk?"

"I belong to an old tradition which has roots in India. I'm a Hare Krishna monk. Our lifestyle is joyful and fulfilling, but we do have some disciplines that we follow."

That seemed to get their attention, so I continued.

"First of all, we are vegetarian, so we don't eat animals."

The words had barely left my mouth when I realized I perhaps shouldn't have put that subject at the top of the list when addressing a group of deer hunters.

"Secondly, we avoid gambling. Thirdly, I'm not married and made vows that I won't get married, so that makes me a rare bird. Most of our members become family people, and the objective is to remain loyal to one person. Lastly, we abstain from intoxicants such as liquor, drugs, and tobacco."

I looked around and realized my not-to-do list had caused a sobering silence in my audience.

"But on a positive note, we meditate, worship the Lord, publish spiritual literature, sing, dance, and do positive community work such as feeding hungry people."

I stopped. Had I said too much? Had I not said enough? Everyone kept silent. I wasn't sure where we were going with this. But then Mr. MacCallum broke the silence. He was staring into the air in a kind of daze. He seemed to be imagining himself as a monk.

"Well, I could cut down on meat… I don't gamble… I guess I can cut down on women," he said before a lengthy pause. "But there is no way I can give up my beer!" he confessed.

I appreciated the fact that Mr. MacCallum put himself in the shoes (or sandals) of a monk. He transformed himself mentally into that of an ascetic, and I imagine the other fellows may have had a similar transformation, at least for a minute. That alone can be of tremendous benefit. Any probing or projecting into the spiritual is good for the soul.

This last day on the mainland, before heading to Canada's youngest province, was indeed unique. A fresh snowfall and a fresh conversation with some 'dyed-in-the-wool' Bluenosers seemed to be a fitting end to my journey across mainland Canada.

And then I was on to Newfoundland at the nation's end!

ANYBODY CAN BE A MONK FOR A MINUTE, A DAY, OR A LIFETIME.

CHAPTER 35

ENDINGS AND THE GHOST ON THE ROCK

"I have heard (but not believ'd) the spirits of the dead may walk again: if such thing be, thy mother appeared to me last night; for ne'er was dream so like waking."

–William Shakespeare

Newfoundland has always fascinated me. It is separated from mainland North America, and when you arrive there, it seems like you have landed on another planet. Newfoundland is often referred to as 'The Rock' because of its rugged terrain. I love the name New-Found-Land; it conjures up images of explorers searching for adventure in the New World! During my marathon walks through Canada, I often wondered what it must have been like for the First Nations Peoples and European explorers when they first walked the land I was walking.

Human habitation in Newfoundland dates back to at least 9,000 years ago. The Maritime Archaic Peoples who relied on sea mammals for their existence were the first known residents; the Beothuk and Mi'kmaq people settled here later, spending summers along the coast before moving inland for the winter. The Inuit, who live mainly in Labrador, were also among the first people to reside in this remote region of Canada.

The Vikings arrived in Newfoundland approximately 1,000 years ago. L'Anse Aux Meadows, near St. Anthony on the northernmost tip of the Great Northern Peninsula, is the only known site of a Norse or Viking settlement in North America. Archaeologists discovered it in 1960, and it was declared a World Heritage Site in 1978. Perhaps Leif Erikson actually visited this historic site.

It is interesting that Newfoundland was the first part of the country to be visited and settled by Europeans, but became the last province to join the Canadian Confederation in 1949. After World War II, there was much debate as to whether to join Canada or remain a Dominion of the British Empire. In the end, the pro-confederation side won out, but to this day many Newfoundlanders still have differing points of view when it comes to this issue.

'The Rock' has an amazing history, but it is also known for its wildlife and natural beauty. Colourful puffins make Newfoundland their playground, especially along the Labrador coast, and if you like icebergs and whale watching, this is the place to visit. Newfoundland is beautiful and attracts thousands of tourists each year, even though it is a little out of the way.

I love listening to Newfoundlanders talk. Most have a thick, distinctive accent, and hundreds, if not thousands, of local sayings. The people, especially those from the countryside, are charming, and you have to listen very carefully, because between the accent and local sayings, it is a challenge to try to understand them. Frankly though, it's a joy to hear them speak. Locals will tell you there are two categories of people in Newfoundland. 'Townies' are from the capital city of St. John's, and 'baymen' are from everywhere else on 'The Rock'.

SPEAKING TO AN ENTHUSIASTIC BUNCH AT MEMORIAL UNIVERSITY IN ST. JOHN'S–"TALES FROM TRAILS."

There are ferries which take you from the mainland at North Sydney in Nova Scotia, to Newfoundland. The ferry to Port Aux Basques on the south-western tip of the island, runs year-round, and the crossing takes about six hours. In the summer months, you can sail to Argentia, around the coast and south-west of St. John's, which takes seventeen hours.

Because summer had already passed, we had to take the ferry to Port Aux Basques, and from there, Madhai, Brian, and I drove to Placentia Bay, a ten-hour journey across The Rock. This was to be my starting point for a three-day stretch to the finish line at the city of St. John's. A police officer informed me before I began my first Trans-Canada trek, that marathoners go to Argentia, and then walk up the Avalon Peninsula to St. John's. It is about 130 kilometres, and I would have to make good time to complete the trek in three days.

So, there were three of us on that last leg of my first journey across Canada, but somehow or other, a fourth personality tagged along with us. The best way to describe this 'extra' is, what shall I say, a disembodied being—a ghost who seemed to target Madhai.

The waves of the mighty nighttime ocean rocked a whole lot of passengers to sleep on the crossing from the mainland. Several people decided to leave their chairs in favour of sprawling out on the floor for a comfier doze. Madhai, Brian, and I liked that option, and were all in deep slumber when Madhai felt a very subtle but strong energy pressing down on him.

Brian, lying on the floor next to him, heard Madhai's attempt to scream. The sound was like that of a man being choked by a rope, and it was hard to discern what he was trying to say, but it was an obvious plea for help. Brian rescued Madhai from his slumberous situation and managed to calm him down. All was well, or so we thought.

The attacking ghost, as Madhai described it, came to haunt him once again. It was late the next night when we arrived at Argentia after enduring the long drive across the island. Madhai had reclined in the passenger's seat, while Brian and I found places to lie down in the back of our small van. There was baggage and other paraphernalia piled up between the front seats and the rest of the vehicle. Our deep sleep was once again disrupted with Madhai desperately trying to call out for help. It was as if someone was strangling him, and it was difficult to comprehend what he was saying.

"Madhai! Madhai! Wake up! Madhai, get up!" Brian and I shouted at the top of our lungs.

We could see Madhai struggling and could decipher what he was trying to say.

"Maharaja!" he said over and over again. It was obvious he was attempting to address me (in the traditional manner of addressing a *swami*).

Our shouts had not awakened him, so Brian and I started chanting the *maha mantra* in a frenzy, feeling we were executing some sort of exorcism.

Brian eventually broke through the barrier of luggage, and with a tussle, woke Madhai.

"It was him again," an exhausted Madhai uttered as he came back to consciousness. "He was holding me down and pressing on my mouth so I couldn't breathe; it was horrible!"

Indeed, it was a freak show for the three of us at this predawn hour. We hoped the ghost had finished its business and would leave us alone forever.

Through the windshield we could see a glimmer of light starting to appear over the horizon, but no sun, just clouds. The day began, and it was also the beginning of the end of my first colossal walk across Canada. The weather conditions were gloomy, grey, dull, and wet, as they often are in Newfoundland in the fall. I surrendered to the elements, donning rubber boots and a plastic rainsuit. I hadn't walked too far before beginning to sweat like anything, causing as much moisture inside the rainsuit as out. I couldn't blame the few motorists there were for staying inside their dry vehicles instead of stopping to talk to The Walking Monk. I must admit to praying for the sun to at least crack through the clouds dominating the morning sky.

One meagre consolation was seeing the sign for Butter Pot Provincial Park. When I saw the words 'Butter Pot' it immediately brought to mind the playful pastimes of God. Krishna *loves* butter, and as an infant He was extremely playful with the substance. The mischievous Krishna would steal butter and share it with His monkey friends.

The thought of Krishna and His butter pots cheered me up, but the weather remained dreary and overcast. After three days of grim Newfoundland fall weather, I finally reached the finish line in St. John's. It had taken seven and a half months to walk across Canada, and I dreamed of an eventful, glorious finish.

It was December 8th, 1996. There were no marching bands, no parade, no angels gliding down from the skies, no throng of supporters, no sun, and no news media. In all fairness, the fine folk of Newfoundland were unaware of my cross-country journey and were just going about their usual daily business.

But a handful of people did arrive at the last minute to cheer me on for those final few steps. Dr. Singh and his family came out, as well as Jan Peters, the proprietor of the very nice bed and breakfast establishment where we stayed. And of course, Brian and Madhai, who supported my trek for so long, led a hearty applause chanting, "*Jaya!*" and "*Haribol!*" to express victory.

THE LAST STEP OF MY FIRST WALK ACROSS CANADA AT THE EDGE OF THE ATLANTIC OCEAN.

I was happy to be surrounded by such good friends and well-wishers, but with persistent rain continuing to pour down, I had ambivalent feelings that the end was more bland than grand. On the other hand, I thought I should just lean into my own intuition and register the positive aspects of the finale. After all, being optimistic always makes a person feel better.

"Count your blessings, Swami," said my inner voice, so that's exactly what I did.

We retreated to our cozy bed and breakfast and had a scrumptious meal to honour that first successful marathon walk. No cork from a champagne bottle was popped to mark the occasion because we monks don't do that. But we *did* enjoy the food that was prepared, and love pervaded the moment.

I no sooner finished walking from British Columbia to Newfoundland than it dawned on me that perhaps this was not the end of the project. Maybe I should consider a complete loop, going full circle by leaving the east coast and returning back to the west coast. *But not right now.*

Seven years later, it became apparent to me, and other pilgrim enthusiasts I confided in, that it might be wise to accommodate the seven-year itch and retrace the steps going westward this time.

Turn around and do it all over again.

On May 1st, 2003, I began the second Canadian trek, this time beginning at Cape Spear, on 'The Rock'. Six months later, on October 30th, walk number two wrapped up in Victoria, on Vancouver Island, with a small walking party accompanying me along the streets to the finish. It was another dark and gloomy day, a kind of *deja vu*, as I touched the plaque reading "0 miles" at Beacon Hill Park. I had come full circle, but not quite fulfilled in spirit.

Must I do it again and again until my heart gives its full nod of approval?
Perhaps so!

I hit the trail again for a third trek completed in 2006 at the iconic location of the continent's eastern-most point, Cape Spear, in Newfoundland. During the last thirteen-kilometre stretch, heading east from the city of St. John's, I could finally sense a proper closure to the walking project as the sun came up. The Canadian Broadcasting Corporation (CBC) responded with a colossal camera in my face and a mic at my mouth. The local newspaper also did a great story, labelling me, 'Canada's Forrest Gump'.

Timing could not have been better as a tourist bus from Montreal had just stopped at the vista view by the lighthouse before heading west in my direction. The tourists had not finished their sightseeing when the driver spotted this monk, and that was fascinating enough for him to stop the bus. The tourists had numerous questions which I answered as best I could.

"I'm walking for my soul and the soul of the country!" was the basic theme of my response.

We all parted by singing that old familiar song together, "Happy trails to you, until we meet again…"

The finish line was just metres away, and entering the parking lot with my last few steps, I heard, then saw, a caravan of vintage cars heading my way. Dozens of souped-up shiny old automobiles had made the trip from Toronto, and their timing could not have been better. It was a tie at the finish line, and I thought I was in fantasyland.

This time nature also displayed a graceful affirmation for my walk. When I took the stairway to the Cape Spear Lighthouse, I peered over the cliffs to see a panoramic view of the Atlantic Ocean. That, in itself, was a wonderful sight, but then I noticed a family of whales frolicking in the water. It was an amazing display of three massive mammals spouting water from their blowholes. Grand finale or what? How could all this be?

I felt so light, almost light enough to tread across the water or waltz with ghosts. Incidentally, there were no signs of a ghost this time around. I was greeted by Daruka and his parrot, Billie, who has a welcoming habit of saying, "Hello!" especially when you place a potato chip in front of her beak.

Unlike the first two walks, the latter two were done in segments. Walking was based on my availability in adhering to other obligations in the priestly category, such as presiding over marriages and festivals. Summertime was the most favourable for walking, and I made sure that when I returned to the road I picked up where I last left off. I walked each step of the way with every inch covered.

Jumping to Sunday, June 29th, 2014, it was the final day of my fourth trek across Canada. I was walking with companion monk, Karuna Sindhu, through a wet west coast drizzle. There was no plan for a major reception, no pomp and ceremony. Karuna Sindhu and I walked to the entrance of the Krishna temple at 5462 S.E. Marine Drive, in Burnaby, British Columbia. Admittedly, I was tired, but reverentially forged ahead to make my way to the deity of Krishna, Sri Sri Radha Madan Mohan, to offer my prostrations. We were close enough to the Pacific coast, with the finish line a mere twenty kilometres away. This was a home run and an authentic place of pilgrimage, a sacred space.

I had been contemplating very deeply, comparing the various walks, and arrived at the conclusion that each successive trek got better by dint of mere experience. I was getting more comfortable with the ways of the land, the elements, the people, and the creatures. I believe I came to terms with acceptance on this fourth trek across Canada, meaning I now understood that whatever conditions arose of their own accord, must be accommodated.

The time had come to kick off the shoes, or in my case, the Crocs, and take some rest. But it wasn't long before thoughts began to enter my mind, thoughts about a new opportunity that lay ahead. In between the Canadian treks, new frontiers had already been explored, including Guyana, Trinidad, Mauritius, Ireland, Israel, and Fiji—all ghost free.

CHAPTER 36

IRELAND AND RAIN THE RIPPER

"Rain is very difficult to film, particularly in Ireland because it's quite fine, so fine that the Irish don't even acknowledge that it exists."

—Alan Parker, Filmmaker

Ireland. I really think it should be renamed 'Indraland'. That's because Indra is the Vedic name of the rain god. It rains in Ireland practically every day. They say you can tell it's summer in Ireland when the rain gets warmer. Even though I'm from Canada where weather is a constant topic of conversation, I never got used to the continuous Irish mist. However, on the bright side, the rain does account for the beautiful greenness of the place.

The Irish have several words for rain, depending on the severity of the precipitation. A 'grand soft day' is pretty normal because it's not too cold, and there is just a thick mist, but it might rain hard later on. 'Spitting' means it is definitely raining, but not hard enough to keep you from going outside to carry out your business. A 'wetting rain' is deceptive because it doesn't look too bad, but is coming down hard enough to soak through your clothing. 'Rotten' means it's the kind of day where it just keeps raining, never turning into a downpour, but relentless, nonetheless. 'Bucketing', 'pelting down', 'lashing', and 'hammering' are a few other words the Irish use to describe their rain.

It was September of 2008, well over a decade since my first marathon walking excursion across Canada. I had become a veteran trekker, and my latest adventure took me across the pond. By looking at a map, I figured I could walk from Belfast, in Northern Ireland, to the southern city of Cork, in a couple of weeks, but I didn't anticipate so much moisture. Two local monks, equipped with an RV, provided support for my trek. They were a big help and great company, too.

The Irish are a resilient lot—they have no choice—and soon after taking up the walk, I, too, realized I would have to be resilient.

One day I actually spent hours wandering, wondering where I was. And then it came to me, I was lost. I couldn't find the local monks, and they couldn't locate me either.

After a while, I spotted them parked on the side of the road. I stepped into the RV, relieved but drenched from the latest in a long series of downpours, and 'knackered' (Irish for exhausted).

"How do you deal with these constant rainstorms?" I asked.

"What storm?" replied one of the boys.

After several days of trudging through intermittent rain and always carrying an umbrella, I asked them, "Is there ever a day when it doesn't rain in Ireland?"

I waited for a response, but there was none. They both put their heads down, as if ashamed, or as if to apologize. At that point, I also started to feel ashamed for criticizing their homeland and thought it was I who should apologize.

"It's okay, Ireland is beautiful" I reassured them.

The confirmation of regular precipitation in this grand land came when one of the monks told me he was once going door-to-door on what we call *sankirtan*, the distribution of spiritual books on *bhakti* yoga. He came to one household, knocked on the door, and a woman answered.

"Hello! I'm a monk and I..." he began to say.

But she interrupted and asked, "What kind of monk are you?"

"I'm a wet one" he responded.

I've travelled a lot, mostly on foot, but I have never been to a place where I've seen so many discarded umbrellas. Broken and battered, they litter the streets, rejected and abandoned by their owners after being snapped by gusts of wind. When something is destroyed, the Irish say it is 'in tatters'.

The image of dysfunctional umbrellas did, however, remind me of an important pastime of Krishna. I was swept up with nostalgia as I recalled readings and discussions shared in an *ashram* of monks, regarding the tale of Krishna holding high the hill called Govardhan.

Transcending the laws of gravity, the young Krishna, the ultimate weightlifter, made light of the hill's heaviness by lifting it over His head like an umbrella, protecting the villagers of Vrindavan from the torrential rains summoned by an irate Indra. Torrents of rain fell for seven days and seven nights, and all the while, patience was demonstrated by this 'boy wonder'. He was a hero to the people of Vrindavan, and to those who reflect on this pastime of hope.

Once, while staying overnight in a kind gentleman's apartment, I woke up early and went outside. My two-monk support team and our host were still inside as I prepared for another day of trekking. Lo and behold, I looked up and saw a clear sky. What's more, there were stars, the first I had seen since coming to Ireland.

"*Prabhus* (a respectful address), come out here; you won't believe it, the sky is clear!" I exclaimed.

They came out and were almost as amazed as I.

On two occasions during my trip to the Emerald Isle, I was victimized by a weather-related wardrobe malfunction. It was a bit embarrassing for me personally, but other folks may have found it somewhat entertaining. The dynamics of wearing flowing robes during constant rain results in the garment pressing tightly against your legs. And then as you stride forward, the material rips. This particular rip started from the base of my *dhoti* (lower robe) and travelled all the way up to my thigh. My attire looked like one of those swanky evening gowns which ladies sometime wear, with a revealing slit up the side.

This remained an inconvenient little problem while I was in the countryside. I walked along the edge of the road where motorists couldn't see my bare leg. However, it became a larger nuisance when I entered a village where people could see me from all directions. Before reaching the monks in the RV, I timidly trudged along for several blocks holding onto the fabric. I remember delivering polite "Hellos!" to pedestrians, hoping they wouldn't notice the erotic look. God knows they rarely see a monk, let alone a weird one.

This happened twice in one day, and I was overwhelmed with anguish which turned to joy once I caught up with the monks and stepped into the vehicle to change into dry clothes.

While I really gained a profound appreciation for the landscape when trekking through Ireland, my biggest lesson was tolerance. Maybe a dash of transcendence would also apply.

My good friend, Praghosa, who is also a follower of Krishna, decided to come and join me for a day on the road. He brought the sunshine with him. The sun literally showed itself, in addition to Praghosa's own euphoric self. He and I have worked on plenty of live theatre productions together in Mayapura, India, the hub of the now popular *kirtan*, or group chanting. I author the scripts, which are of a Vedic morality genre, and direct the plays, while Praghosa is a star actor. He has this great vibrancy about him and a sensational showmanship. The second he hits the stage he receives an awesome response from the audience. Often, it's laughter.

If anything, Praghosa might embody the vibrant spirit of an Irishman, even in the midst of a groggy day. To elaborate, we were walking once, and the sun had eventually hidden itself behind the clouds. I told him of my challenges on the narrow shoulders of the road, the blackberry vines clinging to my robes, the night a woman hurled a full bottle of beer at me as I was passing through Dublin (just blocks away from the famous Guinness Distillery), and, finally, of Indra's disbursement of rain.

Praghosa just laughed as I narrated my stories. No sympathy from this man! But as *karma* would have it, after trekking together for some distance, his inexperience at 'walking warriorism' came to fruition. Something went wrong. The big toenail just fell right off his left foot. He was in some pain, but I smiled and thought it served him right for his insensitivity to my Irish trials and tribulations.

"Not used to the speed and stride, right Praghosa? Enjoy the next downpour, okay?" I chuckled.

Seriously though, Praghosa is a true friend. He's married to a wonderful woman, has two teenage boys, and brightens up a lot of lives with his jovial nature. It's routine for him to do so, and I deserved a few seconds of retaliative fun.

Even though it seems to rain every day, Ireland is a beautiful country. The people

MOIST IN IRELAND.

are toughened by the elements, but kind of heart. To this day, no matter where I am, if it starts to rain, I feel a little less intimidated walking through it because of the experiences I had in joyful, but moist, Ireland.

Although Ireland has more than its fair share of rain, the folks who live there are appreciative of what God has provided them. The following version of "An Irish Blessing" confirms just that:

> *May the blessing of the rain be on you—the soft sweet rain. May it fall upon your spirit so that all the little flowers may spring up and shed their sweetness on the air. May the blessing of the great rains be on you; may they beat upon your spirit and wash it fair and clean and leave there many a shining pool where the blue of heaven shines, and sometimes a star.*

CHAPTER 37

TRINIDAD: TREKKING FOR THE DESTITUTE

"Not all those who wander are lost."

–J.R.R. Tolkien

It was 5:00 a.m. local time when my Caribbean Airlines flight landed in Port of Spain, Trinidad. I wasted no time picking up my luggage and going through customs, excited to begin my latest walking excursion. I was eager to meet a driver who was being sent with instructions to deliver me to the Longdenville ISKCON temple. But, the driver wasn't at the airport and it turned out he thought I was arriving at 7:00 a.m.

"Don't *waddy*; I'll be right there!" said the driver when I reached him on the phone.

His accent seemed more Indian than Caribbean, and his kind reassurance made me feel comfortable, so I took his advice and didn't *worry* too much.

While waiting for him to arrive, I realized my feet were restless and anxious to move after enduring several hours on a jet plane some 30,000 feet up in the air. I hankered to touch, stand, and move upon the earth, but only had a two-day window in which to trek Trinidad. My route would go from the large city of Port of Spain to Debe, a more modestly sized community.

I was rather zealous about walking Trinidad, the birthplace of *limbo*, a unique dance also known as the 'under stick dance'. As a child, I loved to *limbo*, and also enjoyed the steel drum and calypso music craze which originated in Trinidad. Carnival, the nation's festival of sound, featuring scantily clad females and males gyrating, doesn't attract me in the least, but is a big draw for the more worldly.

What was of greater importance to me, however, was the news of the catastrophic earthquake that hit Haiti on January 12th, 2010. At a magnitude of 7.0 on the Richter scale, the earthquake devastated the country, leaving the death toll in the hundreds of thousands. I resolved to dedicate my walk to the suffering Haitian citizens.

The driver picked me up and we had barely left the airport when I made a spontaneous decision.

"Stop the car, let me out, I'm going to walk!" I said. "Hold onto my luggage and please just drive ahead to the next major intersection and wait, then show me which way to go."

He smiled and agreed to this unique request.

I was tired. Tired of flying and tired of being shuttled around in motorized vehicles. I had virtually no rest on the overnight flight, which is not unusual because it is hard for me to sleep at the best of times, let alone while zooming across the universe. Nevertheless, in that fatigued state, I was determined to go on foot and 'mooch it up'—a slang term we sometimes use on our marathon walks. It means not taking the time to have a shower.

Trinidad is a hot place on Earth, at least for me, and as time ticked on, the sun's power increased while *my* power quickly decreased. I sometimes tell people that I'm a polar bear from Canada and prefer the northern clime. But, here in Trinidad, close to the equator, I soon realized I was perhaps too close to the sun. My small compact umbrella provided some shelter from the sun's rays, but did little for the humidity. In preparation for the walk, I had procured a brand-new pair of Crocs. The challenge of breaking in new footwear has its downside, especially with the hot sun, a sweating body, and soon enough, blisters. However, I was doing what I wanted to do and had come here to walk, so onward I trudged.

TRINIDAD'S A HOT PLACE. WE MANAGED TO FIND AN OCEAN CAVE TO COOL DOWN IN.

I was trekking on what they call Main Road, but it didn't seem like a major highway to me with just two lanes lined with tiny shops. Later on, I found out there's a major freeway shooting straight through the country, notorious for nightmarish gridlock. I also observed that Trinidad has a very high density of automobiles.

My mission in part, as usual, was to encourage people to use their feet more often and give the automobile a break. Cars are somewhat useful, but most of the time they are just a nuisance. Horses are more fun. People sometimes challenge me saying we can't live in the past and we must constantly strive to progress and move forward. But sometimes I wish we could go backwards. Hummingbirds fly backwards, and incidentally, Trinidad and Tobago are known to be the 'Land of the Hummingbird'.

I continued walking, witnessing the crazy and chaotic traffic with cars whipping around corners with incredible intensity. It reminded me of the old Sonny and Cher song, "The Beat Goes On."

And while the beat went on, so did the heat as I passed homes, shops, a few factories, and several food stalls where they sell *bhara*. This famous local snack consists of chickpeas with dragon-hot chutney smacked between two thick slabs of bread. Sounds and looks vegetarian, but I wasn't going to take a chance on anything that hot and spicy. I was already sweating profusely and couldn't imagine what would happen if I consumed a *bhara* or two.

I saw lots of people, mainly motorists and pedestrians. One pulled his car over and jumped out with a quick question. "What's your mission?" he demanded.

"Haiti!" I replied. "My walk is dedicated to the destitute people of Haiti."

Just days before, a massive earthquake with a magnitude of 7.0 shook and shattered the nearby nation of Haiti.

But the questioner wasn't interested in hearing about my reasons for walking in Trinidad. He was more interested in telling me, and the world, as it turned out, about his own mission.

"Jesus!" he blared out. "Jesus is the only answer!"

It was obvious this man had been blessed with an extraordinary set of lungs.

"It's Jesus and ONLY Jesus!" he roared again and again, almost drowning out the rumbling sound of traffic.

The man's booming voice started to attract a crowd and the public attention he so badly wanted. I guess the presence of a Hare Krishna *swami* attired in saffron robes wound him up. If he hadn't had a car to tend to, I believe he would have trailed on behind me for quite some time. I could appreciate his strong sense of determination, but after a few minutes, he turned and went back to his vehicle.

Eventually, a couple of devotees from the Longdenville temple came along and joined the walk. After four hours and almost twenty kilometres of trudging along on foot, I finally reached my destination. The merciless sun and its accompanying humidity seemed to be warning me to stop. I became overwhelmed in gratitude when I reached the end of the road. I was well looked after and relaxed for several hours in a cool home. My hosts provided me with an excellent vegetarian meal, which, by the way, did not include the aforementioned *bhara*. A masterful massage therapist worked on my limbs, feet, and back, and I later laid down in a comfortable bed for a great sleep.

Before retiring, Kamal, the massage expert, received *diksa*, the Sanskrit word for 'initiation'. Kamal sat down by a *havan* fire to receive his initiation, a formal ceremony where one vows to honour a commitment to a mentor or *guru*, which in this case was me. The student, or *shishya*, agrees to take inspiration and direction that helps set stability in his or her life. The *shishya* accepts a new, and spiritual, name. In this case, Kamal accepted the additional name of Kartamasha, a name for Krishna which refers to Him as being the boss in the rural settlement of Vrindavan, India.

The truth of the matter was that on day two of my walk in Trinidad, Kamal/Kartamasha was the real boss. He lives on the island and knows his way around. Furthermore, he had been in the military for twenty years and is a fitness trainer. He became my walking partner for the day and led the way. I was more than happy to have such an experienced guide.

We were enthusiastic about getting an early start and covering some distance before the sun became unbearable. We began walking from the Longdenville temple at 2:00 a.m. Very early on in the trek, we were confronted by stray dogs more or less lined up across a dirt road. Anyone who walks knows that dogs are part of the equation, but in this case, they were no match for the walkers. With Karta's military background of fearlessness, and my meagre faith in Krishna, we penetrated the territory of the pack of four dogs and, despite their snarls and barks, marched on.

As the night finally waned and the sun started to rise, people began noticing my robes and addressed me with a hearty, "*Haribol!*" That is what some of the folks in the Caribbean call Hare Krishna monks. *Haribol* is an affectionate greeting and is often sung at the end of a group chanting session as the grand finale to a Sanskrit song. We are happy to be known as monks who sing in the streets.

Five hours passed and Karta and I were keeping a good pace of more than five kilometres an hour, covering the better part of thirty kilometres by 7:00 a.m. We were steady and strong, but I must admit it was difficult keeping up with such a physically fit military man. I soon needed a break and spread my upper cloth on the ground and lay down in a mangrove. Those new shoes were really giving me a hard time. Blisters began appearing on both feet, and the early morning heat resulted in rashes that turned bloody. This is the kind of austerity monks are accustomed to, and right or wrong, we feel austerity builds toughness and character.

While I was taking a brief break, Danial Maharaja, a reporter for one of the national newspapers, phoned Karta. She requested an interview and wanted to know the reason for my walk.

"I'm promoting pilgrimage, a simpler way of life," I began, "and am dedicating it to the victims of the Haitian earthquake who have suffered immensely and are living through challenging times. There's been a tremendous loss of life, homes, and belongings, so my little walk is just a trivial sacrifice compared to the hardships these people are enduring."

Other folks soon came along and joined our two-man walking team. One was a police officer, and another was a big-time oil man. As we moved through the streets we charmed local shop keepers by singing the magical song of "*Hare Krishna*." Motorists acknowledged us and honked their horns in support. We chanted for some time, but it came to an end when Karta and I stopped to attend a *sangha*, a devotional gathering in the city of Debe.

I was honoured to be the guest speaker and told the enthusiastic crowd about my walking experiences in Canada, and of this walk dedicated to the earthquake victims. The members of the audience were particularly attentive when I told them about the adventure of encountering bears in Canada, and an attack of black flies, which I referred to as black, swirly snow.

The gathering ended happily with a much-appreciated meal of Indo-Caribbean veggie food, featuring a delicious *dhal puri* with spicy lentils embedded in flat bread. Soon after this feast we hit the road because we had another eight kilometres to complete before finishing our mini-Trinidad marathon. We walked until 11:00 p.m., completing forty-three kilometres for the day, before having the best rest ever.

It was a difficult day, but our difficulties paled in comparison to what the Haitians endured. Three million people were affected by the devastation and almost a quarter of a million souls lost their lives.

The ancient *Bhagavad-gita* uses the Sanskrit word *dukhalayam* to describe our world as a place of suffering. The *Gita* also encourages us to add a spiritual component to our lives which will enhance our ability to cope with life's calamities. Calamities are an inevitable factor of life, and it is natural for us to seek solace during times of despair and confusion.

I believe walking with prayerful intent alleviates pain for victims of catastrophic experiences. Dedication through walking and prayer helps also the healing process. Helping is always healing, and I hope, in some small way, our little walk in Trinidad helped the victims of the terrible earthquake in Haiti.

CHAPTER 38
DELICIOUS MAURITIUS

"It's no use walking anywhere to preach unless our walking is our preaching."

–Francis of Assisi

I will never forget my first visit to Mauritius in 2011. It was autumn, which coincided with spring back home in Canada. I am still baffled about all the enthusiasm my arrival generated when I ventured to this beautiful island.

Mauritius is an exotic place surrounded by the refreshing waters of the Indian Ocean, and somewhere just under 3,000 kilometres east of Africa. It's about 2,000 square kilometres and has 150 kilometres of white sandy beaches surrounded by the world's third-largest coral reef. It was a Dutch colony from 1638 to 1710, a French colony from 1715 to 1810, until it became a territory of the British regime. Mauritius finally became an independent nation in 1968. Around 1.2 million folks call it home.

My first surprise when I landed was the way I cleared customs at Sir Seewoosagur Ramgoolam International Airport. I was spotted by an airport official who insisted I move to the front of the long queue. My passport was reviewed, and I was quickly admitted. Wow, I had never been treated like a celebrity before.

Then the terminal doors opened, and just as the tropical air greeted my skin and nostrils, I was approached by a huge camera. A man was at the controls and a lady reporter thrust a microphone in my face.

"Hello, can you tell us why you will be walking the whole of Mauritius?" she asked.

I explained that I wanted to encourage a walking culture, a situation where people take time for introspection. The interview with the national TV station was brief, but I think most people in the island nation must have seen it. In the days to come, I met hundreds, perhaps thousands of the friendliest people on Earth.

After the interview I was greeted with an incredible outburst of joy from members of the local Hare Krishna community. A massive garland of fresh tropical flowers was placed over my head, embracing my neck, shoulders, and torso. I was soon whisked away by that eager bunch of devotees to our destination—the farm in Bon Accueil.

The devotees first came to Mauritius in 1975 and were immediately enchanted by the beautiful green subtropical paradise island surrounded by the transparent waters of the Indian Ocean. During his visit that same year, Prabhupada instructed devotees to acquire land for the establishment of a Krishna-conscious community based on simple living and high thinking.

"It will be easy walking in Mauritius because there are no big animals here," said Kala, a Mauritius native of French descent.

"No big game, no large wildlife, that's no fun; I'm fascinated by large animals, and back in Canada we have moose, grizzly bears, and caribou," I replied. "Of course, you have humans here, who are the wildest of them all."

Good-natured Kala had a great chuckle.

I was startled the following morning when I saw a safari of sorts taking shape. It was 4:00 a.m., and seventy-four people, including some young children, came to join my first day of walking. Enthusiasm was oozing forth, even though it was extremely early in the morning. For some of these folks, having a *swami* come to their island was a special treat, and I guess they were equally excited to have a chance to walk with one.

They formed a circle, like a garland of people around me, and each person came forward to offer the standard reverential obeisance, which I would reciprocate. You might define such prostrations of respect as divine push-ups.

All of this took a good half hour, but by 4:30 a.m., we set off on our journey. To my surprise this routine continued every day, and I soon looked forward to being sent off accompanied by so many happy smiles and faces.

I have walked many places around the world and have seen a wide variety of plant life, but the grassy giants of Mauritius are unique. Tall sugar cane plants grow right next to the asphalt, leaving little, if any shoulder to the road. Motorists were courteous and respectful, reducing their speed as soon as they spotted our throng of spiritual walkers.

Those early mornings would see headlights cast shadows and spookily distorted images of walkers against a backdrop of sugar cane. All the while, we continued moving along chanting softly on our *mantra* beads. When the sun came over the horizon, we would burst into Sanskrit songs dedicated to *guru* and God. I loved it, and so did my fellow devotees and the villagers and townsfolk from Port Louis, the major city.

Hinduism is the dominant religion of Mauritius, and when the sun comes up, if you are lucky to see over and above the sugar cane, a temple often comes into view. Most of these countryside and village temples are not very large, but have splendorous pyramid-like shapes, multiple stunning colours, and gods decorating their exteriors.

My fellow walkers and I always acknowledged the spiritual power which emanated from those temples and offered gestures of *pranams* (folded palms) to these gorgeous edifices of devotion. Frankly, they are the country's most aesthetically pleasing structures. Just beautiful! Unfortunately, they were often closed to the public when we walked by. I guess this was because we were such early birds.

One morning, it poured. The rain came down profusely in buckets. Figuring this might be a deterrent to our walking mission and concerned the children might get cold and sick, I thought maybe we should delay the walk until the weather cleared. It was still dark, but I could see there weren't enough umbrellas to go around. The rain was not only wet, but noisy. Its splatter against the asphalt created an overwhelming hissing sound that was borderline deafening.

CHANTING ON JAPA MEDITATION BEADS ON THE INDIAN OCEAN, MAURITIUS.

"It's raining hard and we have a choice, either we go back home and return when the rain stops, or we stick it out!" I yelled at the top of my lungs. "What do you want to do?"

"STICK IT OUT!" they all hollered back in unison.

"Alright, Troopers!" I replied. "Tally-ho and away we go!"

One day near Port Louis, a strong wind swept across the island causing havoc. A massive *arjuna* tree, whose medicinal bark cures numerous health issues, was struck down and left lying across the road. This tree of much herbal power had met its untimely end. We stopped, admired the tree, and some walkers climbed over and under it, while others detoured around. I took the opportunity to tell everyone the ancient story about baby Krishna who mystically pulled down two such trees to reveal their actual spirits.

There is much to learn and to contemplate while out on the road, and Mauritius is one of those places where the experience offers many such benefits. I always looked forward to a dip in the ocean, or places like La Petite Riviere Noire, at the end of a day's walk. When we were in the mountains, we munched on wild red and yellow guava, smelled, tasted, and felt the texture of the cinnamon tree, and observed pink pigeons. The divine artistry of nature always left us in awe.

Belle Mare Plage and Flic en Flac beaches became favourite places for me. The cool waters would wash away the sweat and toil of another day of marathon walking. We always ended our daily adventure with chanting, some delicious *prasadam* to eat, and reading of and discussion on the ancient *Bhagavad-gita* and *Srimad Bhagavatam*.

From the diverse routes and trails, to the encounters with the weather, the outings proved to be enriching for body, mind and soul. It was the people of Mauritius, however, who made this cross-island trek sensational. We created a strong bond.

However, not all was joyous. A tiny sector criticized my walk. The complainers claimed the early trekking was in some way non-conventional; that it was a form of *maya* (a term we sometimes use to indicate a deviation). That's because our walking schedule conflicted with the normal 4:30 a.m. temple service called *mangal arati*. It was suggested that it was wrong of me to take attention away from temple functions.

I was a bit taken aback by this criticism, although I tried not to take it personally. I knew that only one percent of our walking group might normally attend the traditional *mangal arati*. On top of that, to have so many come out, put on their sneakers and have a full spiritual workout must count for something. We were chanting, eating *prasadam*, associating with each other, as well as reading and discussing the holy Vedic scriptures. In my mind, we were becoming an active moving temple.

I didn't make a big deal out of it, and soon the criticism waned. Since I began power walking in Canada back in '96, I have always sensed an echo of contention by a minority peer group. What can be done?

"Let me never fall into the vulgar mistake of dreaming that I am persecuted whenever I am contradicted," the famous writer, Ralph Waldo Emerson, once remarked. Emerson and his contemporary, Henry David Thoreau, were both nature lovers and avid walkers.

"Criticism is something we can avoid easily by saying nothing, doing nothing and being nothing," is how Aristotle responded to criticism.

"One who criticizes me is my friend, while one who praises me is my enemy," said *Bhaktisiddhanta Saraswati*, one of the teachers in the line of the *bhakti* tradition.

That initial visit to Mauritius in 2011 was the start of something truly special. The country and its people are amazing. Year after year I return to see familiar friends while making new ones. We find new trails. The routine is set, and the building blocks of community power persist.

The various Hare Krishna centres celebrate *kirtan* together. Festivals such as *Janmasthami* and *Gaura Purnima* are big draws. The walks on the trails and beaches are something to look forward to. We have also managed to assemble sizeable theatrical productions involving the youth. It's a chance for the community to see how talented the kids are and what the next generation can do. I'm hoping that future succession planning will evolve as a result of local leadership witnessing the bright youth of their community being active on the stage and on the road. Talent and brainpower are precious!

My walking has indeed become my preaching!

Mauritius, I love thee!

CHAPTER 39

ANGELS AND GANGSTERS IN GUYANA

"He will give His angels charge of you to guard you in all your ways. On their hands they will bear you up, lest you dash your foot against a stone."

–Psalm 91: 11-12

I've walked in several countries around the world, each one offering up its own joys and challenges. Such was the case during a trek in Guyana, a small nation right at the edge of the Amazon rain forest on the northern coast of South America.

My plan was to walk part way across Guyana in 2007 and complete the trek when I came back in 2008. This story begins on the last leg of the journey, with four grown men holding me face down on a bed. I was struggling for my life, or so it seemed at the time. Would they succeed with their nonconventional operation while I was in so much excruciating pain?

"This is going to be done the tribal way," threatened a man with a tight grasp on my foot. "This razor blade is going to fix you up."

Rama Lila, a native of Guyana, tightly held onto the sharpest, shiniest, and newest razor blade he could find as he prepared to slash my foot open. But this episode had nothing to do with torture or any kind of sadistic activities. These big men were trying to help me by treating a serious poisonous infection that had attacked one of my much-needed feet.

Rama wanted to cut into the infected foot and personally suck out the poison. I believed he could do it, after all he's from Guyana and they can do these sorts of things down there. He also had a certain amount of experience since he had been a victim of all kinds of bites and infections in a wild country crawling with multiple kinds of stinging insects and venomous snakes.

As a poor boy, he had supported his family by braving the unknown waters in the land of piranhas, electric eels, and snakes. He would dive into the murky waters wearing nothing but shorts, and after casting a net, pull in whatever he could catch to sell in a local market.

Since those humble beginnings, like many Guyanese who left for America or Canada, Rama has done well for himself. He got himself educated and became a successful accountant in Toronto.

He had already helped me out tremendously on this trip by taking me out each morning to get an early start. I always wanted to cover as many kilometres as possible before the intense heat hit the roads and trails of the country.

One day, after dropping me off, he had come back when the sun was at its pinnacle to bring me some water. I stood by his van quenching my thirst and admiring the Demerara River, which runs almost 350 kilometres from the central rainforest to Guyana's capital city of Georgetown, perched on the edge of the Atlantic Ocean. All of a sudden, I felt intense needles piercing my legs. I raised my *dhoti* to view a swarming army of red ants crawling upward.

"Those are *fire ants*!" said an alarmed Rama. He quickly brushed off the aggressive little flesh-eating monsters. These particular ants are unknown in Canada, but Rama told me they were common in his homeland of Guyana.

But, back now to the poison predicament, and Rama's attempt to cut into my foot and suck out the poison. That process failed because of the sensitivity of trying to operate on the inflamed area, which, by that time, looked more like an overinflated football. The whole thing was way too much for me to handle. I literally screamed in pain and the four men couldn't hold me down, so they gave up, determined to try something else.

It all started when Virat Rupa, a New Yorker, and I were putting in long hours and feeling the fatigue of walking through such humid temperatures. We decided to leave the road and head to the beach to walk by the ocean. The beach seemed clean, and nice and breezy. So, we went barefoot and strode along in the salt water.

We always made a point to sing our standard morning *bhajans*. We were singing praises to the *guru* when, suddenly, a lance-like object pierced its

IT'S SOMETIMES A ROUGH COASTLINE AT GEORGETOWN, GUYANA.

way into the base of my right foot. Up came my leg in response to the stab, and I observed a dead catfish dangling from my foot. The fish was longer than my foot and even though the sting hurt pretty badly, I shrugged it off. Rama told me later that if it happened again to urinate on the infected area. *Yeah right!* Maybe, if it happens again!

Virat and I continued walking, but the beach suddenly ended, and we were left to navigate through trees, brush, and thorny creepers. There was no trail at all, and eventually we were forced to wade through some rather nasty contaminated creek water. Finally, we made our way back to the main street.

It was then I realized my foot was swelling up and I started visibly limping. Within an hour, my foot had ballooned to an abnormal size and people who saw it said it was a 'whopper', far from being lotus-like. Something had to be done, and so the four men came to the conclusion that they had.

I toughed it out as best I could, hoping for the swelling to go down, but the next day I was taken to an emergency walk-in clinic to meet a doctor fresh out of India. He had a nerdish haircut and a pretty cool moustache. He examined the wound and determined I needed a tetanus shot. I was scheduled to fly back to Canada the following day and needed a wheelchair to board the aircraft. I had only nine kilometres left to complete my walk. Oh well, I planned to be back to finish the balance the next year.

When I got home, I saw a doctor right away and received intravenous treatment for two weeks. That cured my ailment, but it was tough being injected so much.

Despite my painful foot experiences, I reminisced about Guyana and the country's hospitable people. They lead a nice and simple lifestyle, and both races, the Blacks and Indians, get along well. I seldom saw any other races of people. The rare Caucasian, I assumed, was a missionary making efforts to convert locals to Christianity.

Before the catfish incident, I walked each morning in Guyana, and in the evening, I participated in an organized *padayatra*, a chanting procession throughout various villages. We came to a neighbourhood in Lusignan where, one night, a year earlier, gunmen mercilessly stormed several homes killing eleven innocent people while they slept. Men, women, and children were victims of the massacre by those cowardly gangsters! Our *padayatra* group paid homage to the victims of this sad, senseless crime.

My travels on foot have led me to believe that many people are good at heart and well-intentioned. I would go so far as to say they are sweet and innocent; I would call them 'regular angels'. And then there are others that are 'lost angels', a confused lot, sometimes doing the wrong things, but in their hearts, meaning well. And then there are just blatant 'bad angels', mean-spirited, filled with resentment, and always lashing out at the world.

In the ancient Vedic texts, we read about these three divisions of mindsets, states of behaviour. They are referred to as the three modes of nature. The first type, the one's I call 'regular angels' can be described as being in *sattva* in Sanskrit, which means thoughtful, kind, and good. The second group is influenced by the mode of *rajas*, passion and restlessness. They are the 'lost angels', but are capable of becoming 'found' should they gain the company of people in *sattva*. Finally, in category three, we have the 'bad angels'. The Sanskrit word for the mode of these people is *tamas*, ignorance, darkness, and self-destruction. They are irresponsible, blame others when things go badly, and have a sense of entitlement. Gangsters and marauders fit neatly into this box.

Everyone is a 'good angel' deep down inside, but for the most part, *rajas* and *tamas* have been allowed to enter into their hearts, leaving the individual deeply confused, entangled, and with their vision clouded.

I see traces of the three modes everywhere I walk, and Guyana was no exception. Remember the clean beach where we encountered the sting of a catfish? It was during that trip Virat and I came upon a *tamas*-type beach full of empty plastic bottles. We couldn't see the sand in some places and were skipping and tripping over the garbage. That was a tough place to traverse, and just to add to it, it was a tear-jerker to see the mess, the carelessness, and downright gangsterism lodged against Mother Nature.

WALKING IN GUYANA IS NOT COMPLETE WITHOUT TREKKING ITS SEAWALL.

There are plenty of good things to say about Guyana. There are qualities of *sattva*, goodness, emanating from this great land. One of its visually appealing features is the lotus flower that grows in abundance. We find reference to the lotus flower in the *Bhagavad-gita*. It sits resiliently on the water yet is never drenched by the water. Even if storming rain comes upon it, it never becomes water-logged. It remains aloof from its surroundings. There's a saying, "Be in the world, but not of the world."

One interesting place where I stopped on the course of my walk on a very hot and particularly sweltering day, was at Demerara Distillery, known for its El Dorado rum. It is situated on the main coastal road. One of the managers of the place spotted me on the highway as I was coming near. He invited me into the front office where I could cool off.

No, I did not go for a shot of rum! Monks don't do that, but I did accept a cold soft drink as a gesture of reciprocation. I was treated nicely.

This man was like an angel to me. Let us all try to be like an angel. Like a lotus.

CHAPTER 40

FANTASTIC FIJI

"People always said to me, 'Why would you leave civilization to go to a place like Fiji?' Fiji is a far more civilized place than California or New York City."

–Raymond Burr

I was enthusiastic to explore a country which is known world-wide for its exceptional bottled water. The word 'Fiji' in bold print on a blue tinted container, stamped with the signature hibiscus flower, is pretty much all I knew about the South Pacific island.

But I learned that Fiji is more than just one island, it's an archipelago of more than 330 islands including a total land area of about 18,300 square kilometres. Almost ninety percent of Fiji's 900,000 residents live on the two major islands, Viti Levu and Vanua Levu. The capital city of Suva is located on Viti Levu and serves as Fiji's principal cruise port.

I started from the city of Suva. The sun was beaming down; it was thirty degrees Celsius and the Pacific Ocean was right next to me providing a little bit of relief with a cool breeze. I was accompanied by three congenial walking companions on the Queen's Road, which would take us from Suva to the city of Lautoka. The road twisted a bit; spectacular mountains were in the background. My health was super. My legs were eager to move. What more could I want?

'*Bula*' is the local word for 'hello', with the 'u' sounding like the two 'o's in 'ooze'. Fijian folks love to be greeted with '*bula*'. The people look healthy, especially the native Fijians because most of them don't have cars and use their feet for transportation.

First-time visitors might be a little surprised to see some of the men wearing skirts called '*sulu*', which fall just below the knee. I was told that before the Europeans came, these men's skirts were made out of grass. Today's version of the *sulu* is made from cloth and reminded me of the Scottish kilt. Interestingly enough, I met some young Mormon missionaries wearing *sulus* with their patented white shirts and ties. These nice young men were trying to blend in culturally and looked pretty smart in their outfits.

The native Fijians found my attire interesting. When stopping for a break, residents would slowly poke their heads out of their homes and stare. One of the members of our walking group would meet those stares with a smiling, "*Bula*."

Soon after I arrived, I learned there was a history of cannibalism in Fiji. Legend has it that one insatiable chief by the name of Ratu Udre Udre, used stones to count the number of humans he had as meals. The total was more than 900! Also shocking, in July of 1867, the same month and year Canada became a nation, Reverend Thomas Baker was on the chief's dinner menu.

I was told not to worry, however, because cannibalism hasn't been practiced in Fiji for more than 100 years. The closest you'll get is a meal of mongoose, a rodent introduced by Indian indentured labourers when they were employed in the sugarcane fields. In India, cobras are known to frequent sugarcane stocks, so they brought the rodent to kill the snake.

Mongoose was actually the only roadkill I ever saw during my trek through Fiji. That's a huge contrast from my native Canada where roadkill of all kinds is a daily occurrence. Moose, deer, bear, raccoon, porcupine, skunk, squirrels, and other unfortunate species are regularly being reincarnated. These days, you're not likely to find a single snake on Fiji's main island. I did, however, keep hearing stories about the huge Degei, a serpent of an extraordinary kind. Situated on the northern section of the island is a place called Rakiraki, and near Nakauvadra Hill, there is a lake in which resides the Fijian version of the Loch Ness Monster. Native Fijians consider this area a forbidden zone and do not want to disturb Degei who is considered the creator of the Fijian Islands.

Our *guru*, Prabhupada, referred to this creature as 'Kaliya'. During Krishna's time, Kaliya escaped the waters of the Yamuna River in northern India. This multi-hooded snake was danced upon by the feet of Krishna; it was His way of admonishing the serpent for poisoning the inhabitants of His village. Thus, Kaliya was sent away, fleeing, or rather, slithering into the ocean, and finally heading to Fiji, where he currently resides in some aqua cave. I love these stories, far-fetched as they may seem to some.

It was Radha Madhava, a Fijian-born person of Indian descent, who brought me to his native country and did the trek with me. Our dream was to follow our *guru*'s instructions to share the sacred sound and catch the ears of people in 'every town and village' on the planet. Chanting sacred names is traditionally known as *kirtan*. An added feature of our program would be to share *prasadam*, sacred food, whenever possible. Radha Madhava told the villagers that I was an *italatal'a*, a priest.

We met Elike, a fifteen-year-old boy, at the Pacific Harbour. He introduced himself and told us his older brother, Daniel, used to live as a monk at the Hare Krishna *ashram* in Suva, and now lived in a tent on the beach close to the road we were walking on. We soon met the free-spirited nineteen-year-old native Fijian fellow, and he reminded me of an older version of Disney's *Jungle Book* character, Mowgli. I invited Daniel to join our walk.

"If you are available, would you consider walking with us and helping with the food and entertainment program that Radha Madhava and I have in mind? We can bring our message of peace and joy to your village, and if you have a good hand at the drum, you can be our percussionist as well as a co-walker."

Daniel accepted the offer, took up the challenge, and in a carefree way, started his walk with us the next morning. It was 4:00 a.m., and we soon entered into an area of Fiji known as 'The Salad Bowl', where plenty of papaya orchards and fields of cassava and taro can be found.

At Sigatoka, we met two dynamic women. Gita Kirti and Guru Smaran are dedicated to seeing to the construction of a new Krishna temple. They were at a farmers' market where we held our first outdoor *kirtan* in Fiji. It was exhilarating to know that the cross-country trek through the islands was taking on a new meaning by incorporating the chanting of *mantras* in every town we walked through.

In this hub of market activity, we prudently started to play with Daniel on the *mridanga* drum, and I on *kartals*, hand cymbals. Curiously, we waited for a response. It is not an exaggeration to say that people stopped what they were

WALKING SOMETIMES TOOK ON SINGING, DRUMMING, AND DANCING IN FIJI.

doing and were attracted by our chanting. They wondered what the sound was, and a few thought it was something Hindu. Well, not quite, but it was something different, something spiritual!

Hindus and Christians alike, manning their booths, stopped what they were doing to check us out. Some walked over to us offering Fijian dollars. Customers came over and tourists responded to the sacred sound of the *maha mantra* with warmth and smiles.

We are not professional musicians, but somehow through the mercy of Krishna, I believe, we touched many souls that day. Our *kirtan* seemed to relieve a burden, a burden that is routinely felt by people all over the world. After all, people here struggle with the pangs of life just like they do everywhere else. *Bhagavad-gita* spells out four traumas which all souls face—birth, disease, old age, and death.

The breakthrough we encountered at Sigatoka built up our confidence and provided the necessary fuel for us to hold public chanting programs in every town we came upon. In the city of Nadi we planted ourselves under a massive tree. I began chanting while Daniel was away for a washroom break. A curious crowd formed and a few immature younger kids began to snicker and laugh at us, but when six foot, two inches tall Daniel came to join us, the mood changed. When the younger crowd saw one of their own amongst us, they relaxed, were more accepting, and able to genuinely enjoy the chanting.

That evening our party was accommodated in a simple farmhouse nestled about two kilometres from Queen's Road. The facilities were semi-primitive, but quite suitable for a monastic person, as austerities are the wealth of a renunciant. I rose the next morning at 2:30 a.m., and after my routine shower, headed for the highway, leaving the others to sleep in or get cleaned up. By 3:00 a.m. I made my way down a bumpy stony road bordered on both sides by sugarcane crops.

Only a distant barking dog broke the silence. I had a small 'torch' (flashlight) to help me find my way in the dark. The streak of beaming light startled two creatures tucked away next to the edge of the towering sugarcane. Their sudden presence shot a jolt up my spine, and their dark hue, blending into the equally dark leaves of the crop, revealed the shining whites of their eyes. *Hyenas?* No! The humble mongoose is the only game here. My torch soon revealed they were local natives in work clothes, and they were shivering in fear.

"What are you?" one of them demanded.

"*Bula!*" I said. "I am a walking *italatala*."

He cautiously edged forward to examine this foreign creature and looked at my bald head complete with the *tilak* marking on my forehead. He then dropped his gaze to my orange robes, eyes wide open in wondrous fright.

"Do you have legs?" he asked.

I lifted my *dhoti* to show my ankles and feet and let the fellow know I wasn't a ghost. Gradually, his tension subsided. I flashed a friendly smile and said, "Hare Krishna."

"What?"

"Sacred sound."

Obviously, this fellow, who identified himself as Rocco, hadn't tuned in to the latest news concerning a walking *italatala*. The National TV station and local newspaper both had done stories about the walk, but these guys obviously hadn't seen the media reports. Meanwhile, Rocco's friend decided to remain semi-hidden in the safety of the sugarcane. It was Rocco who accepted my handshake after he decided I was neither ghost nor foe. We finally hugged. He broke into a smile.

"Where are you from?" asked Rocco.

"Canada," I replied.

"Take me there," he insisted.

"No, no, we need to work our way back to God," I replied. "Our soul must prepare to move on and we must eventually leave this planet."

He nodded in agreement before leaving me to carry on toward Queen's Road. Moments later I concluded that the two sugarcane workers were probably high on *kava*, nicknamed, '*grog*', a muddy earthy beverage which calms the consumer but can create hallucinations.

The following day, I met another worker in the cane fields who went by the name Tukes. This young father of Southeast Asian descent asked what I was doing. He was just standing there by the road in deep despair because he had just been dismissed from his job, and was now unemployed.

"I'm walking for purification," I told him.

"Do you believe in Christ?" asked Tukes.

"Yes. Jesus is the son of God and Krishna is His father. This relationship between father and son is very strong, and in a sense, they are one."

I told him I was raised Christian, but added Krishna to my life, so I now have both Jesus *and* Krishna.

Tukes decided to accompany me to the city of Lautoka which was quite some distance down the road.

I pondered. *What will be Tukes' destiny? Will he become a piece of driftwood like me, always moving?* Not likely; he's got a family to provide for.

Our destination was the Krishna Kaliya temple in Lautoka. We arrived to a warm greeting and the temple administrators arranged for Tukes to shower and clean up. They also provided him with some fresh clothes. Minutes later I found him cleaning pots in the community kitchen. He looked like a new man with restored hope. All he needed was some attention and direction. I hope he continues happily in his service to family and the Divine. I felt good to have met Tukes and felt even better to see that another soul had taken some positive steps forward.

A second fulfillment soon came my way. I had been aspiring to see the real Kaliya at Rakiraki, that massive and terrifying snake, both feared and revered. Maybe I would be able to feed him some of that scrumptious and sacred *prasadam* so well prepared by the Fijian devotees at the temple. By the way, I consider Fijian cuisine to be the best ever.

But time was slipping away, and two more islands were part of my itinerary. I thought I could satisfy my wanderlust by having a serious *darshan* (viewing) of the deities in the Lautoka temple. There they were, two figures—a venomous multi-headed serpentine creature, and on top of him in dance pose, the charming young Krishna, chastising and subduing the epitome of evil beneath His lotus-like feet. I firmly believe that divine powers rest even in inanimate forms, because there's life and feeling in all things.

Now, back to Daniel. With great help and planning from two stalwart *bhakti yogis*, Jai Ram and Vishvanatha, our dream for *kirtan* in Daniel's home village of Navutulevu came true. Rasamandala, a local *brahmachari* monk, played his *djembe*, I sang, and Daniel served the *prasadam*. We were thrilled that Navutulevu's chief was in attendance, and he danced along with all the villagers to our spiritual music. It was a feel-good occasion for everyone involved and a huge success. "More! More! More!" my inner voice cheered, referring to more of this for the villages, towns, and cities in the Fiji Islands.

The walk along Taveuni, one of the smallest islands, put the finishing touch to the Fiji trek. We took the small cruiser, *The Princess*, to get there. I had a following in Taveuni, a group of walkers. I even carried a young fellow, maybe four years of age, on my shoulder for a good length. The kid had the thrill of his life, and so did his parents. How

WALKING AND SWIMMING GO HAND IN HAND.

many people can say they rode on the back of a monk? At Tavoro Falls, the entire group of us did more than splash around in the natural springs. With the humidity up high, swimming was most rejuvenating. And then rain came down. Water was everywhere.

It was also a sensation touching the mark at the International Date Line at the 180th meridian. It is at this location that we register the sun's first appearance for the day on planet Earth.

Heat persisted and it was almost time to head off to the airport by way of a mini-aircraft destined for Suva. I was tempted to go for a last dip, this time in a pristine shoreline ocean dock along the walking path. The water was waist-high and most enticing. I told Radha Madhava that I intended to jump in, saffron clothes and all, but one of our locals said, "You don't want to do that. Last week a shark killed a man right at that spot."

Okay! That was a deterrent, so off we went to the airport, leaving the clear blue water for the clear blue sky.

While up in the air, I contemplated how walking conjures up the best of dreams which then hover about wanting to materialize. If you simply apply patience and planning, those dreams will come down for a landing.

My time in Fiji soon came to an end. It was a walk I'll always remember. The beauty of the islands was grand, but the people were grander. Living a simple life and learning to become high thinkers, these folks from Fiji are certainly some of the more civilized people I have met in my travels.

CHAPTER 41

ISRAEL: WHY NOT?

"When I was a child, Israel was a legend more than a reality. She emerged from a dream and today she has surpassed that dream."

–Shimon Peres

It was Sunday, November 7th, 2010 when I arrived in Tel Aviv after a restless flight from India on El Al Airlines. Fatigue overwhelmed me by the time I reached the home of my hosts, a Russian family in the community of Ari'el. Just before my head hit the pillow for an anticipated deep sleep, I had a chat with the man of the house, Radhikatma. Israel was my final stop before returning home to Canada, and I was here to share some teachings on *bhakti*.

However, there may have been another reason for my coming to this land of rich history. A thought came, and then a question.

"What is the distance or length and breadth of Israel?" I asked Radhikatma.

"About 420 kilometres or 260 miles from north to south," he answered, looking very curious.

It just so happened that a sudden seed of pedestrian passion sprouted within my heart. And when Radhikatma pulled out a map for my perusal, it triggered an adventurous lust for the land.

"If I'm doing some speaking engagements in the evening, what will I do in the morning?" I asked before saying, "It's doable."

"What are you talking about?" he questioned.

"I think I'll walk across Israel while I'm here. Can you drive me to a place where I can start trekking?"

"Anything is possible!" he said with a slight smile.

Radhikatma was a terrific host, and after my penetrating sleep, he set gears in motion for the first steps on a trek through this ancient land. He had soon talked to several people who volunteered to accompany me along different segments of the walk. Vrkodhar and Boris joined me the first day as we ventured to Tel Aviv, our starting point. This is not exactly the northern or southernmost point in the country, but it was a natural place to literally get my feet wet. The beach is the place to be in order to touch the Mediterranean Sea, a body of water shared by many different countries.

After a two-hour exposure of sun, sand, and water, our group converged with Israeli and Russian followers of *bhakti* yoga to celebrate the popular *Govardhan Puja*. This festival acknowledges Krishna's great heroic weightlifting power. The faithful believe that He actually lifted a hill to protect villagers from torrential rains.

On day number two, Ekavirya, a soon-to-be father of twins, became my walking partner and led me along the Mediterranean's eastern shore. We started with a quick pace and maintained that momentum for most of the day. We saw hundreds of friendly walkers, runners, and cyclists. I would utter an occasional 'shalom' to these well-wishers while chanting the Hare Krishna *maha mantra* on my *japa* beads.

I have always felt walking and meditative chanting are the perfect marriage that will never know divorce. As usual, nature showed off its splendour in unique ways. In the dry desert terrain, we noticed multitudes of white-shelled snails resembling cotton balls, latching onto long green grass. We admired unique birds and smelled aromatic wildflowers, all in a shared co-existence.

Our final steps of the day took us to a place which confirmed you can never trust a coastline, either by nature or man's imposition. At Apollonia National Park, trekking was hindered by a fence put in place to protect ancient Roman ruins.

The next day, at Netanya, my companions and I soon realized how out of shape we really were. Our walking began with a sprint-like stride, but before long we transitioned into a trudge. The loose sand of the beach is not the easiest place to trek, so we moved to the harder-packed sand next to the water's edge and found a meandering trail leading us through a Kibbutz settlement.

It was hard work walking under a hot sun on the slope of the beach, but we were soon rewarded. My hosts organized a trip to the Dead Sea, and during the drive through the Judean Desert, I received a call from a monk friend of mine. American-born Kavichandra Swami, who pays regular visits to the devout followers of *bhakti* in Israel, heard I was there, and by the magic of mobile phones, found me.

"How are you, Maharaja?" he asked.

"I'm fine!" I said.

"So, I hear you are in the desert. It's a great place to be for a *sannyasi* monk because there's no sense gratification there, just sand dunes."

"That's a good point" I replied.

Kavichandra Swami then offered a little advice and wished me well on my trek across Israel.

After a drive of an hour and a half, we arrived at one of the most therapeutic natural bathing spots in the world. The dense, dynamic, and mineralized water makes you extremely buoyant. Fish don't occupy this body of water as the minerals are too intense for them. However, tourists gravitate to this location like anything. My hosts warned me to be careful not to immerse my head, eyes, or lips for fear of receiving an immediate and extreme burning sensation. I heeded their advice as I bathed in the Dead Sea.

After all of this physical activity we spent the evening in reverence to our *guru*, Prabhupada. By lunar calculation, November 9th was the anniversary of his passing. Devotions were heightened as we reflected on his great contributions to the world. He pioneered the now popular *kirtan*, the non-meat diet, and the non-violent way of life.

Early the next morning, our team, now consisting of four, ambled along the oceanside following the Israel National Trail. It eventually leaves the ocean and ventures inland going through very rough terrain, requiring some challenging climbs. Ekavirya, called the path 'The Paramatma Trail' which means 'God-led', or perhaps, 'go with your gut feeling'. The signage and twisting trail are confusing in spots, especially to newcomers.

HIKING UP THE ISRAEL NATIONAL TRAIL.

Later that afternoon after a twenty-kilometre trek, our special treat was a stop-over at the Jordan River. Jesus had bathed at Yardenit, a Baptismal site on the River Jordan, but it was crowded with pilgrims, so we took our dip in the coolness of Jordan's waters at a more secluded spot just a few metres away. It was more than a bath, perhaps a baptism—a cleanser. It was there that a distant memory came to me when as a child I prayed, "Hallowed be Thy name." As we swam in the Jordan, we started singing

God's names, not in Hebrew, but in Sanskrit. We were swimming in sacred waters and swimming in sacred sounds.

November 11th is Remembrance Day in Canada, a day to mark the end of the First World War. It was on this anniversary that we left Tel Aviv to venture along the seafront once again, but this time we reversed direction in order to end up more strategically near Jerusalem. It was there in the evening that I would speak to a group of Russian *yogis*. The sea was now to our right, and we carried on giving our hips a break by walking the slope of the beach in the opposite direction. All was well until we hit a major obstacle—an army base.

Off we went to Jerusalem to meet Eli and friends, who acted as our tour guides, claiming this city has never drawn people for an abundance of water or oil, but for being a beacon for the religious. Eli showed us the layers of stone put in place by different empires over the ages.

Father Michael, who happens to hail from Timmins, Ontario, in Canada, took us on a tour of his church of St. Anne, dedicated to the mother of Mary. He sanctioned our chanting of *mantras* in that acoustic wonder.

We also veered over to the Jewish sector where I went to the wailing wall and chanted softly with intent to wail or cry in the spirit of a baby yearning for its mother or father; factually—a cry for God. There I met a Hasidic Jew who recognized my robes.

SHARING SPIRITUAL PATHS AT THE WAILING WALL.

"I was a *guru* once back in 1972 in Central Park and hundreds of people watched me do my *siddhi*, but I went back to my heritage, Judaism," he said. "You know what Krishna said to Arjuna 'You have to follow your *dharma*.'"

I really enjoyed my first visit to Israel, but I met so many nice devotees and visited so many historic sites that I didn't have time to complete my cross-country walk. On my flight back to Canada, I was determined to visit Israel soon to complete the journey. It was late October of 2011, when I made it back and resumed the walk in Ashdod.

I am used to greeting devotees with '*haribol*', a combination of two Sanskrit words: *bol* means 'to say' and *Hari* means 'the One who takes away the negative'. I continued to greet people with 'Shalom'. Either way,

I made these addresses in a low tone. I was a little uncertain which greeting to use, even though I preferred '*haribol*', which is from my chosen path. I can also honestly say I would be most uncomfortable if I were to come across as too evangelical, as if I had the *only* answer, and that all other paths are those of ignorance. Perhaps as a novice in the earlier days of my renunciation, I exhibited a trace of fanaticism. That was immature, but I was young, and since then, age has mellowed my mind and allowed me to be more accepting of differing points of view. I revel in the position my *guru* took because he openly admitted that any channel that invokes a love for the sacred is valid. And as the Buddhists say, "There are many paths to the top of the mountain."

Jagannath was my walking partner on my first day back in Israel. The Mediterranean Sea is very much alive and clean, or so it seems. There were many signs of life, including a crab on the shore slothfully moving toward the water. But we also saw a sea turtle who had washed up on the shore, leaving his skeletal armor behind after his soul had moved on.

Later, when approaching the Gaza Strip, we came upon ancient ruins from the Byzantine period, around 600-1000 A.D.

"Let's stop here," Jagannath said. "I think we've walked far enough for the day and maybe we should have some *prasadam* and take rest." That sounded like a great idea to me, and I was soon glad I took Jagannath's advice. Early the next morning, the news reported a bomb had exploded and nine people were killed on the very trail we were about to trek.

Our next stop was Caesarea, where King Herod walked the aqueducts in that ancient place. His patron was Caesar Augustus, hence the name of this city, completed in 9 B.C.E. Crowds of more than 30,000 used to cram into the hippodrome to watch the chariot races, an ancient version of today's NASCAR.

Bala Krishna, my latest guide, walked with me through ruins of palaces, ancient bathhouses, and a major temple which reflected a more prosperous time. Like all places in this world, conquests never seem to cease, and there, from Herod's time through to the Crusades, in the early days of Zionism, and onward to today, doing damage to others has been a constant reality. Will a future Herod ever reappear? Hopefully not. But lest we forget—history often repeats itself.

Going through Harish, I was joined by an enthusiastic group of walkers, and together we left the coastline and headed inland toward Nazareth. We eventually came to an intersection and a myriad of trails going gradually from uneven terrain to orchards of fruit trees including figs, carob, and olives.

We were charmed to meet up with a herdsman who kept four dozen curious goats moving along in line. Also sharing the raw trail was a Zionist group of about sixty young men blowing bugles. And as they were making their mark, we also made ours by chanting many of the songs of devotion that our *guru* taught us—songs of the soul's yearning.

All of this walking and singing made us hungry, and a family of the Druze tradition provided a meal which more than satisfied our appetites. After a joyous repast, we soon broke into *kirtan*, something we did every evening. This *kirtan* was extra-special because it involved a group of Israeli-born members of Vaishnavism. I was also invited to give a short talk and spoke about the sweet pastimes of young Krishna before concluding with a few stories about my own joys walking in pilgrimage.

Over two short visits I walked across a major portion of Israel. There was no media coverage, but the people were sincere and seemed to appreciate my efforts. Israel is a place of contention, socially and politically, but I didn't feel it while amongst the people there. Only at the airport did I feel momentary uneasiness when my saffron robes attracted attention and I was singled out and sent aside for questioning.

All went well, and the last remark from a female officer was, "You better go, or you're going to miss your flight; and by the way, you smell like incense."

CHAPTER 42

A SLICE OF NEW ENGLAND: MASSACHUSETTS AND CONNECTICUT

"If Americans paid more attention to their spiritual life they would be happier."

–Srila Prabhupada

Pilgrims from the United States, Canada, Europe, India, and many other places around the world, united at the Commonwealth Pier in Boston in great anticipation of celebrating the 50th anniversary of a unique historic event. It was here that a tiny five foot, three inches tall brown-complexioned *swami* from India first landed on American soil, disembarking from the Jaladutta, a cargo ship, at 5:30 a.m. on September 20th, 1965.

This jubilee celebration was held under clear blue skies and most of the participants were *yogis* of the Krishna tradition and disciples or followers of the *swami*. I was among the pilgrims and we all credited him with making a huge difference in our lives. His name was Srila Prabhupada, and he demonstrated the values and concepts of a peaceful existence, embracing the techniques of *mantra* meditation. He taught us how to lead a karma-free lifestyle and encouraged us to simplify our lives with a back-to-the-land way of living. He also told us about reincarnation and helped us address our identity crises. He gave us a Vedic perspective on life.

Prabhupada authored many books on the science of devotion and even influenced the members of the Beatles, the world's most popular music band ever. For all these reasons and more, the gathering of pilgrims at Boston Harbor took place—the best and most appropriate way to express gratitude. We reflected on his achievements while sailing on a boat in the very place of his arrival.

The boat, *The Province Town II*, was a 900 passenger vessel which set sail for a three-hour cruise. It was a time to immerse ourselves in the pastimes of the Founder-Acharya of the International Society for Krishna

Consciousness. During this wonderful time of appreciation, I felt intense eagerness to express gratitude in my own unique way by putting feet and heart together.

My official kick-start to an ambitious walk across America was on this day, September 20th, 2015, when a group of international travelling monks, the Harinama Ruci, led a *kirtan* chanting session through Boston's downtown to Commonwealth Pier. The theme of my trek was 'Walking for Our Teachers'—teachers being a sector of people who, in my opinion, are somewhat underrated and underappreciated. In an ancient Vedic context, the *guru* is revered and honoured for the austerities undertaken and wisdom imparted in an effort to guide and advance the spiritual life of the seeker. In exchange, services are offered to the *guru* as an expression of gratitude and indebtedness. This context and approach, common in Krishna's time, is somewhat alien in today's world.

On Monday, September 21st, the day after the walk to the Commonwealth Pier and the cruise in Boston Harbour, I set out for the west coast of the United States. That day, I walked to the town of Natick with the support of Vivasvan, a Ukrainian-born Michigan resident. Also joining us were a couple of Canadian supporters: Karuna Sindhu, monk extraordinaire, and Pradyumna, a young French-Canadian musician.

We began what became a consistent routine, one which would see us starting our trek in the early morning hours, well before the sun rose. Vivasvan drove our support vehicle three miles ahead, about an hour's worth of walking. He was our team's navigator, while Karuna, Pradyumna, and I were the walkers.

At the end of each hour, we approached the parked support vehicle and took a short break for water and sometimes a snack. We repeated the pattern for several more hours. By 9:00 a.m. that day, we had completed well over ten miles and decided to take a nap at a nice grassy area shaded by trees. This location just happened to be the starting point for the very first annual Boston Marathon in 1905.

We took our rest under a stately oak tree, and I awoke after one of the best snoozes of my life, poised to continue the trek. I noticed a man and woman setting up chairs by the park's gazebo, and soon many seniors made their way to the chairs, some with the aid of various walking support devices. Vivasvan went to see what was going on and was inspired when he met Rachel, an aerobics instructor. He immediately volunteered me to assist her with the senior's stretch session, and I was quick to accept.

"You're on," said Rachel. "Let's see what you got."

Many of the elderly participants were restricted in their ability to walk freely, so I realized the '*swami* step', a simple back and forth swaying of the legs, would be too difficult for them. Spontaneously, I came up with the '*swami* swerve', a similar movement that would allow the seniors to be active while remaining seated.

Rachel played some music to help motivate the participants and first up was Willie Nelson with his rendition of Irving Berlin's "Blue Skies," followed by "Fly like an Eagle" by the Steve Miller Band. Karuna, Pradyumna, and Vivasvan joined in the fun, swaying and swerving along with the other participants.

After the class, Jennifer, one of the facilitators of the program from the seniors' care unit at Golden Pond, invited us for lunch. It turned out we were fasting until noon that day in honour of Radha, Krishna's eternal consort. It was her birthday, which is known as *Radhastami*, and by noon we were going to be extra hungry, so we gladly accepted the invitation to eat in style.

Kelsey, the chef, asked for our menu preferences, and we specified no onions, garlic, eggs, or animals,

LEADING SOME SENIORS IN SWAMI AEROBICS.

including fish. Our tummies were empty, yet filled with anticipation as Kelsey and his assistant, Emma, went off to prepare a delicious feast. Our impromptu time with the senior's group was not only the highlight of the day, but one of our most cherished memories of the entire trek across America. A few days later, Rachel sent me an email to say the seniors liked the '*swami* swerve' so much that she had added it to her repertoire.

With full bellies, we still had some walking to do, so off we went. Even though it was late September, the sun was still quite hot. After a while, Pradyumna and I became quite exhausted and covered in sweat. We also became preoccupied with some beautiful ponds along the way and were tempted to go for a refreshing swim.

Vivasvan and Karuna, who were in the support vehicle, read our minds and found a perfect body of water in which to cool down. When Pradyumna and I reached the boys, they led us to the edge of the water and a nice place to jump in. To our surprise, they found a treasure in the shallow water near the edge of Pratt's Pond.

"Look! It's Ganesh!" Karuna said. "What in the world is he doing here?"

And sure enough, there was a statue of the adorable Hindu elephant god submerged, but easily seen through the clear water. It was hard to believe that he was right there in Massachusetts. I suggested we pull him out of the water, dry him off, and bring him along as a passenger in our van. Ganesh is revered for removing obstacles on one's path, and we took his appearance as an affirmation of our trek. He became an inspiration for all of us, and from that point on, the one-foot-tall Ganesh travelled with us in the second-row passenger seat, minus a seat belt, colourful, bright, and optimistic. We were happy cruisers.

It took less than three days to cross Massachusetts, which was just eighty kilometres wide, or about fifty miles. I had to get used to converting kilometres to miles, but Vivasvan was able to help me with that.

FOUND IN A BEAUTIFUL LAKE OUTSIDE OF BOSTON, THIS LOVELY GANESH.

I was gradually getting accustomed to new experiences in America. New England is graced with many trees. Fallen walnuts and acorns are aplenty and some of them ended up under our feet, creating nature's acupressure treatment—'good for the soles'.

There was also an abundance of wild concord grapes which we discovered on vines dangling from fences and trellises along the roadside. Poison ivy came right up to the shoulder of the road in many places, and because I am an easy target for their rashes and subsequent itching, I had to steer clear of this infamous plant. So, I discovered some favourable and unfavourable circumstances along our walking route in New England. It reminded me of the blessings and challenges we encounter along life's journey.

One of those blessings was a chance encounter with Peter J. Reilly, a semi-retired accountant. One day, this man of numbers invited our small party to join him and his wife for lunch. It was unbelievably spontaneous.

He saw me. He stopped. We ate. We bonded.

The blessings always seem to outnumber the challenges and we were truly blessed to connect with a meditation group headed by Jeremy at Brown University in Providence, Rhode Island. I always get up early and do the majority of my walking before mid-afternoon which allows time in the evening to meet folks and talk about spiritual matters. Jeremy's group was receptive to our message and kind to our group of trekkers.

Tom Nappi, news director of HCAM-TV in Hopkinton, was curious about the walk across America, and what was supposed to be a five-minute interview went on for the better part of twenty minutes. Tom gave me ample opportunity to explain my desire to walk as a monk in a modern-day setting. As I was leaving the TV studio, I noticed a poster for the Orson Wells classic, *Citizen Kane*, one of the all-time most popular films in movie history.

"Isn't *Citizen Kane* a story about greed?" I asked.

A few of the friendly folks at the TV station who heard me nodded in agreement. I guess greed is something that we all consider evil. Similar to the 'seven deadly sins' listed in the Bible, Vedic texts reveal that in addition to greed, evil traits also include—but are not limited to—lust, anger, envy, the illusioned mind, the propensity to cheat, false pride, and false ego.

After completing our quick hike through Massachusetts, we crossed the border into Connecticut and walked to Hartford. It was here, just like in Boston, that there is a haven of *bhakti*, a devotional centre aloof from the mundane. Here we were charmed and inspired by Pyari Mohan, an American practitioner and teacher of *bhakti* yoga. He's also a magician who can produce white doves from his sleeves and hat!

I also met Tre'von Stapleton at the Hartford ISKCON temple. Nineteen-year-old Tre'von resembles Bob Marley with his tall, lanky frame and dangling dreadlocks. It was his first visit to ISKCON, and he listened intently to my talk about the goddess, Radha, the consort of Krishna, and to the story of our discovery of Ganesh in the pond. I was especially enthused about Radha on this occasion because it was her birthday. As I wrapped up the talk, I mentioned something about our cross-country walk and that seemed to move Tre'von.

"I want to go with you guys!" he immediately said.

"How do you think you could manage that?" I asked curiously, especially after he mentioned that he lived with his mother, had a steady girlfriend, and was the top salesperson at a men's clothing store.

"I'll talk to mom and my girlfriend, and take a leave of absence from my job," he replied quickly.

With the power of his conviction, Tre'von soon became a team player with our little group. His enthusiasm and spontaneity took me back more than four decades to when I met the devotees for the first time, and shortly after, joined the Hare Krishna movement. It has been a great forty-plus years, albeit with a few trials and tribulations, but I have never regretted the lifelong decision I made back in the early seventies to leave my arts studies in college and become a monk.

FIRST DAY WALKING WITH TRE'VON. HE LIKED THIS CAR IN HARTFORD, CONNECTICUT, BUT IT WASN'T GOING ANYWHERE.

Tre'von needed a day or two to get his leave of absence straightened out, and while waiting we went for a stroll through Hartford. I found out he and I share the same birthday—October 5th. We were getting along nicely and becoming quick friends.

He showed me the home of Harriet Beecher Stowe, the best-selling author of *Uncle Tom's Cabin*. This classic novel contributed largely to the sentiments of the public at the time of the American Civil War. Just across the street was the home of Mark Twain, renowned for his witty sayings like, "Don't go around saying the world owes you a living, the world owes you nothing. It was here first." He also said, "I don't like to commit myself about heaven and hell. You see, I have friends in both places." My favourite is, "Anger is an asset that can do more harm to the vessel in which it is stored than to anything on which it is poured."

WEATHER CONDITIONS WOULD NOT DETER US.

Tre'von exhibited the inquisitiveness that is often inherent in the young. I say young, because after all, when it comes to age, I could be his grandfather. I began telling Tre'von the essence of the teachings of the ancient Vedas from India regarding self-identity.

"We are not these bodies. We are spirits. I am not white. You are not black. We are the spirit within the body. That is a fundamental aspect of Vedic wisdom as was taught by Prabhupada when he came to America fifty years ago," I explained.

"What's his name again?" Tre'von asked.

"His Divine Grace A.C. Bhaktivedanta Swami Prabhupada. He was the Founder-Acharya of the International Society for Krishna Consciousness."

And then, I recited a poem I had written to honour my teacher.

TO MY TEACHER

Your arrival to the USA
Was a draw to pull us away
From the culture of the gun—
All the trigger-happy fun

You set our finger to bead and string
Gave us a song that we could sing
A different tune, a different drum
A magnet to which many would come

We turned down fish, fowl, and cow
Our palate knows better now
Food became not just food
But a product of a devotion's mood

Life became a makeover—a reversal of ways and thoughts
It was an untying of prejudicial knots
We even denied denim pants
For in robes and saris we now dance

The word 'service' has now a different meaning
Even the toilet is appealing at the time of cleaning
In that spirit the sun always rises
It is in giving we observe endless surprises

You direct us where pilgrims go
To lands sacred that sages know
The land of India has become an attraction
As is America where my feet now have traction

CHAPTER 43

HAIL MARY AND HARE KRISHNA! PENNSYLVANIA, NEW JERSEY, NEW YORK

> "When the sun comes shining, then I was strolling, and the wheat fields waving and the dust clouds rolling. The voice was chanting as the fog was lifting, this land was made for you and me."
>
> –Woody Guthrie

Trees were going nuts shedding their fruit while squirrels were in ecstasy collecting the fallen walnuts and projecting all forms of communication through squirms, squeaks, and barks. Who could blame them? It was harvest time, and the sweet sounds of the bushy-tailed rodents and nuts cracking became a persistent feature within the glow of autumn's panorama.

For each fallen specimen, one or two branches engendered a snapping sound accompanied by a shaking of leaves as each nut descended from the top of a giant tree before landing on the ground. Whether with companion or in solo flight, we were lucky not to get struck by one or more of the gravity-induced, high-speed nuts.

Near Union Vale, our party crossed another border and entered New York State. On Monday, September the 28th, I received a phone call from a friend who is a sports coach. He is the author of several books on personal motivation, so in the course of

SUPPORT PERSON, MANDALA RAM, OFFERS COMFORT TO SORE FEEL WHILE I TAKE CARE OF ADMINISTRATIVE DUTIES.

ambling along, I candidly asked him for advice for a follower of *bhakti* who is living in the contemporary world which is fraught with degrading influences.

"Appreciate, appreciate!" he said. "And never think that because you are spiritual, good things will always happen to you; don't feel entitled, be grateful!"

That was great advice, and I did indeed feel grateful for his call, and was appreciative of his wise counsel.

New England is heavily populated, and we were always meeting people along the way. Near Sylvan Lake, during a picnic break, an older runner came up to our small party.

"I saw you in Connecticut, and I'm curious what you're all about? I'm a retired professor interested in UFOs, and I'm writing about the positive experiences people have had in encountering beings from other spheres and planets."

I told him the Vedas from India are full of information about evolved life on other planes of existence. I handed him a pocketbook by Prabhupada, entitled *Beyond Birth and Death*. I didn't feel he would want a colossal book on *bhakti*, given the fact that he was jogging. Before he resumed his run, I also gifted him with a strand of *japa* meditation beads which fit around his neck perfectly. I felt like I was presenting a gold medal to an Olympic marathon star.

"I've got this left brain that wants to know in a scientific way why these beings are coming," he continued. "Apparently some people who have been in contact with them have had good experiences, transforming their lives and making them wise."

He was focused on unidentified flying objects while I was committed to *bhakti* yoga. I suggested perhaps we shouldn't over-analyze, but instead come to an advanced point of loving, giving, and serving.

So, there you have it—a runner and a walker becoming friends.

Tre'von, the young lad I met in Hartford, had a momentous first full day with me out on the road. We had the thrill of walking from Montgomery to Newburg and crossing over the Hudson River. It was the first of several great rivers I would cross in America, including the Mississippi and Missouri. But on this day, Tre'von and I enjoyed the view of the Hudson River and surrounding landscapes in the middle of a rather lengthy bridge when a motorist cajoled, "Don't jump; it's not worth it!"

We had a chuckle while continuing to admire the vista.

We soon resumed our walk, and it took half an hour to traverse the bridge. When we arrived in Newburg, someone told us about a restaurant called Nimai Bliss Kitchen. Owned and operated by a family of the *bhakti* tradition, the restaurant offers blessed food called *prasadam*. There, I met seventy-five-year-old Jimmy who calls himself 'The All-American Boy'. Jimmy was looking for a new path in life, and I felt he had come to the right place.

A program was quickly arranged at the Bliss Kitchen after I agreed to make a presentation about my walking adventures. Newburg's mayor, Judith Kennedy, heard I was in town and came right over. We talked for over an hour and covered many topics. It was she who informed me about the recent shooting of eight people at an Oregon college. I felt a little embarrassed because while doing all of this walking, I was out of the

MAYOR JUDITH KENNEDY OF NEWBURG DANCING IN OUR KIRTAN.

loop in terms of current news events. Some of the concerns which came up in our talk were rampant drug use, Reaganomics, commercialization, and being deeply in debt. Is America the new Rome on the road to self-destruction? Are there any solutions?

Mayor Judith sat down with several other folks to hear my talk, "Tales from Trails." She is a very cool lady because she got up from her chair to dance, chant, and drum along with everyone else when we started chanting the *maha mantra*. With no inhibitions whatsoever, she was at home with her people.

We continued on our way and reached Pennsylvania by October 3rd. We trekked through Delaware State Park where constant rain fell upon Tre'von and me for about four hours. Rivulets of water streamed down hillside roads causing us to have to dodge the flow. There were few motorists, but when they did pass by, we were sprayed and splashed with freshly fallen rainwater. Rarely did anyone stop to talk with us during the downpours, and we had to lower our heads watching our every step as we were pelted from more than one direction.

Fortunately, we were able to take a break from the deluge proceeding to a pre-arranged presentation. It meant taking a drive to a place called Old Forge. The occasion was the opening of a yoga studio situated in an old, but newly renovated railway station. A cargo train still chugs by on a daily basis, but passengers are no more. However, the once-abandoned station is once again busy, smartly done up to accommodate the spiritually curious.

Father Bill, who frequented ISKCON's Laguna Beach Center years ago, and who is a member of the Liberal Christian movement, teaches yoga at Old Forge. He asked if I would speak about the concept of *bhakti/ devotion*, and how it entails a relationship with God. He also encouraged me to express the nature of God as Radha and Krishna, the female and male aspects of the Divine.

I liked Father Bill's suggestions and did as he asked because I believe in the values he brought up. I also conveyed the superior, or essential element of yoga, telling the listeners that it is not just a physical exercise, but an enactment of profound love for the Supreme.

I can say with full candor that, up to this point in my travels in America, I had never met a group of such gracious, smiling, and appreciative people during a talk and *kirtan* session. When the drum pulsated, when the hands and arms spontaneously went up in the air and all were singing in sweet surrender, everyone seemed to feel transported to another realm.

I felt we were neither in a yoga studio, train station, nor any other physical space. It was also a thrill to see a nun in her full traditional regalia, chanting and dancing in our enchanted circle. We were all wonderfully wild, wilder than the fleeting deer, scurrying squirrels, fearless porcupines, or hungry wild turkeys we had seen throughout the hills and forests of sweet New England.

Tre'von was also beginning to show a strong devotional side, and occasionally being a bit aloof from the world around him. He intently listened to my lessons on *Bhagavat* philosophy and seriously chanted on the *japa* beads I had given him. He spent hours meditating on the transcendental vibration of the sacred sounds while strolling along the roads. One day, he chanted over sixty rounds on the strand of 108 beads, keeping himself occupied in meditation for eight hours! I smiled because I could see he was feeling a new higher level of freedom.

"I've never seen the stars like this before," he remarked very early one morning as we started our trek in the countryside.

"You must have spent your whole life in the city, right, bro?" I asked, trying to bridge the generation gap.

"That's true," he said before beginning to rap spontaneously. "Your ego says you're such a big shot. When you see the stars, you ain't even a dot."

While rapping about the insignificance of human beings, he broke into a dance. He didn't seem to care what any passersby might think of him in this very conservative Amish countryside. I didn't dance, but I did contribute lyrics to the rhythm and rhyme of his rap song.

Yes, we were entering real farm country, and being a city boy, Tre'von was not accustomed to the pungent piles that we sometimes inadvertently stepped into while striding along before the sun came up. The Amish use horse-driven carriages, so I warned Tre'von to be on the lookout for the mounds of horseshit.

"Just accept it," I counselled.

Not all areas we covered were rural. At State College, we trekked through the trendy downtown, and out from a café a radio blared George Harrison's song, "My Sweet Lord." With the doors wide open and the restaurateur preparing tables, the chorus of the song was projected to the outside world: "*Hare Krishna Hare Krishna, Krishna Krishna, Hare Hare, Hare Rama Hare Rama, Rama Rama, Hare Hare*." What were the chances of that fortuitous event occurring just as we came along? Another one of those little everyday miracles.

In Tyrone, Pennsylvania, a benevolent bed and breakfast owner invited us into his facility, providing two bedrooms. Paul's B&B is rated first in the state, third in the U.S., and fourteenth in the world. That gave us a feeling of prestige, but there was one catch.

"You have to come to church with me in the morning," said Paul. "And then I'll take you to *The Herald* newspaper to do an interview about 'Walking for Our Teachers'."

Media, on different levels—radio, TV, newspapers, and cyberspace—had all taken an interest in my latest walk ever since we started. At a ribbon-cutting ceremony in Tyrone where a new age health food shop was opening, I met briefly with the local senator, John Eichelberger.

"How are things?" I casually asked him while shaking hands.

"Lots of problems," he said with a smile.

MEETING SENATOR JOHN EICHELBERGER.

From his tone, I speculated that social, and perhaps, financial issues were major problems in the community. Pennsylvania, after all, is a Rust

Belt state with declining industries and aging factories. However, the citizens of Pennsylvania were really good to us. It was here I encountered the Amish, who, at least from my perspective, were transcending the effects of the Rust Belt. I admire their ways of old.

One fine morning I arrived in Butler on foot, as usual. This is a special place for all Hare Krishna devotees because our *guru* came to the city seeking accommodation at the old YMCA, now the Boys Club Center on McKean Street. After having landed at Boston and moving on to New York, Prabhupada was driven to Butler to stay for some time. From here, he established himself as an exponent of Sri Chaitanya, an influential monk and well-known walker from the medieval period in India.

SHARING WITH OTHERS ON A SPIRITUAL PATH.

Vivasvan, our reliable and ever so helpful support person, went to the downtown library where he connected with a local historian who was utterly surprised to hear that Butler was where the Krishna movement began. Also, personally for me, it was quite overwhelming to tread the trail of my teacher who spoke at the YMCA, the local Lion's Club, and Saint Fidelis' Catholic Monastery nearby.

I met up with a reporter from the *Butler County Eagle* to inform him of my trek. I also explained I was celebrating the fact that a half-century ago, a humble man from India resided here under the sponsorship of Butler residents, Gopal and Sally Agarwal. I mentioned to the reporter what had been said

SALLY AGARWAL SPONSORED PRABHUPADA TO COME TO THE WEST.

50 years ago by the *swami* to the then journalist of the same newspaper,

"If Americans paid more attention to their spiritual life they would be happier."

Indeed, I felt choked-up at moments while walking in this historically significant area thinking of the boldness exhibited by this small Indian *swami* in a very strange land.

On Saturday, October the 24th, 2015, the members of ISKCON's New Vrindavan community organized a banquet at The Grand Hall. It was a 50th anniversary jubilee celebration to mark when the *swami* came to Butler. Over 200 attendees came to celebrate and engage in one of those world-famous feasts hosted by Hare Krishnas.

50 YEAR ANNIVERSARY BANQUET CELEBRATION.

Moving on, we then visited the city of Indiana, Pennsylvania, the birthplace and stomping grounds of actor, James Stewart. Indiana also claims to be the Christmas tree capital of the world.

When walking through various lands, you always experience unique human encounters. It was there that a couple of women pulled over, mistaking me for one of the Tibetan monks who were visiting the town to demonstrate a *mandala*.

"I'm not Tibetan, but I am a monk," I explained.

"You mean, there are other monks in town?" she exclaimed. "Oh well, the more the merrier!"

The next day, an officer came and questioned me, and then became somewhat apologetic.

"You're just doing your job as a warrior," I told him.

"A warrior?" said the officer, somewhat flattered by my remark. "I've never heard it put that way before."

A motorist stopped her car in the midst of traffic. With tears in her eyes, she asked if I was the one walking. In the passenger seat was her son whom she explained had to leave the classroom over an anxiety attack. Now she was on her way to a gospel prayer meeting, and when she saw me, she felt I could perhaps offer her some prayer and encouragement.

"Just look up," I expressed to the pre-teen. "There's the Creator. Shine with Him."

With that, they continued on their way, she with a smile, and he still not sure what to make of The Walking Monk and his comment about the Creator.

In Mapleton, I left the beaten path to discover an old area, one that I was told would include a quaint iron bridge that arches over the highway. It was becoming a bit of an ordeal finding my way through. It was one of those lost moments part and parcel of a long trek. I trudged through thorny brush. I arrived at the rather steep bridge, and indeed, it had character. I went up and over the bridge and came upon a creek and got my feet wet crossing it. Then, over train tracks, and finally reached a road. *Whew!* There was a row of houses. I approached the one closest to me, knocked on the door, met Jim, and in an adventurous spirit asked him about my whereabouts.

"You're on Callowhill Street," he said. At that moment his mother, almost like a Jack-in-the-box, popped onto the porch with *The Daily News* in her hand.

"You're on the front page!" she exclaimed.

Jim and his mom asked about my origins, so I told them, and then she sternly said Toronto had just beaten her New York Yankees. I even explained that though I was from Toronto, I didn't follow the Blue Jays or any other major league sports teams. This, of course, was a confirmation that baseball and other sports are where the hearts of many Americans lie.

In Black Log Valley, many congratulations came to us—Tre'von, Mandala (a new fellow from Canada replacing Karuna, who went off to India), and me, the principal walker. I guess the news about our trek didn't quite reach the farmers in the valley, however. They hadn't yet read their newspapers. One such uninformed local fellow noticed Vivasvan parked at the side of the road after having seen something out of the ordinary.

"I'll give you a heads up, the police are back there, and they just caught some prisoners," the man excitedly told Vivasvan through his rolled down window. "I'm tellin' ya, it's like a scene from the movies."

"Is there a guy in orange back there?" Vivasvan nervously asked. "If there is, he's not an escaped prisoner, he's a monk, and his friend is a *yogi*, and they're walking across the United States."

The man was ultra-embarrassed, and his excitement immediately deflated.

I know that Tre'von and I looked like an odd couple with our counter-culture appearance, and we were especially an oddity when singing a Vedic song at the top of our lungs to the cows in the pastures, "*Govindam adipurusam…*" *This* is a song in Sanskrit about God protecting animals. Our interaction with the police on this occasion was interesting, to say the least.

"I'm harmless," I told the officers.

In the heart of Pennsylvania's Amish country, there is a unique little Krishna community, a group of farmers at Gita Nagari near Port Royal. They were extremely enthusiastic when our little walking troupe came up the road. Singing *mantras* and playing drums, they came out to greet us with one of their dancing bulls. The massive sign outside their land implies it's a yoga farm. This is no oxymoron, because animal raising, plant production, and exercise are all compatible as ultimate wellness activities.

At Juniata College in Huntingdon, students were intrigued with a verse I quoted to them.

"Everything that is animate and inanimate in this universe is owned and controlled by the Supreme. Therefore, one should take as one's quota what one needs, not more, not less, knowing well to whom it belongs," (*Sri Isopanishad*).

The students were studying comparative religions and they were so responsive that they insisted on walking with us for a stretch after their class was over, so we had some nice company on this part of the trek.

There is a lot of history in New England, and here and there you'll find plaques erected to honour various people and events. The wording on one of these historical signs at an old fort was extremely alarming. I thought the message was unenlightened and uneducated. I pointed it out to Mandala and asked what he thought about it.

"That's not right," said Mandala.

I took a photo of it and let Tre'von have a look at it later on.

"They've got it backwards," was his response.

The plaque read, "Fort Standing Still—Built to protect the settlers against Indian raids in July 1778—Continental troops and Militia were ordered here as part of a plan of defense against Indian attacks."

I think we can take lessons from the ancient text, *Sri Isopanishad*, regarding proprietorship. When settlers came from Europe to the New

World, they first recognized the Indigenous peoples as warm-hearted souls and able teachers. Later on, the settlers oppressed the Native Americans, and had no interest in sharing the vast space of the American frontier with its original inhabitants.

When travelling on foot there is an obvious need to share, and so one Sunday morning when moving along spritely and pepping up our steps after crossing the state line into New Jersey, we met with other pilgrims. Vivasvan came by in his van to inform Tre'von, Mandala, and me that we were not alone on the trail through Washington Valley.

As we were fingering our *japa* meditation beads while going ever westward, we met about a dozen people heading east in single file while praying on their rosaries. Frankly, it's rare to see a pedestrian anywhere in America in a rural setting, but on this sunny Sunday morning, with fall foliage in our midst, we met other walkers who defied the norm. Fancy that, two sets of pilgrims crossing paths! Our brief encounter with this group of Catholics who routinely walk while praying for others, ended with words from one of the ladies.

"Oh well, we all believe in the same God," she wisely said.

Moving forward in life with a purposeful aim sends out a good message to everyone you meet. *Hail Mary and Hare Krishna!*

We were not long in New Jersey before reaching New York. November 10th marked our last day of the first leg of the U.S. journey. I wanted to start in September to honour Srila Prabhupada's arrival in the west on the same date, fifty years earlier. However, I knew my trek across America would have to be done in two, possibly three, stages because, with fall already in the air, winter would come quickly.

It was day number forty-five of a 983-mile walk (1,582 km). Taking a ferry from New Jersey, we landed at Manhattan under gloomy skies, though, there's always something resilient about New York, regardless of weather conditions. We came upon a monument to honour the Irish who made numerous journeys to the New World as a result of grim experiences in their homeland, including the infamous potato

NEAR GROUND ZERO IN MANHATTAN.

famine. I stood there for several moments in contemplation, and it gripped my heart as I registered the pain, hardship, and suffering that humanity sometimes struggles through.

Just blocks away, we arrived at the site of the great dark hole, Ground Zero, an impactful display commemorating the loss of many lives resulting from the terrorist attack and Twin Towers' collapse on September 11th, 2001. As I stood where they perished, shivers went up my spine, and I read the names of some of the victims, names which are too numerous to imagine.

Finally, with a few new companions from New York, Michigan, and Philadelphia—all of us feeling 'hyped-up'—we marched to our final destination for this leg of the journey. The first stage of 'Walking for Our Teachers," so carefully navigated by Vivasvan from the first steps in Boston, was now completed at Tompkins Square Park. We stood at the

THE HARE KRISHNA MOVEMENT STARTED PUBLICLY AT THIS TREE.

foot of the towering elm tree under which Prabhupada enacted some of the first *kirtan* chanting sessions ever heard on western soil.

My friend, Abhiram, came to join us as we formed a circle, and hand in hand circumambulated that holy tree in a spirit of great gratitude for all of the teachers who offer direction in our lives.

HONOURING THIS SPECIAL TREE ALMOST 50 YEARS LATER.

It is said that a good teacher can inspire hope, ignite the imagination, and instill a love of learning. Certainly, much is learned when every step you take is an open door to greater awareness.

229

As the first stage of this cross-country walk wrapped up, I was already looking forward to returning to begin stage two!

CHAPTER 44

THE GREAT MIDWEST: HELLO OHIO!

"I've damned near walked this world around, another city another town…and it's many a mile I've spent on the road, it's many a mile I've gone."

–Patrick Sky

It was 2016. Spring had finally arrived, and it was now time to resume my cross-America trek in honour of my *guru* and spiritual teacher, Prabhupada. I am not at all superstitious, but I couldn't help noticing it was Wednesday, two days before Friday the 13th.

Our party, now consisting of Gopal and myself, resumed the walk in the eastern end of America's great Midwest. Gopal is a young devotee in his early thirties who hails from the Lone Star State of Texas. We began in Butler, Pennsylvania, close to the Ohio border, a location I had already reached in the fall of 2015. It was as far west as I had gotten, and the extra mileage back to New York City the previous year was to follow the route taken by our *guru* fifty years earlier.

Our first encounter with local folks involved two brothers, mechanics by profession, who were dutifully on their way to work when they were intrigued by seeing a man in saffron robes. Mark and Junior came to a full stop and jumped out of their vehicle.

"Are you really a monk?" Mark asked.

"Yes, I am!" was my response.

"We've never had a 'God experience' before," Junior added. "We're skeptical and aren't ready to convert to anything, but we sure are *damn curious*."

Curious, indeed. But I got the feeling they didn't want me to get too excited about them stopping to meet me, so I took it all in stride and let them know I was happy to just make friends. I never attempt to 'convert' people to my faith or way of thinking. I just try to be a positive person and set a good example. If someone decides they'd like to know more, I'm happy to provide them with information about self-realization and

Krishna consciousness.

Mark and Junior had several questions and comments. They were not the most sophisticated chaps I've met out on the trail, and during our roadside chat, the 'f-bomb' almost slipped out, but Mark covered his mouth just in time. They spent several minutes with me, and we shook hands a few times as they attempted to leave, but then some new question would rise to the surface of their minds.

"So does the soul really travel?" Junior inquired.

"Yes, through new bodies, in order to gain experience and learn lessons," I answered.

"And what about heaven and hell?" Mark quipped.

"Many people live in hell right here on Earth, but you can turn it into a heaven by raising the consciousness of yourself and the people around you."

It seemed Junior and Mark just didn't want to leave. They were very inquisitive and most sincere. Their last two handshakes turned into *pranams* (folded palms), so it appeared they were indeed making some spiritual progress. Realizing how much time had passed, Junior reminded Mark they had better get going or they would be late for work. They departed more informed, and perhaps a little more enlightened.

Walking along the Mahoning River by way of an excellent trail, I embraced the sounds and sights of the most intensely coloured birds I had ever come across in North America. Scarlet tanagers, black-throated green warblers, belted kingfishers, grey catbirds, capped chickadees, and water and wood thrushes were just some of the feathered beings one can encounter in that neck of the woods.

I finally reached the fair-sized city of Youngstown. The heat was rising and along with it, my thirst. So, I stopped at the next convenience store, and upon entering, I couldn't help but notice they were cooking chicken for customers to take out. I made my way to the cooler to select a drink with minimal sugar content when a boisterous fellow burst through the door.

"Hey man, thanks for hooking me up with that hot chick the other night!" he loudly addressed the clerk behind the counter.

"Think nothing of it," the clerk replied.

I am not overly immersed in the material world, but even I realized he wasn't talking about the chicken that was cooking in the pot. I looked around to see if any youngsters had overheard the remark as I'm always concerned about children's innocence being spoiled by so-called adult matters. I quickly got a cool drink, quenched my thirst, and got back on the road, wondering why some folks are so infatuated with things such as exploitation.

Soon after that disturbing dialogue, Gopal managed to secure interest from a polished journalist from *The Vindicator* newspaper. Friday afternoons are always a challenge for media members because reporters usually just want to go home after chasing news stories all week. Bruce Watson was different and showed up in slick attire, from the shiny shoes on his feet to a neat dress shirt and colourful purple vest. Bruce was rather formal in his approach and grave of facial expression. We weren't exactly sure how he felt about a walk dedicated to teachers, and in particular, a small *swami* from India who came to the west to suggest a different way of approaching life. What relevance would that have for the folks in Youngstown, Ohio? But Bruce surprised both of us when he wrapped up a fairly long interview.

"I think it's great what you're doing," he said in a serious, monotone voice. "Can I give you both a hug?"

We obliged, and as he left, I couldn't help wondering how his story would turn out. Bruce's article, "Walking Monk Makes a Stop in the City," appeared on Saturday morning and revealed

THE CHICAGO TRIBUNE-TREKKING PAST THE TOLEDO MUSEUM OF ART.

that he had done his homework. Not only did he write a nice story about my trek across America, but he also included a paragraph to describe the *swami*, who with humble beginnings, came to the west. 'His Divine Grace A.C. Bhaktivedanta Swami Prabhupada' is certainly a mouthful to say for most North Americans.

The next morning, I had the chance to meet an outgoing guy who runs a used car dealership. He had just read the paper and noticed me passing by his lot, struggling under drenching rain. I was just about to turn a corner at the Mill Creek Metro Parks Bike Trail when Gene, beaming like the sun, called out to me, "Hey come on in and take a break!"

Exceedingly helpful, he offered a chair, a coffee, and even the T-shirt off his back. I sat down to rest, but turned down the coffee and shirt. He was concerned for my wellbeing and wanted me to dry off. When I mentioned

I was from Ontario, he told me his best friend was from Wawa. Only 3,000 people live in Wawa, which is located along the Trans-Canada Highway near the shores of Lake Superior. The famous Canada goose statue is one of the most photographed landmarks in North America. Having walked across my native land on four occasions, I am very familiar with Wawa, which means 'wild goose', or, 'land of the large goose', in Ojibwe.

The rain subsided and I bid farewell to Gene knowing his kindness and good cheer would remain in my memory bank. I knew I could never forget him because of his good nature and a face that looked like a cross between the sun and the jolly actor, Burl Ives. Months later, the generous and amiable Gene called me when I was in India. It was clearly a kind follow-up because he just wanted to know how The Walking Monk was making out.

I soon passed by a memorial for William McKinley, the twenty-fifth President of the United States, who was assassinated in Buffalo in September of 1901. Then, as I entered Warren, I walked by the Mini Food Mart and immediately heard a hearty, "*Hare Krishna*!"

Laksmi Narayana and Brnda, the store owners, were from Nepal and had strong ties to Krishna consciousness because Laksmi's father had translated the writings of Prabhupada into the Nepalese language. They insisted Gopal and I hold *kirtan* in the store for as long as we wanted. Laksmi ran home to fetch his harmonium and joined Gopal, who played *kartals* (hand cymbals), and me, keeping beat on the *dolak* drum which we carried in our support van.

PRESENTING "TALES FROM TRAILS" IN A BOHEMIAN STOREFRONT.

Customers had not seen or heard anything like this before. Laksmi would stop his harmonium playing to serve customers who came in for cigarettes or beer, and then he would get right back to chanting and blaring out the droning sound from his instrument as the customers left. Laksmi was grateful we had come, and said our visit invoked fond memories of when he lived in the *gurukul ashram* (children's school) in Vrindavan, India.

Gopal, who was a very good support person, took great care of me out on the road. He drove the van lent to us by a very sweet lady from Ohio who looks after alpacas on her farm. Gopal would often go ahead, park the van, and come back to walk with me for a while, but he justifiably irritated folks with his sometimes-erratic parking style.

"Hey, you're parking on my grass!" people would say. "Don't start spinning your tires on my grass."

Gopal was quite aghast at these kinds of outbursts. One poor fellow became disturbed when Gopal pulled the van over and blocked his driveway. When he explained that he was the support person for a monk walking across America and *for* America, the man calmed right down.

"Oh, you can park just a few yards ahead," he said. "There's room right by that nice rustic lake."

At a farm near Burton, I observed men repairing the roof of a barn and a woman hanging out clothes to dry. This is Amish country with people hard at work. It reminded me of growing up on a small farm all those years ago. Patrick Sky's song, "Many a Mile" from the sixties, also came to mind. Back in my hitchhiking days, I sang that song loudly in the valleys of Canada when I had a break from farm chores. It's a real down-home heartstring puller.

With memories flowing and mind reminiscing, I marched on. I soon met Anne from the *Geauga County Maple Leaf* community newspaper. She heard about the walk and wanted to interview me.

"How are the Amish treating you?" she asked soon after we met.

"This morning I walked by an Amish farm," I said, "and saw some kids having fun playing in the front yard. That gave me great joy because today so many kids stay inside, glued to a screen, playing with electronic devices." I thought it was almost surreal seeing the imagery of children playing outside. It's such a rarity. It certainly brought me back to my childhood.

Anne couldn't have agreed more.

Chris McClellan pulled over. He is a nice guy who builds earth homes. But homes are not for me. I'm a walker!

"Would you like a ride?" asked a woman in tears. "Sorry, I've been crying because I just came from a women's support group."

As usual, I declined the invitation, but felt compassion and concern as folks sometimes become overwhelmed with the trials and tribulations of this world.

Beachwood is an upscale neighbourhood just east of Cleveland, and it was there that multiple motorists stopped with a willingness to help in some way, shape, or form. I appreciated their concern. They smiled and seemed genuinely interested when I told them about my trek across America. I'm not much for shopping, but the one good thing about plazas and retail strip malls is you finally get to see people walking. I must admit I miss seeing people walking, partly because I don't want to be the only one having all the fun.

Right around this time, a friend of mine, whom we'll call 'Charan', joined me for a few short days. A deeply gifted and likeable artist who struggled with painful addictions, he joined to help me, and perhaps find some healing for himself in the process. The walk, the service, and the support involved do generate a lot of positive power.

Charan and I trekked through downtown Cleveland, but our natural flow of movement was interrupted when we had to circumvent Superior Avenue while a stunt was being filmed for the movie, *Fast and Furious*.

"*Fast and Furious?*" I asked Charan, "What the heck is that?"

"It's a movie series!" he replied.

"Do you like it?" I asked.

"Sure do!" he answered.

One of our local friends in Cleveland treated us to a guided tour down memory lane. It focused on someone I have always admired and had a fond relationship with. The late John Favors, aka Bhakti Tirtha Swami, was an African American monk with an outgoing character and the coronated king of a tribe in Nigeria. We drove by his old church and the site where his home once stood, and then drove past Hawken Upper School, the private boys' school he attended.

We met Jeff Briggar, a classmate of Bhakti Tirtha Swami, who took us to see the school and showed us the yearbook from their senior year. I laughed out loud when I read the tribute about my friend:

"With his amazing strut, his flaming, iridescent, tapered, cuffless, beltless, sharkskin electric, spray-paint, skin-tight, orange tubes (pants), his matching four-inch high-rolled-collar turtleneck offset by contrasting sport coat (belted in the rear), and alligator pinstripe shoes, John Favors came to Hawken. Favors' contribution to every class was always impressive. He was one of the few seniors who studied during the day (or studied at all for that matter)."

John Favors, whom many of us knew as a popular *swami*, died from cancer in 2005, leaving an incredible vacuum in the Hare Krishna movement. I went from laughter while reading the excerpt from the yearbook, to tears thinking of his untimely passing. Surely his *atma*, or spirit, is now in a superior place.

On May 26th, Uttamananda from Toronto joined Gopal and me, as did

Abhimanyu Arjuna, a talented musician from Florida. The weather was getting warmer and we now had some opportunities to swim. I've always enjoyed a dip in cool, refreshing water, and it's something I encourage walkers to do to relax and loosen up their aching muscles. Lake Erie offered her welcoming waters for our comfort in this latter part of May.

In some neighbourhoods, the honeysuckle flowers along lakefront properties threw their sweet fragrance into the air along with the more pungent-smelling garlic mustard plant. All plant life seems to offer salutations in their own unique way, especially in spring.

It was at 4:30 a.m. in Sandusky when Uttama and I heard the crash of glass just ahead of us, breaking the silence of an otherwise splendid morning.

AT A RIVER IN CLEVELAND.

"And don't come back!" shouted the voice of an angry woman.

A door slammed, and out onto the street emerged a man with a muscular build. He noticed us and I decided to strike up a conversation.

"Is everything okay?" I queried.

"Yeah, it's alright," he said, somewhat stunned at our being there.

"We're walking to San Francisco," I replied before explaining the purpose of the trek.

"I'll tell ya, I've never met a monk before," he said. "Thanks a lot; you really made my day!"

On a Sunday morning, a motorist of eastern-European origin, pulled over.

"Do you speak English?" he asked as he held up the New Testament and started preaching.

"I am sure we share mutual values and principles," I said. "Let's just concentrate on what we have in common and respect each other's differences."

But he insisted that the differences were important and continued to make a case that his particular faith was the only one which would lead to salvation. After some time, I lost patience and suggested he enjoy meditating on the wall he had just built between us. I make it a practice to respect and appreciate other ways, and not to get evangelical about my own faith, but sometimes I get perturbed when other people insist their way is the only one.

On June 2nd, we entered Toledo, where I crossed a bridge arched over Interstate 80. It was there I met two fellows sharing a bag of popcorn, and one of them asked the classic question, "Are you a monk?"

"Can you teach me howda faht?" asked the other fellow as we met at the edge of the bridge. By 'faht', he meant 'fight'—it must have been a Toledo accent. My attire often misleads, and once again, I was mistaken for a martial arts master.

"I'll teach you how to *avoid* fighting," I suggested. "Consider gentleness, try wisdom first, and if all else fails, then use force, but only if there is no other way."

His jaw dropped and his popcorn chomping stopped.

"Hey bro, that's so cool!" he said.

After over two weeks of traveling on foot, Ohio was now behind us. To our right, Lake Erie appeared now and then with breath-taking sunrises. When walking, one always catches a slice of nature, and trekking through rural and urban spaces, meeting people, or going long stretches in solitude, allow you to absorb all that's around you. Walking enhances one's appreciation for nature, creatures of the wild, people you meet, and the Creator. Ohio provided all of that. Hello and goodbye!

CHAPTER 45

THE THREE '*I*'S: INDIANA, ILLINOIS, AND IOWA

"I grew up in the Midwest, so I have sort of an honorable moral code. But I moved to a city and joined a sort of fast crowd. A lot of people who grew up in the city sort of aren't aware of manners and other ways of life and common decency."

–Derek Blasberg

Indiana, Illinois, and Iowa fall in a perfect line, and they became our next list of states to traverse. If I were to group these conveniently as one, I would refer to them as 'The Three *I*s', or 'The Three *Eyes*'. I would consider Illinois the 'third eye', naturally, because it's the one in the middle, and Chicago would likely be the *fovea centralis*, which means the centre point of, in this case, the 'third eye'. So, the centre of the centre.

Much happened while on the trails of 'The Three *I*s', and it didn't take long to notice the flatness of the terrain. At times I felt inspired by Narada, the mystical sage from ancient India, who roamed flatlands in addition to hills, mountains, valleys, forests, orchards, and villages. There is no mention in India's ancient Vedas of Narada ever traversing massive cornfields like the ones we encountered here. These giant, or soon-to-be-giant corn stalks of ten feet or more,

GETTING SOME NOURISHMENT FROM THE CATTAIL PLANT.

became part of my walking experience in the Midwest.

Heat and humidity were an issue during this segment of the walk, and I found myself almost always thirsty, craving cold water and other refreshing drinks. My go-to food consisted of an entrée of wraps stuffed with hummus, avocados, and olives, all foreign produce in this area. Both Gopal and Uttama became creative road gourmets adding new features to our daily diet. I must say, I never tire of these delicious and nutritious wraps while I am out on the road.

Mike and Kathleen Connell, a kind and courteous couple, had us over to their summer home one day for a nice light lunch. It just kind of happened spontaneously, because I was walking down the road when Kathleen spotted me and issued the invite. Just being out there and being seen draws interest. Had I been in civilian clothes instead of my monk robes, it would not have sparked the same spirit of inquiry.

AT A HINDU HOME PROGRAM WITH SUPPORT PERSON, GOPAL KELLER, ON THE RIGHT.

At Orland, Indiana, Ben, age seventy-seven, was tossing the last stick of firewood into the back of his pickup truck along the side of the road. "I do these physical things so I don't have to go to the gym," he said proudly. "Plus, at the end of the day, I can look at a stack of wood and feel I have actually accomplished something."

In Bristol, Indiana, a sweet middle-aged woman was walking along a trail that converged with the one I was on. We paused for a brief conversation and I asked about the philosophy behind her walking.

"I walk every day because I want to be fit to serve my Lord and others," she happily said, revealing her sensational secret.

"Good girl!" I replied.

On that same road, Highway 120, a businessman, decked out in suit and tie, pulled over and asked if I would share some wisdom. I could feel his passionate energy. Two concepts came to mind, but I knew he was in a hurry and I would have to make my points quickly. "First off, you and I are human, and our human bodies are designed for walking," I advised. "Second, our bodies are also meant for cultivating our spiritual lives."

"Good enough," he said, and he handed over a twenty-dollar bill to help support the walk.

In Mishawaka, a mechanic named Johnny also gave us a twenty. It was rather compelling and casual how it came about, because while working on a vehicle he saw me and just couldn't restrain himself.

"That's an interesting dress you've got on!" he chuckled.

"They're actually robes," I replied. "I'm a monk."

"Oh, yeah! Are you on your way to the monastery?" referring to the Notre Dame campus in nearby South Bend.

I explained I was just passing through on my way to the west coast. He broke away from his work and we struck up a conversation, as best we could, through a meshed metal fence. Uttama tossed a copy of the pocketbook, *Chant and Be Happy*, over the fence. This little book features frank conversations our *guru* had with George Harrison, John Lennon, and Yoko Ono. I left Johnny hoping he would be inspired to read the little book in his spare time after changing a spare tire.

OFF TO VISIT A CHAMPLAIN AT NOTRE DAME.

"Here's a donation; be sure to get yourself some water," he said. "It gets wicked hot out here this time of year."

Soon after my impromptu meeting with Johnny, an edition of the *South Bend Tribune* hit the news stand. It featured a story by Selena Ponio, entitled "Monk Crossing USA on Foot—He Touts Meditative Lifestyle by Walking." Selena wrote that most people tackle the 3,000-mile trip from New York to San Francisco by trains, planes, and automobiles. She claimed, "One man savors every single mile and meticulously chips away at it in a pair of Crocs." She then quoted me concerning the humbling nature of dealing with the elements along the way.

"You develop a tougher skin, and at the same time your heart softens," I explained. "Slowing down, taking life in stride, getting close to nature, and meeting good people is a spiritual experience."

On we ventured through Indiana, moving toward the other two '*Is*'.

It was then we decided to take a slight detour on a parallel route through Buchanan, Michigan. As I carried on with my rhythmic routine of walking, I suddenly became aware of a tall person sauntering along beside me. Dave, a middle-school teacher, was out jogging and had slowed his pace to have a brief conversation.

"I remember you guys in the movies and at the airports back in the seventies," said Dave. "Tell me about Hare Krishnas."

"Well, we're back out on the road again," I said in a tongue-in-cheek fashion, before telling Dave a bit about the International Society for Krishna Consciousness and why I was walking across America.

Michigan wasn't on our original itinerary, but turned out to be an interesting state, even though we only spent a short time there. After another hot morning of walking, Gopal and Uttama drove me to Niles for a lengthy and meaningful interview with reporter, Debra Haight.

Debra informed us the town had some original drawings by Chief Sitting Bull. Gopal and I were particularly intrigued, but Uttamananda, who was born and raised in India, had never heard about this famous individual. In the local museum we admired the Chief's colour sketches of horses. Ernie LaPointe, author and great-grandson of the famous warrior, penned a book about

AN ORIGINAL SKETCH BY CHIEF SITTING BULL.

his grandfather's magnanimous nature, writing, "Sitting Bull or *Tatanka Iyotake* was a special person who cared for his people. He suffered for them in the Sun Dance, fought for their survival and gave everything he had for them."

Back on the road we walked into the city of Gary, a place which has seen better days. It was nicknamed 'Scary', Indiana, by some Americans. The good thing about hitting rock bottom, from a social and economic point of view, is that you can only go up from there. Gary once had a thriving steel industry and was somewhat famous for being the hometown of Michael Jackson and The Jackson Five.

I find it's often a bit easier to talk to people in small towns than some of the folks I meet in big cities. For example, I met Jim sitting in front of a not-so-busy barbershop. I introduced myself as the monk walking to San Francisco, and mentioned that Americans love their cars, but in this 'hood' I notice many people walk.

"Hey man, when ya on an overdose ya ain't gonna git inta a car and start drivin' around; ya know what I mean?" Jim stated. "It's sad, but it's true."

Moving right along, we were starting to get close to the 'Third I'. In an east end section of Chicago, Uttama and I moved through one better 'hood', but even there, *maya* (illusion) raised her ugly head. Two police officers stood outside an apartment complex. There was a man on one side of them, and a woman on the other.

Pointing at him, she yelled, "He tried to rape me!"

The accused rolled his eyes while the lady in distress appealed to the police officers for help. We ventured on, hoping the woman would be protected.

But more refreshing moments lay ahead. Lake Michigan had been a companion since Indiana, but as we neared the mega-city of Chicago, we were enticed by its vast size and pristine nature. In mid-June the waters were still cool, but that didn't deter me. While Uttama refrained, I just couldn't resist. The ticks and flies we encountered along the way were just too much of an agitation, so a plunge in one of the Great Lakes was in order. As I embraced Lake Michigan, words from the ever-present *Bhagavad-gita* came into my mind. *There are dualities. Learn tolerance from them.*

The Windy City is huge with over ten million people living in the greater Chicago metropolitan area. It is the birthplace of the skyscraper and home to a thriving music scene including jazz, blues, hip-hop, and gospel. While walking through the third largest city in America, we were blessed to be able to visit the Chicago ISKCON temple on Lunt

YOUNG NOVICES FROM THE CHICAGO KRISHNA TEMPLE JOINED ME ALONG THE CHICAGO RIVER.

Avenue. I consider this place easily the 'Third Eye' of the city, for it is here that *bhakti* (devotion) is practiced. After several weeks on the road, it was nice to enter a transcendental place, and while there, I met an enlightened sixty-two-year-old soul named Tony. He is a friend of the temple and is a massage therapist who was elated to do some service by working on my cross-country body.

"Your ankle bones are perfect, which is rare for someone your age," Tony said with a grin. "Your bones are dense and strong from all that walking you've been doing."

Tony shared some wisdom about overall wellness and fitness, and told me what he tells his clients when they ask how to take care of their bodies:

1. Walk, don't run
2. Clean the house
3. Do some gardening
4. Eat plenty of veggies and greens

At Joliet, Gopal stumbled upon a unique trail which is part of the I & M Canal National Heritage Area. The I & M Canal was part of a plan to link the waters of the Illinois and Mississippi Rivers with Lake Michigan. The canal was the brainchild of Louis Jolliet and other French fur traders in the 1670s. The old canal, with a walking trail next to it, was dug mostly by Irish settlers and opened in 1848. It had fifteen water locks to transport boats carrying grain, lumber, coal, limestone, and people. Teams of mules towed boats and barges a distance of seventy miles, until they were replaced by steamboats in 1870.

The canal has transformed itself over the years and is now mainly a still water swamp teaming with dynamic energy of a different kind. It is much like a paradise with huge, energy-giving mulberry trees. Every few minutes you see herons and egrets standing frozen like *yogis* in meditation, transfixed on fish instead of God. Bullfrogs leaped and plopped into the waters as I walked along the trail's edge. It's their defense mechanism, but their splashes gave me real joy. The I & M is a true treasure.

Eventually, I came upon a narrow river with a steep slope where I slipped, fell, landed with a thud, and slid along the ground until stopping at the water's edge. No scrapes or scratches, but I bruised my ego and got quite muddied. My cell phone got the worst of it and was out of commission for several hours, cutting me off from my support team. We eventually found each other.

I was soon preparing to continue the trek at Ottawa, Illinois. It was one of those drenching days and my support team was determined not to step out of the van. After some thought, I came up with a plan. I donned my swimming trunks, slid on my Crocs and began walking along the canal shirtless, sheltered by trees and an umbrella. It was June 22nd, 2016. I warned the boys not to take a picture of me in this wet weather attire. They had a good laugh and promised not to take any photos as long as they could stay in the van until the rain stopped. I must have been a sight, but I was able to keep walking and covered many miles that day along the old canal.

I was feeling rather wild and wonderful during this part of my trek across America, especially when I found out that "Wild Bill" Hickok worked on the barges along the canal when he was a teen. James Butler Hickok was born in 1837 and became a folk hero of the Old West, best known as a drover, wagon master, soldier, spy, scout, lawman, gunslinger, gambler, showman, and actor. Just walking on the same terrain that old Wild Bill had tread made me feel rather daring myself.

We were more than a little sad knowing that the I & M Canal would come to an end in Peru, Illinois, but our sadness turned to joy when we discovered a new canal. The Hennepin Canal State Trail was constructed between 1892 and 1907 and played an important role in American history. The Hennepin was the first American canal built with concrete, and today its waterways, locks, aqueducts, and adjoining hiking trails provide an amazing recreational experience. We were ecstatic to find it and enjoyed the solitude and safety it afforded us. On July 4th, America's birthday, we saw some people fishing and discovered coyote scat along the trail. You can tell what they eat by examining their stool samples, and it was obvious these particular coyotes relished mulberries.

CATCHING A MOMENT WITH A FISHERMAN ALONG THE I & M CANAL.

I love to walk along or cross over waterways, and knew I had reached a milestone when the Mississippi River came into sight. It carries so much history and folklore, including the tales of Huckleberry Finn. From Narada to young Huck, I felt like a free spirit seeking adventure. After all, the soul is nomadic, moving from one body to another, and then another, and, well, you get the picture.

Walking along Highway 2A in Iowa, another one of 'The Three *I*s', I started receiving some reaction from commuters. They must have read Emily Wenger's story in the *Muscatine Journal*, entitled "The Walking Monk: Traversing the United States on Foot." I was acknowledged with several honks, some hearty hellos, and a few brief conversations.

"The automobile is cold because you don't really see each other through the tinted glass," I told Emily. "The car makes us impersonal simply by its speed and its closed-off construct."

Just outside Iowa City, I met one of my favourite people. A diligent police officer just doing his job stopped to check me out. When I told him I was out to encourage a 'slowing-down culture', he smiled and agreed. It was nice to see another person was on board concerning the purpose of my walk.

"People are so accustomed to instant everything and want to have this and that, and have it right now!" expressed the officer, who admitted that someone phoned in suspecting me of being an escaped prisoner.

"This happens quite often," I sighed. "Can you please do me a favour and inform the police in the next county that I'm coming their way?"

The next day brought another bout of torrential rain, so I wore sweatpants and a T-shirt. Later on, the rain ceased, and the winds picked up. Just then another patrol car pulled up.

"Hi, I got a call that someone is walking!" the officer said rather apologetically.

"It's not a crime to walk, is it?" I replied.

"I know, I know, but people are people," he said with outstretched arms. "You've got to understand; yesterday you were walking near a penitentiary, and today you're walking near a mental institution."

Soon after my encounters with police, I was joined by some other folks who wanted to keep me company for part of the walk. Rajasuya from Toronto, and Ananta Sesa and his family from Florida made a big effort to come to Iowa to walk with us in corn country.

Most people never walk with me for a full day, which usually amounts to at least thirty-two kilometres (twenty miles), but they do what they can to assist in that most cherished activity—service. Heartfelt service is the essence of *bhakti*.

The path of *bhakti* yoga encompasses several activities including *mantra* meditation—chanting the names of God. We chant, either alone on our *japa* beads, or accompanied by music in kirtan—a congregational setting. *Bhakti* yoga also includes the study of sacred texts such as the *Bhagavad-gita* and *Srimad Bhagavatam*, associating with other aspiring spiritually inclined folks, eating sanctified vegetarian food, and living in ways that embody the principles of truthfulness, mercy, austerity, and cleanliness.

"What prompted you to do this walk?" asked Dann Hayes of the *Iowa County Market News*. "Does it have anything to do with the current political situation, ISIS, and so forth?"

"Much to do with it," I answered, before going on to explain that ancient yogic teachings encourage gentleness and service to others.

Great news came to us during the trek through Iowa when we were roasting like marshmallows (it was 107 degrees Fahrenheit!). *The Chicago Tribune* had published an article by Urvashi Verma, entitled "Swami Embarks on Transnational Walk across the USA to Commemorate 50th Anniversary."

I always appreciate news coverage and go out of my way to accommodate requests for media interviews. Many come from small town daily or weekly newspapers with an occasional radio or television interview. But this story, in one of the major papers in the United States, came from the centre of the 'Third Eye'—Chicago!

This article reached an incredibly large audience and helped us spread our message of upliftment and leave our mark. It made me think of a saying: "You can't leave footprints in the sands of time if you're sitting on your butt. And who wants to leave butt prints in the sands of time?"

We soon wrapped up this segment of the walk and left 'The Three *I*s' behind.

Stepping into Nebraska, I was excited about reaching the midway point of America. The city of Lincoln is just that place, but Mandala, my new support person, and I managed to end our day slightly west in Seward, a smaller city. Given the almost unbearably hot daytime temperatures, we decided to change our strategy and routine. It wasn't easy, but we began sleeping during the day and spending nights walking from around 9:00 p.m. to at least 3:00 a.m.

Indiana, Illinois, and Iowa provided some great memories and inspired me to continue to walk toward the west coast and see what new experiences were waiting along the way.

CHAPTER 46

BIG LONG NEBRASKA

> "Anyone who spends time on the road knows there's something special about being in the middle of Utah or Nebraska—you sit with it, and there's a peace about it. You can go left or right, and it opens up all kinds of doors. You take your own path."
>
> –Jason Momoa

I began the third segment of my walk across America in Nebraska, the Cornhusker State. It felt good to get back on the road, and it was nice to start in a state with the motto, "Equality Before the Law."

I got back into the routine quickly, reacquainting myself with the open road and randomly meeting police, journalists, and people in pickup trucks. I was assisted in this portion of my U.S. trek by a small but vibrant support team consisting of two young Canadian monks. They were enthusiastic to take to the road for a brand-new experience and their enthusiasm helped encourage this veteran long-distance walker.

Hayagriva, a monk of seven years from Quebec, and Marshall, a Krishna novice from Halifax, both yielded to my particular way of approaching this marathon. We would get up before the sun, shower, get dressed, and hit the road. Their wardrobe was casual while I dressed in the traditional robes of a monk, the *dhoti*, *kurta*, and *utariya*.

It was 4:38 a.m. on May 16th, 2017. Police lights flashed ahead just minutes after we began to trek for the day.

"What a start!" I thought. "Police? Already? So early?"

It didn't take long to convince the authorities we were harmless and that our walking mission was a wholesome one. They happily moved on, and so did we.

By 8:00 a.m. Hayagriva and Marshall jumped into the van and left me on my own. I like company while walking, but also cherish time by myself, especially in rural areas. My support team hadn't abandoned me; they were on a mission to see if they could attract the attention of the local media. They were successful, and Emily from the *Seward Independent Weekly* newspaper came by. Well done, boys!

Just before Emily arrived, I had already met O'Ryan and his son, Chad, who were curious as anything.

"So, what's your story?" asked O'Ryan just after he pulled over and parked along the side of the road.

"I'm walking across America to encourage the culture of introspective walking," I responded.

"Do you believe in reincarnation?" he asked.

"Sure!" I said. "The Creator gives everyone a second chance and maybe a third or fourth to address the demons within."

He nodded in agreement.

It would appear that God's policy of 'another chance' is driven by some form of compassion for the human condition.

Steve Moseley of the *York News Times*, a small Nebraska daily, also came out to see me. Steve wanted to do an interview because, by complete coincidence, their columnist, a local pastor, had just published a story on the many benefits of walking. That was a case of blind luck, or perhaps, divine intervention. Either way, Emily and Steve were anxious to let folks know The Walking Monk was in their midst.

My contact with the elements, the pavement, and the people made me feel like I had never left the road at the end of the previous summer. That first day was a day of recharging and restarting, but it was so familiar that I felt I had not missed a beat.

Onward we went! Coming up to Aurora, the three of us admitted we had never heard so many thunderclaps nor observed such numerous lightning flashes in our lives. Suddenly, the thunderstorms were right on top of us, ripping through the countryside. A radio newsflash reported that a tornado had touched down just behind us and torn through the Omaha region. Heavy rain poured down before turning to hail the size, look, and feel of diamonds. I decided to jump into the van to wait it out, practicing patience in the inundation.

INFINITE CORN IN NEBRASKA.

When the storm was over, I resumed walking and soon an officer pulled over after spotting me on the road.

"Is everything alright?" he asked as he came out of his patrol car.

"I'm fine," I replied.

And as I was about to tell of our pilgrimage and our purpose, I took two steps toward him ready to offer a handshake.

"Don't come any closer," he warned, stretching out his hands, ready to grab guns from both holsters.

Well, that was a unique response. I've had many encounters with police during my walks, but this was something I hadn't experienced before. Of course, I didn't go any closer, and soon enough the officer was satisfied that I didn't pose any sort of threat to him or the fine folks of Nebraska.

At Elm Creek, a fellow stopped wheeling his bicycle out of sheer inquisitiveness. He introduced himself and then said, "I am Sioux," referring to his Tribe.

"Well, you're the first Native person I've met on this trek since I started from Boston," I said.

"And you are the first monk I ever met in my life," he quickly responded.

It was a few days into the walk, and I was starting to get well known in this rural part of the state. The media was most interested in my journey and generously interviewed me for radio shows and newspaper stories. Soon after these started appearing, motorists began waving, honking their horns, and sometimes stopping to chat. Most were interested in my walk and encouraged me, but not everyone was a happy chappy. When Hayagriva and Marshall stopped to photograph over 35,000 beef cattle crammed into a feedlot at a nearby ranch, two suspicious elderly men quickly arrived on the scene in their pickup.

"Having vehicle trouble?" they asked.

"No, we're with The Walking Monk who's just passing through on his walk across America," one of the boys answered.

"Not anymore he ain't. You guys go pick him up and get the f— outta here before he gets shot!" they demanded.

Those two 'neighbourly gentlemen' then drove up to where I was walking.

"Listen, thieves come here all the time and they've got guns," they said. "There are bullets flying through the air, and we've got mean dogs on both sides of the road, so you had better get outta here."

Did I get out? Yes, but not right away. I informed the two 'gentlemen' that I was just finishing up at the next intersection anyway.

Whew, rural America is a lot different from rural Canada!

Hayagriva and Marshall came to my rescue and drove me to another parallel road to continue my trek. Soon afterward, we got a chuckle out of a roadside sign that read, "PRAYER is the best way to meet the Lord—but—TRESPASSING on this property...is the faster way."

Evidently, trespassers do come around and create problems for local farmers. Farmers with any livestock or fowl also consider coyotes to be trespassers. Coyotes are not a problem for those of us who walk in the early morning, and their yipping and yapping is most welcome, although a little haunting. I am always in a state of ambivalence when I hear coyotes howling. They remind me of the *mantras* monks chant at the *brahma muhurta* hour just before the sun rises. Actually, the coyotes harmonize quite nicely compared to some of my monk friends!

Further on down the road, a nice welcome came from a state trooper at Brule. He pulled over, opened his trunk, and with a firm grip grabbed two bottles of water to give to me. Perhaps that was a celebratory gesture because, as one motorist put it that day, "Congratulations, you're halfway across the USA here on the Old Lincoln Road." It was indeed a milestone to be midway on my trek across the United States.

At Chappell, Hayagriva and Marshall began to experiment with public *kirtan* (chanting). Even in this relatively small place with a population of less than a thousand, Hayagriva began playing the harmonium on the main street while Marshall pounded out the beat on a *mridanga* drum. As they were playing and chanting, two local women approached them.

SOMEHOW OR OTHER, WHEN WALKING, NUMBERS BECOME IMPORTANT.

"Stop! What are you guys doing?" they asked with animated gestures. "What's going on?"

"We are travelling monks sharing sacred sounds and spreading spirituality," Hayagriva replied.

"What do you mean by 'spirituality'?" they shot back.

251

"Understanding who we are and our relationship with God," answered Hayagriva.

The ladies seemed satisfied, especially with the reference to God. And so, my two bold boys in this tiny midwest town were then given permission to go up and down the residential streets to sing away to their hearts content. They had received the stamp of approval—a green light— and their chanting became a celebration.

The landscape began to look more and more desolate as we trekked westerly along the trail. It was the same road traversed by exiled Mormons who made the long haul with horses and wagons back in 1846. Bullsnakes and antelope, who are comfortable in this terrain, caught our curiosity, and I am sure we were a novelty to them, as well. Hayagriva picked up a turtle whose defense mechanism was to release a good flow of urine on his hand.

Peggy from the local library brought her granddaughter, Rhonda, to check out my stride and mood. They walked with me for quite a stretch. In Sydney, I met Aaron, a rather typical young American fellow who showed some fascination with the renounced order. He asked if I was Buddhist—a very common question. Aaron ended up trekking with us on a daily basis until we got too far from his hometown of Lodgepole.

Also in Sydney, a well-tattooed fellow came out of Legion Park, seemingly better informed and recognizing that I was not a Buddhist. "Hey, are you a Hare Krishna?"

"Yes, I am."

"You guys were all over the place in the movies in the eighties. I always wanted to meet a Hare Krishna. Can I get a picture with you?"

"Sure, why not!"

IN JACKSON TELLING KIDS AT A SUMMER CAMP ABOUT "TALES FROM TRAILS."

The town of Sydney was a great rendezvous place for us as we were nearing the end of Nebraska. It was there that we met the kind Patel clan from India. They owned a local motel and generously gave us accommodations. We were invited to give a presentation at the North Elementary School summer camp for kids. Colleen, the principal, asked me to tell some tall tales about my walking experiences. I included some yoga breathing exercises, and then delivered the grand finale in the form of chanting and dancing. Dozens of children, with parents alike, participated in this new twist to summer camp.

Leaving Sydney, we unexpectedly stepped into another delectable piece of history. At least half-a-million migrants came through there in the 1800s on their way out west in an ambitious search for gold. I believe that Hayagriva, Marshall, and I actually struck gold in the town of Sydney. We met a lot of nice people who were genuinely interested in our mission.

We even made the front page of the *Sydney Telegraph* in an article written by Brandon L. Summers. To enhance our satisfaction even further, two members of our Denver community came to join us near the town of Potter. Nidra and Jaya Gauranga gave us their loving companionship. Their visit on the road, coincidentally, marked the end of our travels to the dusty, but dreamy, second segment of Nebraska.

We left the state behind with fond memories of clear and ambient sunrises, even though our first steps were met with ominous cloud cover and drenching rain showers. Ranchers and cowboys became new sights for us, as well as bullsnakes, both living and dead, on the road. Before leaving the Cornhusker State, I fondly remembered the hospitality of the place, particularly the residents of Sydney.

As I sat on a bench in front of Dudes, a popular steak house, the manager of Dudes noticed me and wished me well. They had read all about me in their local paper and offered up one of their famous hamburgers. With thanks, I declined, informing them I was a vegetarian. They again extended their kindness by offering a veggie burger made with black beans! I politely refused with the utmost gratitude because, frankly, my tummy was already full.

Nebraska, we do love thee. We were like tumbleweeds bouncing around and hitting a few objects along the way, but the wind tossed us farther along to new treasures. There is certainly a peace about this state which allowed us to take our own path.

May our memories of Nebraska last forever.

CHAPTER 47

COLORADO COOL – SWITCHING ROADS

"Now he walks in quiet solitude, the forest and the streams, seeking grace in every step he takes. His sight is turned inside himself, to try to understand the serenity of a clear blue mountain lake."

–John Denver

"**D**o you sleep in the ditch?"

"No, I'm not quite that austere, because someone has sponsored rooms for me and my support team."

The question came from a police officer who, along with his partner, listened attentively as I explained why I was walking along the highway at such an early hour. I imagine the police see all kinds of folks out on the road, including hitch hikers, drifters, marathoners, cyclists, free spirits, and an occasional monk. The two policemen expressed concern for my safety considering the high speed of the traffic and the narrow shoulder along Highway 40 near Ault, Colorado. Traffic and lack of space weren't my only challenges, because out there between 5:30 to 6:30 a.m. was no happy hour—it was mosquito hour! You better believe those little critters were aggressive. I've encountered my fair share of 'skeeters' in my native Canada, but those tiny fellas in Colorado were the most aggressive I've ever experienced. They were out for blood and they didn't cut me any slack!

Walkers are always concerned about high-speed truck traffic, but on this morning, I was glad to hear the big rigs coming up from behind. The gusts of wind they created brushed those little pests aside, at least for a moment or two. Despite those welcomed blasts of air, the traffic became too much to handle and our little team of three decided to pay heed to the officer's advice.

Highway 3 merged with Interstate 80, which was *truly* unwalkable. At times like that, we switch, or jump, to parallel roads which are usually much quieter and slower paced. We transferred over to Highway 14 which runs through Wyoming and Colorado.

Later, Marshall, Hayagriva, and I jumped again, this time to Highway 86, a dusty gravel road. We soon realized we were intruders in a prairie dog habitat, and they were quick to let us know they were displeased with our presence. Interestingly enough, prairie dogs don't really resemble dogs and they don't bark. They look more like ground squirrels and sound a lot like those squeaky toys that kids love to squeeze. On this more tranquil path they could hear the unwelcome sounds of our footsteps which sent hundreds of them into a frenzy, producing intermittent cries of warning to their families and friends.

"I can make noise, too!" I blurted out. You may think my efforts to communicate with Colorado's prairie dogs a bit strange, but when walking long distances, you can't overcome the urge to talk to the animals and be a little bit of a Dr. Doolittle.

We were scheduled to have a *kirtan* at an Interfaith Center on the campus of Colorado State University that very afternoon. The *kirtan* (chanting and drumming session) was splendid. The students formed a dance circle with a mix of *mantra* and madness, creating a release of good energy, a congenial bond, and the satisfaction of body, mind, and soul.

"So, what do you think of Krishna?" I asked one of the students.

"I think He's great because He's a party God, and it's fun to chant His name and dance," he replied.

I reflected on his point, as this was the most ecstatic chanting session we had experienced since visiting the kids' summer camp in Sydney, Nebraska. We were releasing a lot of energy and having some good clean fun without booze, drugs, or sex. It was an absolute beatific and organic explosion—my kind of party!

ENCOURAGING ANNUNCIATION FOR KIRTAN AT CSU.

The next day back on the road, two different officers came across us on County Road 74. We were still trying to stay away from heavy traffic, but the prairie dogs' gravel road had turned into a paved highway before dead-ending, so we had to find another route. The officers made it clear that the rate of car accidents is very high in Colorado compared to the rest of the nation.

"At least you're wearing the right colour!" one of the officers joked. "Drivers can see your flowing orange robe from way down the road!"

They went on to advise us to head toward and beyond Fort Collins to Cache La Poudre River, as it would be safer and more scenic there. My team and I listened and took advice from the friendly pair of authorities.

AIN'T NO MOUNTAIN HIGH ENOUGH...

Soon we entered a new landscape. Colorado is known for its mountains, and it wasn't long before we left the frantic oilers and farmers with their monster trucks behind. It was quieter now with the area being populated mainly by vacationers who had come here to go fishing, hiking, picnicking, and white-water rafting. We were surprised to see some semi-isolated, very posh mansions tucked away among enclaves of smaller dwellings.

A sign on one of the long lanes read, "WARNING. You are entering a RED NECK area. You may encounter American flags, Armed Citizens, and The Lord's Prayer."

Aaron, who had recently joined our small group for a few days, had a good chuckle while the roar of the Poudre River next to us provided some comfort. The boys boarded our support vehicle and left me alone on the road, climbing upward and ever westward. The altitude increased, the air began to thin, and the wind whistled a haunting hiss as it filtered through the needles of jack pine trees. Patches of snow left over from the previous winter started to appear, and the steep grade and thin oxygen made me tired, so I took a nice nap between two pockets of snow.

I hadn't actually seen Hayagriva, Marshall, and Aaron for a few hours, but I did meet Brian and Amy from Fort Collins. The couple spotted me on the road a day or two before, and again earlier that day as I ambled along past their cottage. They were a blessing as they provided me with some much-needed human interaction. Brian wanted me to stop for a chat, and I was more than willing. Our conversation didn't penetrate very deeply in a philosophical sense, but that's okay. I simply made a couple of new friends. They offered me water, grapes, and granola bars, and admitted jokingly that they had jumped in their car to go 'monk hunting', and had made their catch.

The family owners of the Trading Post Resort kindly gave us a cabin for three days to rest our weary bodies. It became a base camp as I would walk my twenty miles (thirty-two kilometres) or so each day before being driven back to the Trading Post. Hayagriva and Marshall did accompany me for portions of the walk, but their main efforts involved driving the support vehicle, organizing speaking engagements, and finding accommodations. They also prepared nutritious meals, transformed through *mantra* into *prasadam*, right there by the side of the road.

Heading farther west, the sun and wind became more prevalent. At the town of Walden, at a major turn in the highway, young Michael Fry, a local resident, asked about my clothes.

"I'm a monk," I said.

"That's what my dad told me," Michael replied. "He said you're a Hare Krishna monk, and that's pretty cool. Can I get you some water?"

He soon came back from a convenience store with a massive bottle of H2O. I was extremely grateful.

That day it grew really hot, and when the heat was most intense, we visited a library which, thankfully, had air conditioning. We met the lovely lady in charge and donated a book, entitled *The Teaching of Krishna*, by Pierre Corvieu, with the preface by yours truly, Bhaktimarga Swami, The Walking Monk. It is a publication that constantly refers to *Bhagavad-gita As It Is*, by our *guru*, A.C. Bhaktivedanta Swami Prabhupada.

Rabbit Ears Pass is not the highest elevation in Colorado, but at 9,000 feet, it's a unique watershed along the Continental Divide. A local person told me that if you

NEAR SLEEPING BABY ELEPHANT MOUNTAIN. CAN YOU SEE IT?

pee at that spot, some of it goes to the Pacific and some to the Atlantic; in other words, from there water flows to the oceans on America's east and west coasts.

Toby Shaw from Denver sent me an article about Eric Brown who was also trekking across the U.S. Eric's mission was to spread love and peace.

That's pretty cool, but what's more inspiring is that he was being accompanied by a goat. I can see it now, Eric walking on his feet, and the goat on his hooves. Back in Canada, we say fast-paced walkers are 'hoofing it', and in this case, that's exactly what Mr. Brown's goat was doing!

In Steamboat Springs I was thrilled to see more people walking for a change. In this town, you have it all—walkers, joggers, cyclists, and hikers. Mount Werner and the Yampa River are nearby, and the 12,000 folks there seemed to be more laid back than their fellow Americans in larger cities.

Audrey Dwyer from *The Today*, Sasha Nelson from *The Craig Daily Press*, and Matthew Shuler from the paper in Walton, all wrote stories about the pilgrimage. Yoga studios were very receptive hosting presentations of 'Tales from Trails' followed by *mantra* meditation. Hayagriva played the harmonium, and Marshall, the drum, while I generally was the lead crooner.

But we weren't the only ones singing in the Colorado highlands. Hawks, eagles, and crows also sang their *mantras* while performing their daily aeronautics. That was something we couldn't do, but wished we could. Back on earth, jackrabbits, coyotes, and foxes were quite active as prey and predator. There was also a lot of human interaction, and the remarkable response from the kind mountain people was in large part due to the positive media attention we received.

WITH REPORTER, MATHEW SHULER, FROM WALTON.

"You know, everyone's Facebookin' ya!" said one fellow with a big grin on his face as he approached me at the corner of Yampa and Fifth Avenues in the town of Craig. "Can I take a selfie with you? Me and my little daughter?"

I, of course, agreed and smiled for the camera, which in this case was a cell phone.

Another chap stopped and told me he had read all about my walk in the local paper. Then Luke and his wife came up to me and asked for advice on the purpose of life. I did my best to say something inspirational before trudging onward. Scott and his friend also wanted me to provide some advice, so I suggested they slow down the pace of their existence and address the needs of their souls. As humans, we have an obligation to take care of the physical and spiritual sides of life—to strike a balance. Here in Colorado, I felt I was really reaching people as they were responding positively to my reasons for walking across the United States.

Beyond Craig, the interaction with people continued, although now it came mostly from motorists. A man from Boulder offered water, as did a fellow who was from back east in Maine. Surprisingly, I then met a Canadian from Saskatchewan. He pulled his truck over, walked right up to me in a small place called Elk Springs (a ghost town of sorts), and wanted to know if I could come and visit him.

I thought it was an odd request and asked him where he lived. He pointed to his truck and then let down its tailgate which is his sofa. It was a convenient place for a chat, but I soon saw that he was about to break down and cry.

"Why is there so much pain in the world?" asked the heartbroken man. "I thought a monk would know."

"Suffering is part of this world," I responded. "All of us will suffer at some point, but I think it is important to count our blessings and the gifts we are given in our lives."

He seemed happy to have unloaded an internal weight by speaking, being heard, and accepting a small piece of advice. He was very genuine, and that's what came across to me and my companions, Hayagriva and Marshall. When there are true moments, people do shine. When an opportunity arises, they shine just like the stars we encounter when we begin walking before the break of dawn. During those quiet times, we are under millions of stars set against a jet-black backdrop. We feel fortunate to tread our trail in this world of awe-inspiring wonder—moving in nature's pleasantly-imposed humility, feeling small in our own insignificant way.

"Are you guys familiar with music composer Holtz and his masterpiece, 'The Planets'?" I asked my two companions.

"No," said both Hayagriva and Marshall.

I switched on my phone and played it for them. "Venus, the Bringer of Peace" played as we walked under the stars. Our ears bathed in celestial sounds, truly enhancing those precious moments.

Later that day, we realized the soil upon which we tread was once the land where the notorious Butch Cassidy and The Sundance Kid galloped on their ponies, conducting less than holy affairs. We felt like renegades too, but not like the outlaws of the 1800s, because simply by walking, which is almost non-conventional these days, we felt we were doing something daring. It was like we were living off the grid, which perhaps made our marathon walk somewhat different from the normal way of getting around. It is definitely an out-of-the-box type of pursuit, scouting the land endlessly, and hitting trails or roads which we had to 'jump' for practical reasons while staying as loyal as possible to the direction of the Old Lincoln Highway.

Unlike Butch and Sundance, we were chanting on our *japa* meditation beads, often with a clarity of consciousness that is generally hard to come by these days; another reason why being out there in the early morning hours with so few distractions is so peaceful, calming, and uplifting.

As we were nearing the end of Colorado, we could see the desert looming ahead of us—big, beautiful, and dry, while our dear friend Surya, the sun god, began to intensify his rays even more upon the earth.

CHAPTER 48

UPS AND DOWNS IN UTAH

"I'm a man of means by no means, king of the road."

–Roger Miller

Back in the nineties when I first started these marathon walking excursions, I had little support, few walking companions, and only occasional media interviews. After years of experience, I have learned that a capable support team is essential for a successful trek. I've gotten a little better at doing media interviews, and as a result, more people are aware of what I am up to and sometimes folks even like to join me for a few days on the roads and trails. Although I enjoy the solitude of walking alone, it's nice to occasionally have someone to share the joy and challenge of long-distance walking.

Curtis is from Calgary, and I have known him for some time, so I reached out wondering if he might like to join our small walking brigade. I was sort of in his neighbourhood—he lives in Alberta, and I was in Utah on my walk across America. Curtis was glad I called and figured a good walk might be just what the doctor ordered because he was having a few ups and downs in his life. Walking just might be that breath of fresh air he was yearning for. As it turned out, the adventure would bolster his spiritual quest, and the fascinating countryside that we walked through provided incredible inspiration.

Curtis flew to the Salt Lake City Airport on the first day of August in 2017. As we started walking together along Highway 6, we watched a frustrated mother deer become separated from her two fawns. With pride, the doe cleared a fence next to the road with ease, but she couldn't seem to understand why her two youngsters were unable to make the same leap. The poor mother was puzzled when she plodded on and her offspring weren't tagging along behind her. It reminded me of a similar situation in British Columbia when a moose cow became separated from her two calves—déjà vu, indeed. In any event, just viewing this scene pulled at our heartstrings.

Curtis startled us after that first day of walking when he left us for hours after we had settled into a humble motel room in the town of Helper. He disappeared unannounced, but came back to let us know that he had been looking for potential engagements at several venues where I could speak. He had spent that time researching and scheduling. He certainly has *bhakti*, devotion. That evening I realized a dear friend lived in the area and I gave him a call. His name is Charu.

Charu lives near Spanish Forks, Utah. "You must come visit and spend a little time with us while you are here," he said. "And by the way, the area near the town of Helper is the most intriguing part of Utah because of its mountain formations."

Helper is located beside the Price River on the east side of Central Utah's Wasatch Plateau. In the early 1880s, the Denver and Rio Grande Western Railroad came through, and trains travelling west had to climb a steep fifteen-mile stretch of track up Price Canyon to Soldier Summit. Helper engines were required for the trains to ascend the big hill. The additional engines were stationed at the foot of the incline, and as a result, the town was named, 'Helper'.

My friend, Charu, and his wife, Vaibhavi, settled near Spanish Forks several years ago, and they operate a successful llama farm, restaurant, and boutique. This is the heart of Mormon country, and interestingly enough, Charu and Vaibhavi opened a Krishna temple that resembles the architectural wonder of Kusum Sarovar in Northern India.

MY FAVOURITE STATE.

A visit with my friends was in order since they live right on the route we were taking on our journey west. This is a land of rock and desert with roads and trails ascending to mountain peaks and descending into deep valleys with incredible salt flats. We had a lovely visit enjoying the company of other Krishna-conscious folks.

One day, after staying at the motel in Helper, I woke up and left in order to tackle the early morning road. My team members always took their showers after I left and would catch up to me later on with our support vehicle. On this particular morning, it was very dark and a forceful wind was funnelling through the incredible rock alleyways, causing my robes to misbehave. Then a teasing intermittent rain came down with very cold drops. I forged ahead like a soldier on a mission, or so I imagined.

While trekking on this dark, dreary, and sometimes rainy morning, I received a call from Montreal.

"He's gone," said Anubhava. "Basab passed away."

Basab was a thirty-two-year-old member of our community there, a gentle, big-hearted bachelor. His death came so suddenly.

Minutes later, an email message showed up on my phone screen. "Could you please pray for my father, eighty-four, who just left his body this morning?" requested a friend. "It was cancer."

These communications reminded me of Krishna speaking in the *Gita* about how this world is temporary and full of suffering. I realized that His statement was truly profound and an absolute reality; the theme of death and turbulence lingered in my mind during the early morning.

Those thoughts were punctuated by a dead deer on the side of the road. The car that caused this gruesome roadkill scene was also in shambles. Not yet towed, it just sat there abandoned near the lifeless deer with a broken grill, dented hood, fender, and a front wheel snapped off its axle.

What could be next on this day of death? The list of tragedies seemed to be piling up, and when the boys finally caught up with me, Hayagriva said he spotted a black bear crossing the road.

WE ARE A SMALL SPECK IN THIS WORLD. THE STUNNING UTAH LANDSCAPE.

Oh Providence, please spare the bear and not have him be a casualty, too.

Trouble sometimes lurks ahead, though once in a while, it can provide an opportunity for service. Later that day, we came across Luke from Washington, D.C., and his girlfriend from New Jersey, who were stuck on Highway 6. A flat tire left them in a helpless situation because their spare tire was useless and mobile phone reception was non-existent. The sun would soon descend, and we seemed to be in the middle of nowhere. Fortunately, Hayagriva had our support vehicle and assisted the young couple. Service was done. Yes, this is what it all boils down to—service to others. The sun will never set on service.

Speaking of service, reporters often render service to the cause of walking by letting the public know what we are up to. Rick was no exception, and the following day he found me out on the road and seemed genuinely intrigued with my walking adventures.

"The tremendous benefit of moving one foot forward," I told him, "and then swinging the adjacent one forward—the simple stepping procedure is something we take so much for granted."

Rick, a senior citizen, was an employee of *The Sun Advocate*. He appreciated my pep talk and admitted he wasn't walking enough. We were lifting each other's spirits—a kind of mutual service. His story would let people know about my walking excursion, which also encouraged Rick to make a commitment to do it a little more himself!

Marshall, Hayagriva, and Curtis, my small but capable team, were always looking for opportunities to book media interviews or speaking engagements to promote the cause of walking. They arranged for me to speak live on AJB FM Radio in Price City on August 3rd, with Frank and Taylor.

"How did this all begin?" asked Frank during the broadcast.

"Well, I became a Hare Krishna monk in 1973," I began to respond.

"Wow, that's before I was even born," replied Frank.

"When you were in another body," I added.

With that, we shared a laugh before Frank asked about some of my adventures on the road. It was then that I noticed a colour poster of a beautiful badger pinned to the wall and my mind flashed back to the huge badger I recently saw out in the wild.

"I came upon a badger, my first one ever, but he didn't make it across the road," I said. "It was some vehicle that was the culprit, or rather, the driver."

This seemed to be the perfect opportunity to 'badger' cars, so I talked about how we live in a car culture, how we're obsessed with them, how they have taken away our sense of neighbourliness, and how they do so much damage. Frank and Taylor actually loved what I was saying, and at the end of our talk they asked me to call back for another interview once I finished the walk in San Francisco.

Before arriving in the state with 'The Greatest *Snow* on Earth', I knew

Utah had many mountains and a few lakes. There are high points and low points, just like life, but you have to keep on moving if you want to get somewhere. This is an obvious metaphor on life itself.

One afternoon, I grew tired just as I was approaching Eureka, birthplace of Frank Zamboni, inventor of an ice resurfacing machine. Zambonis are found in rinks across my native Canada and beyond, so Frank is a pretty famous guy.

I would have enjoyed the coolness of a Canadian hockey rink on this day because the sun was merciless and the constant ups and downs of elevation, although gradual, were wearing me down. The angle of the road's shoulder was challenging my ankles. Comfort came when I saw our support vehicle approaching with Marshall behind the wheel exhibiting his cautious demeanour. Hayagriva had filled my thermos with iced almond milk, and Curtis was making preparations to massage my feet and calf muscles. These services were performed right there on the side of the road. Curtis put his firm fingers between my toes and provided comfort to this walker's tired feet. I offered thanks, appreciation, and gratitude to my small team.

ON THE LONELIEST HIGHWAY IN THE USA, BUT I'M NEVER TRULY ALONE.

Eureka is frightfully quiet and has seen busier days, but it did offer some mental calm. Practically the only business operating was a small convenience store, and inside, hanging on the wall, were these one-liner puns:

"I tried to catch the fog, I mist."

"I didn't like my beard at first, then it grew on me."

"I'm reading a book about anti-gravity; it's impossible to put down."

"Why don't programmers like nature? It has too many bugs."

"I don't trust these stairs because they're always up to something."

Somehow, these silly one-liners rendered service by making us laugh.

On the evening of August 5th, I spoke to a group of people in Salt Lake City, on *Bhagavad-gita* (2.40). The topic: "How to overcome fear through service." After the talk, our party decided to get some walking done in the coolness of the night. Victor, a twenty-two-year-old Brazilian who helps out at Charu's llama farm, joined us as we walked toward the city of Delta. With traffic so subdued and the lateness of Sunday evening, we all felt like kings of the road. However, greater than us were the moon up above and the clouds expressing their superiority. We were just a few insignificant souls in this vast part of the Earth, but we were looking up. In this metaphor of life, we cannot avoid being touched by both its ups and its downs.

In the course of our nocturnal trek, we found a small furry ball of love, a kitten who just manifested from out of nowhere. She was weaving through our moving legs and we had to be careful not to trip over the little girl, whom we speculated was about four months old. She was yellow in colour, and since she appeared to have been sent to us by the wind, we called her Tumbleweed. Orphaned, left alone, and lucky to be alive, we adopted her and accepted her as another casual walking partner. We fed her milk and offered lots of petting, but eventually decided to leave her at the llama farm to mingle with the other temple cats. *Adios!*

WE SAVED TUMBLEWEED FROM THE COYOTES.

Beyond the village of Hinckley, a sign declared, "Next Services: 83 Miles." The desert is evermore, and several motorists pulled over to convey the reality of the situation, just in case we hadn't seen the sign. No gas, no humans, very little water, and whatever water does exist is filled with minerals and salts. "Don't let those flat salt lakes deceive you!" I was warned.

Having a vehicle on a cross-country walking excursion is pretty much a necessity. Like a horse, it could always lead us to water. Hayagriva, Marshall, and Curtis were *my* horses, and during the hottest hours of the day they drove me to Delta where there is a unique dredged-out lake. This awesome body of water is swimmable and has a bottom of butter-like mud that squeezes between your toes, so we couldn't resist also taking a mud bath.

Barbara Clark, from *The Millard County Chronicle Progress*, also came by the mud-bottomed lake just as we were finishing our consumption of *kichari*, the ideal road food cooked up on our trusty little stove. She asked many questions for the article she was going to write, but her last question was off the record. "What do you think of the U.S. President Donald Trump?"

"I'm all for making America great again, but greatness lies in becoming more spiritual," I replied. "There's a lack of spirituality everywhere in the world, and we are all essentially spiritual beings, but we find ourselves doing so many mundane things which are incompatible with our natural constitutional position."

One day during our midday break, the local sheriff came over to talk to us. He told us that he gives classes to adolescents about morals, values, and self-esteem. We gifted him with a copy of *Bhagavad-gita As It Is*, commentary by His Divine Grace A.C. Bhaktivedanta Swami Prabhupada.

Looking at the cover and pointing to the images of the two people, he said, "So this must be Krishna, and this is his warrior friend, Arjuna." We were glad to know he was familiar with the two special people on the cover.

I should not forget to mention a couple of my more favourite live radio interviews. I met Amy at KLCY 105.5 Eagle Radio, and Jennifer on Channel X94. Amy's station played country music while Jennifer's played pop. We were having a light conversation, when suddenly, Jennifer said, "Okay, Swami, put on the headphones, we're going on the air!"

Jennifer started speaking to her listeners and mentioned her special guest at the studio, "The Walking Monk. The *swami* said that the word 'pop'

CELEBRATING INTERNATIONAL SUNGLASS DAY AT KLCY.

in Sanskrit—as in pop music—means 'sin', and that's why we have the *swami* here today, to deal with our sins," she said facetiously.

The interview went smoothly, and Jennifer was great. I showed her a copy of *Bhagavad-gita* with the two famous figures on the cover. I explained to her that the subject matter was about the ups and downs of life and how to transcend them.

"You know, I have that book!" she said. "Now I'll have to read it."

Of all the states I've trekked through, Utah was unique and pretty special. In this harsh, but beautiful territory, there lives a population of spiritual disciplinarians called The Latter-Day Saints. I believe the culture in Utah contributes largely to a more passive environment.

As we were edging our way closer to the Nevada border, Hayagriva, Marshall, Curtis, and I, were extremely moved by Ron, who worked as a pizza delivery person. He felt a great inspiration from our walking project. He asked for an extra Walking Monk *mantra* card, and out of his own volition, approached people, his customers, for donations toward our project when making his deliveries. He came back an hour later with forty dollars. Ron was kind, and from his actions we could discern that he was not a 'downer' but an 'upper'—an optimist.

There are two ways to be in life, upbeat or beat up. Take your pick. The people I met in Utah were some of the most upbeat folks I have ever encountered.

CHAPTER 49

NEVADA – AND A POOCH POOJA

"Petting, scratching and cuddling a dog could be as soothing to the mind and heart as deep meditation and almost as good for the soul as prayer."

–Dean Koontz

Hare Krishna monks and *swamis* follow four regulative principles, one of which requires us to refrain from gambling. So, you might imagine how I felt when I entered the State of Nevada, home of Las Vegas, the gambling capital of the world. I had never been to 'the strip' before, with its colossal array of flashing neon lights, but I imagined it might be quite the sight.

I didn't have to go to Las Vegas for a spectacular light show because it began soon after I entered Nevada, but it wasn't man-made. Meteor showers were forecast for the night sky and that provided the motivation for getting up extra early. I am an early riser, normally getting up around four in the morning and hitting the road soon after. On this occasion, my entire team and I rolled out of our beds extra early to take in the sensational sights.

Under a sparkling sky, Hayagriva, Marshall, Curtis, and I began to gaze upward into the heavens. In a way, we were committed to multi-tasking—walking, *mantra* meditation, and looking up and being awed by the light in flight. But these weren't the bright flashy lights of the strip at Sin City; they were nature's light show in Osceola on the morning of August 12th, 2017. We were humbled by the experience, knowing full well that what we were witnessing was far superior to any concocted creation of man-made ticky-tacky twinkles. The meteor shower was sure worth rising early for, but soon the sun crept up behind us, dissipating what had been a sensational night. With the first rays of the sun, local plant life began to reveal itself—shrubs by the name of winter fat, salt brush, and Indian rice grass. There's also something called halogeton, which is poisonous to livestock. Curtis was bold in taking one of the herbs, which

I had presented for a sniff, into his mouth.

"I gave it to you to smell, not swallow," I said. "Please, be careful."

Junipers also became prevalent with their cedar-like scent, yet plants weren't the only living beings out there. Jackrabbits and chipmunks dominated the landscape, while crows and hawks patrolled the skies. These creatures have their lodgings in burrows and trees respectively. What did we, the walkers, have for refuge at night? Well, our team had it fairly good because the motel owners of Gujarati origin often offer free accommodations, and sometimes even cook for us. Looking after 'Swami-ji' is part of the custom. We were, of course, grateful.

FIGHTING THE SUN.

"Are ya broke down?" asked a man with a very strong southern drawl.

"No, I'm doing a walking pilgrimage and have almost completed my daily goal of twenty miles," I responded.

"Do ya read the Bible?" he asked.

"I'm reading a cousin book called the *Bhagavad-gita*, which complements all that the Bible says," I answered. "In fact, every morning our group chooses one verse from the *Gita* to reflect upon, and today that text is 13.31."

I paraphrased, "When one ceases to see different identities which are due to different bodies, and sees how beings are expanded everywhere, one has reached the platform of self-realization."

I explained these passages help me to see the sacredness in all things around me. Jackrabbits and junipers are alike because plants and animals both have spirits inside of them. He seemed satisfied with our conversation and soon went on his way.

What is interesting, or perhaps disturbing, about the state of Nevada, is not just the all-pervasive dynamics of the desert, but the presence of rampant slot machines. Every town, even the most broken-down ones, have these gambling devices. Some places which were once thriving mining towns, are now practically left to the ghosts and slot machines. I found it strange when I was asked to speak at a casino on more than one occasion. Bugsy Malone, the gangster behind the whole dream or scheme of Vegas, might be happy to know a monk came to talk in a prominent casino in the city of Ely. Yes indeed, the local justice of the peace, High Court Judge Stephen Bishop, invited me to talk about the tales of the road, the holy way to travel, and the holy way to live. The venue was the Jailhouse Casino, and the presentation was for members of the local Lions Club.

While in Ely, I was asked to go on the air at KDSS 92.7 FM, with Chuck, the morning talk show host. Chuck opened his program naming famous folks who were born on that day, August 15th. The list included Napoleon Bonaparte, Princess Anne, and Oscar Peterson, Canada's sensational jazz pianist.

Chuck's birthday list provided a perfect opportunity for me to announce that on this day, Krishna was born. Luckily, Chuck knew who Krishna was—the chariot driver for Arjuna, the warrior—and how He spoke of overcoming despondency in life.

Chuck also shared some dark humour; for example, when I mentioned that large numbers of jackrabbits were being run down by cars on the infamous Highway 50, he remarked that being the 'Loneliest Road in America', the animals were likely committing suicide. And when he asked if there would be a big Krishna bash when I reached the end of the walk in San Francisco, I said yes, to which he responded, "They're not likely to have tequila at the party."

I must admit, Chuck was actually a smooth operator and gave me the opportunity to put out a spiritual message to his listeners across the airwaves.

Later that day, it became obvious that not all humans have a sweet sense of humour. We were startled when we heard a commotion outside the door of our modest room at the Ruby Hill Motel. Curtis opened the door in time for us to see an actual brawl involving two grown men. Kids and adults were circled around the scene, shouting and screaming at the chaotic combatants. Lola, the motel owner, called the police, and things soon settled down. Later she explained the cause of the turbulence—a biological dad was trying to take away his child when the adoptive father resisted.

Other than that episode, I definitely had my *shanti*, my peace, on the trail. Clouds would roll in at times, creating diverse colourful hues which reminded me of angel hair and swimming jellyfish. Rainbows arched across the sky between intermittent showers. The Nevada ether offers wondrous surprises with such imagery. Who needs an IMAX screen? I had it all around me. While relishing the out-of-doors, it always comes to mind that the aesthetics of nature should be shared.

Curtis, who had been with us for several days, had to return to Calgary, and we were sad that his vacation ended and our temporary travelling companion had to go home. But soon after Curtis left, we met Mark from Austin, Nevada. He'd been struggling with alcoholism, and after a little persuasion, he decided to spend some time with the three monks who were moving through his town. It was a breath of fresh air for Mark to see nature from a pedestrian perspective. It was a good experience for us too, and he became our new friend.

WITH HAYAGRIVA FOR A MUDBATH IN DELTA.

On a Saturday night in late August, we were invited to an outdoor party put on by the Nevada branch of the Lincoln Highway Association. The shindig was held at the historic Leland House, and folks from miles around came together to celebrate their road. It is here that the Lincoln merges into Highway 50. There was live music featuring Bob, the mayor of the town, who played a pretty mean saxophone. Many of the revellers drank beer, wine, or liquor, while we sipped ginger ale—as monks, we refrain from taking any intoxicants. We had lots of fun at the party, and several really good souls were curious about the monks who were trekking

FRIENDS OF THE LINCOLN HIGHWAY ASSOCIATION INVITED US TO THEIR OUTDOOR PARTY FOR A COOL DOWN.

along their highway.

We also met Devon from Flint, Michigan, who was on his own walking mission. He's another one of those rare long-distance walking addicts who was taking bold steps from east to west. Devon was just three days behind me and had been driven into town for the party. I was surprised to find out that he had been chanting the *maha mantra* while walking mile after mile across Nevada. He acquired a Hare Krishna *mantra* card back in Utah. I had given it to a group of free-spirited people, and they in turn passed it on to him.

Devon was clever and practical. He didn't have a support team like I did, but he had a baby buggy to carry his possessions—clothes, tent, sleeping bag, and food. He told me some people think he is a father pushing his baby down the highway, so they stop to offer assistance. He camps by the side of the road, and, like me, enjoys the mosquito-free environment of Nevada. Even though there are clouds in the sky, they are more teasers than anything else as it rarely rains. So, with such little precipitation, there are no mosquitoes. *Yahoo!*

GIVING MARATHON WALKER, DEVON, A BREAK FROM HIS BUGGY.

The walking excursion now led us to 'Burning Man' country, that bohemian style desert festival which promotes itself as a 'global quantum kaleidoscope of possibility'. We traversed from Austin to Cold Springs, to Rawhide, and then Fallon. With little traffic to worry about and an expansive landscape, I thought this was a good opportunity to memorize a Sanskrit verse or two. After all, I'm in the desert, there are no trees to look at, no people, no barns, no cows, no houses, not even a 7-11 convenience store! And as mentioned, it *is* The Loneliest Road in America, so what are you going to do?

I decided to memorize a new verse that I could sing out to my heart's content and project it into the empty space of the desert ether. I chose verse 7.11 of *Bhagavad-gita*, originally sung by Sri Krishna: "*Balam balavatam caham, kama-raga-vivarjitam, dharmaviruddho bhutesu, kamo 'smi bharatarsabha."*

It certainly has a nice ring to it. The English translation reads, "I am the strength of the strong, devoid of passion and desire. I am sex life which is not contrary to dharma (principals), O, Arjuna."

By the way, regarding the interesting appetite known as sex, motorists sometimes ask me if I'm married or have a girlfriend. To them I say, "No, of course not, I'm a monk, but I *am* married to the meditative walking mission."

It may sound like I have a disdain for the desert, but truly, it is a space of splendour and mystery, and any trails running through it offer incredible surprises. And just when you think you've seen it all (or have not seen *anything*), you are bound to encounter something unique. While I was learning the verse from the *Gita*, a van hauling a trailer carrying an eight-foot tall, 800-pound Buddha, pulled over.

Virginia, the sculptor, felt a compulsion to stop and perhaps see a living Buddha walking along the side of the road. She had constructed her Buddha in such a way that the various *chakra* points in his body would light up at night from the bottom up. Virginia and her partner were on their way with their Buddha to the Burning Man festival.

A woman from New York also en route to Burning Man, pulled her vehicle over, as well. She stopped far enough ahead to give herself time to prepare a special greeting. She laid out her yoga mat and placed upon it a carton of coconut water, a plastic zip-lock bag full of sweet snap peas, a bag of trail mix, and a banana. She did this very neatly, leaving enough space on the yoga mat for her to assume the lotus pose. As I approached, she declared, "Breakfast is served!" with her two palms clasped in *pranam* format.

"*Namaste*," she said.

First Buddha and now this! My heart melted. There was still space for another person on the mat, which I supposed was intended for me. With introductions complete, I explained my position as a monk on foot with a message for national healing. She understood I wasn't going to sit. In frankness, I explained that if I were to sit, I would find it hard to get up. Walking 20 miles a day makes me very stiff, and it's dangerous to sit while out on the road. She understood completely and made sure I had some goodies while I continued on my walk. This dear lady had, what we say in *bhakti* circles, 'a real service attitude'.

At the famous Sand Mountain, a man bearing the iconic look of a wise Indian Chief pulled over. No horse, unfortunately, but like the yoga lady, he also displayed a nice level of devotional service. His name was

Chief Johnnie Bobb, and he was Chief of the Western Shoshone National Council. His face was framed with long ponytailed whitish hair, and he began to offer prayers in his native language. Figuring I could use some help, he opened his trunk and pulled out water to sprinkle on me.

"Just face the sun," he said, tossing water in various directions, while reciting the Shoshone version of *mantras*.

"What does it mean?" I asked.

"May your legs and feet be strong," he said, "and may you be protected and successful in your journey forward."

He then presented me with a sage smudge stick for good luck. In reciprocation I gave him a card with the *maha mantra* on it, which has similar therapeutic and protective effects. Truly, between the two of us, I felt he was the big giver, and I was the major recipient of goodness.

Chief Johnnie's friend, Lorraine, a member of a dog rescue group, noticed me as well. She was a soft-hearted person and burst into tears when she pulled over to meet me. She asked if I could do animal blessings, and I agreed, thinking she would want to get several friends together for such an event. So, it was arranged, and on the first Saturday of September, we met at Fuji Park in Carson City. It was a hot, dry Nevada afternoon, and around fifteen pet owners showed up with their dogs of various sizes and ages.

I planted myself on the grass under the shade of a tree. In front of me was a picture of our *guru*, Prabhupada. To my right was a *thali*, a tray holding *pooja*, or worship paraphernalia, a blowing conch, incense, a ghee lamp, a water conch, local herbs, and Chief Johnnie's smudge stick. The dogs were spread out in a semi-circular fashion about fifteen feet in front of me, and behind each of them, their owners. The dogs were so passive sitting there, just as calm as *yogis*.

The ritual began with the sound of the conch and the ringing of a tiny brass bell in my left hand. Then,

A DOG BLESSING.

keeping my right hand free to mobilize the items from the tray one by one, all was done in orthodox style, just as I was taught to honour deities of Krishna in temples when I became approved as a full-fledged monk years ago.

The dogs were so attentive in watching my every move, whether it was the wave of the smoking incense, or the sprinkle of water that landed on their snouts. It was amazing how they responded as I explained to their owners what each of the paraphernalia items meant. Then Hayagriva, Marshall, and I began a *kirtan* chant which turned out to be the ultimate pooch *pooja*. When the chanting ended, I quoted from the *Gita* (5.18). This is one of a number of Sanskrit passages that I have memorized by heart and would sing in the desert: "*Vidya-vinaya-sampane, brahmane gavi hastini, shuni caiva sva-pake ca, pandita sama-darshinah.*"

The pet owners loved the language and its translation:

"The wise see with equal vision a learned and gentle priest, a cow, an elephant, a dog, and an outcast."

This verse defies human arrogance. It helps us understand that from the spiritual perspective, all entities are equal, and from the physical perspective, all are complementary.

Much of the coordination for my travels, media interviews, and speaking engagements in Nevada was carried out by Annabelle Younger, aka, Anavadyangi Dasi, my dear god-sister from Stage Coach, Nevada. She met up with the boys and me on the parched highway. The sun was merciless that Saturday afternoon as temperatures reached 107 degrees Fahrenheit. There weren't any trees to provide shade at that location, so we sheltered ourselves inside a huge conduit set under the highway. It was there that we experienced cooler temperatures while enjoying the vegetarian wraps brought by Annabelle, and to make our desert picnic even more pleasant, we also indulged in some of her home-made cherry juice. Tommy and Serenity, her grandchildren, indulged along with us.

WALKING ON THE SALT FLATS WITH COMMUNITY YOUTH.

Annabelle looked after us and lined up many speaking engagements in Nevada in locations like seniors' centres, various media outlets, Hindu gatherings, and the Satyachetana *ashram* in Silver City. Meeting people and having the opportunity to hold programs is like drinking ambrosial nectar that springs forth from the heavens. These activities are an important part of my walks.

Our journey through Nevada was a hot one. I was glad to be able to make good use of an umbrella to protect myself from the blazing sun. I felt, at times, close to the *avatar*, Vamana, who is known to always carry a parasol, and who is also renowned for taking three giant steps which covered the entire cosmos.

We ended our walk in Nevada with a ritual and the wagging of dogs' tails, which are often interpreted as signs of joy. The dogs at Fuji Park were the happiest pooches in the world. We learned much from the canines. At the top of that list is loyalty. It is the quality which is demanded by royalty.

CHAPTER 50

CALIFORNIA: IT'S SMOKING!

"This land is your land, this land is my land, from California to the New York Island. From the Redwood forest to the Gulf Stream waters, this land was made for you and me."

—Woody Guthrie

As I entered California, I knew I was on the homestretch of my journey across America which began in September of 2015 to coincide with the 50th anniversary of Srila Prabhupada's arrival in the United States.

To recap, I made it as far west as Butler, Pennsylvania, in the fall of 2015, before trekking back to New York City to celebrate Prabhupada's establishment of the International Society for Krishna Consciousness. Then, it was back to Butler in the spring of 2016 to carry on ever westward to Seward, Nebraska. In May of 2017, I headed back to Seward and started west to San Francisco where I would finish the walk almost two years to the day after I had begun.

California was my fourteenth and final state, and as usual with these mega-walks, I had mixed feelings about approaching the finish line. For the most part, I was lovin' the walk, but at times each step proved downright painful. The 'DH' (desert heat), the 'TT' (terrible tilt of the road), and the 'NS' (no shoulder on the sides of some roads) caused considerable physical pain and mental anguish. Overall, however, I felt fit and reveled in the celebration of each new day dealing with the challenges of marathon walking and looking forward to the people I had yet to meet.

Walking along Highway 88, I came across one of those famous signboards featuring the iconic image of Smokey Bear, guardian of the forest. I felt comforted by his presence as he was a familiar symbol from my childhood. Smokey was created by the U.S. Forest Service, and his message is embedded in the minds of several generations: "Only You Can Prevent Forest Fires."

Seeing Smokey was a relief because the sight, shade, and shape of trees always give me strength and fortification. You see, I had been missing the comforting presence of trees since Colorado, and Smokey's presence in California meant I was now back in the forest. The loveable mascot who turned seventy not so long ago, was issuing a stern warning. The gauge in Smokey's hand indicated the danger of forest fires were at their highest levels near Kit Carson in the Sierra Nevada Mountains—elevation 7,300 feet.

Unfortunately, fire loves trees, and the city of Jackson, which I was approaching, had been covered with smoke blowing in from several wildfires in the surrounding area. In the western parts of the United States and Canada, trees, grass, buildings, wildlife, and people are at risk due to forest fires.

The imminent danger reminded me that 2016 was also a bad year for forest fires. Back home in Canada, a major fire had forced almost 90,000 people to flee their homes. The Fort McMurray fire burned over 1.5 million acres of land, destroying over 2,000 homes and causing more than 3.5 billion dollars in damage. As is the case with ninety-five percent of forest fires, the big one in northern Alberta was caused by humans. Interestingly enough, while the west was tinder dry and ripe for wildfires, the east was almost fire-free. Reports from back east confirmed there had been an abundance of rain in the spring and early summer. The west sure could have used some of that precipitation.

Forest fires weren't the only cause of smoke in California. Soon after entering the northern part of the Golden State, several motorists and bikers stopped to pay me visits. They were all very kind and laid back, but almost every one of them were smoking up. 'Where there's smoke, there's fire' is an old saying which out here could be slightly adjusted to read, 'Where there's smoke, there's desire.'

In California, there appears to be a strong and natural compulsion to feel good and get high, as *ganja*, dope, weed, pot, marijuana—whatever you want to call it—grows in abundance. When Prabhupada went to California in the psychedelic sixties, many young people drawn to the sound of his *kirtan* initially continued their experimentation with hallucinogens and *mantra meditation*. Many of those same 'far out' folks soon found a 'higher' calling and straightened out to became official members of the Hare Krishna movement.

Chris pulled over on his motorcycle when he spotted me in the gorgeous Sierra Mountains. Overjoyed, he introduced himself with a firm handshake and fondly remembered his glorious past.

"Hey, I miss you guys. I grew up in the Haight Ashbury area of Frisco with some Hare Krishna people," he proudly stated. "By the way, do you smoke weed? 'Cuz that's all I got to give."

I thanked Chris for the sentiment and wanted to let him know about an amazing alternative.

"I get high from my constant striding through the mountain pines and cedars," I explained. "Take a whiff of that scent, chant your *mantra* as you walk, and soon you'll enter another zone."

Chris smiled and we talked a bit more before he cranked up his bike and disappeared down the road. We parted ways, both 'stoned' on our own brands of inner peace.

The next day, a man and woman pulled over near the town of Pioneer, asking if I wanted a ride.

"No thanks. I'm walking for healing and have walked here from Boston," I said.

Instead of a ride, they handed over a bottle of water, and after a brief conversation, gave me a thirty-dollar donation which was used to help defray some of my expenses along the way. They were definitely in the mode of giving, and before I knew it, they had offered me a chunk of hash. I informed them of my pledge to be 'hashless' and thanked them for making me no longer 'cashless'.

It seemed like many unique and colourful folks wanted to talk to The Walking Monk and were interesting conversationalists. I came across two men who were out in a field loading their pickup truck with firewood.

"Hey! I like those clothes! Are they comfortable?" one of them shouted. "By the way I'm a Satanist, but also admire Shiva, the lord of destruction, because when the world flushes out, he'll come to dance."

I smiled a little smile knowing these guys were just having some fun. Perhaps they were trying to shock me with their rhetoric, but after years of being out on the road, I have pretty much heard it all.

On that same day, September 4th, 2017, an all too familiar sound caught my attention. It was another van with a couple inside who pulled over to offer a ride.

"It's interesting what you're doing," the fellow said. "Life is alright; I'm just tryin' to stay outta jail."

"We're also having difficulty having a child," the woman confessed. "Do you have a prayer or something that could help us?"

I could tell by looking into their eyes that their parental instincts were strong. I told them that I was a chanter in a traditional Vedic style, and if they wanted, I could chant some *mantras* right then and there as a kind of fertility blessing. After all, I had just completed a dog blessing a few days prior, so why not add to the repertoire of blessings? They happily agreed and I chanted one *mantra* beginning with, "*Namah om vishnu padaya…*" and asked if they liked it. They were very charmed at the musical tone of the Sanskrit *mantra*, so I continued with a second one. When I wrapped up the chanting, I asked them if they would get back to me and let me know if anything happened. They promised they would.

"I read the *Bhagavad-gita* and loved it," said a man who pulled over to stop on the shoulder of the eastbound lane. "What do you get out of all this walking?"

"Appreciation for nature and life," I began. "Humility and seeing that the source of the *Gita* is in all things, everywhere, and at all times."

Rachel Norris of the *Amador Ledger Dispatch* newspaper came to interview me on a restaurant patio. She confirmed that the roads in these parts are the worst in America. Her article about my cross-country trek was top-notch with a front-page headline, several pictures, and an extensive word count. I liked the fact she concluded by quoting from the *Gita*, where God says, "I am sex which is not promiscuous."

Rachel went beyond the barriers of being a good journalist and extended her hospitality. She and her partner, Clayton, opened up their home for Hayagriva, Marshall, and me to stay the night. We were blessed with great company and appreciated their kindness and acceptance of our approach to life.

This form of California kindness also came through with Patti, who owns and operates Pause Yoga & Meditation studio. After a presentation at the studio by the boys and me, we explored a 'gonging' session for re-laxation. We lay on the floor facing the ceiling, listening to the continuous resonance from a massive circular metal gong. It was an extravaganza of sound which had a grounding effect and put me into a deep sleep. I was

CHILLING AT A YOGA/MARTIAL ARTS STUDIO.

certain it was much more calming than the after-effects of smoking a joint.

At Detert Park in Jackson, a large group of people came to hear my talk, "Tales from Trails." Jackson was inundated with a lot of smoke from the forest fires, but it was there that Hayagriva and I became teachers for a group of high energy six-to-ten year-olds at the Hub Center. We told of our encounters with wild animals and demonstrated fun physical and voice warm-up exercises culminating in *kirtan*.

"I bet you see God lots of times when you're walkin'?" a man at Detert Park asked genuinely.

"For sure, in multiple shapes and forms," I replied.

In the Linden area of California, a fruit-belt district, I did see God in a more light-hearted manifestation. It occurred on Highway 26, right next to the edge of the asphalt, where a perfectly round green ball was laying there all by itself. From a distance, I wasn't sure what to make of it, but curiosity got the better of me, so I picked up the pace.

As I moved closer, I observed some semblance of an umbilical cord attached to the object. The cord was actually a vine and had borne a beautiful watermelon! Somehow, a single seed had made its way to a small patch of fertile earth right beside the road and grew something totally out of place, yet conveniently positioned as Krishna's gift for a solitary walker. I believe He delivered the melon just when I needed it most. Despite my thirst, I felt I had to share this great find with the boys once they caught up to me.

There was a large amount of U-pick fruit in the area. One vineyard owner came out to see me on the roadside, saying his daughter heard about my trek from her schoolteacher. He was so enlivened and enthused about my walk that he insisted I enjoy the fruits of his labour.

"You can help yourself to anything from my orchard!"

I later found a nice way to deal with the heat by walking through other orchards, often pear and plum, usually about five rows in from the highway. I would naturally select the ripest specimens possible and just reach out and pluck as I was walking. How could I resist? This was somewhat reminiscent of when I was an adolescent growing up in one of southern Ontario's fruit belt areas. I worked in the orchards, and it was often cherries I picked and ate all day.

I see all kinds of signals coming from the Supreme, the Source of everything, in the form of lush forests or the beauty of a barren desert. At times, He allows rain, sun, and other elements to beat down hard in an attempt to crush our monstrous egos. At the same time, I believe God can be seen as the energetic force behind our sensory powers of smelling, tasting, seeing, hearing, and touching. The Divine is everywhere.

Perhaps the most profound and thoroughly fascinating thing I find on these treks is the divine power invested in people. I have witnessed many powers and miracles shining through those I meet. Somehow, we have to go beyond whatever darkness lurks inside us, and just pull at the wings of the angel within. There's a spark of devotion in everyone, and it simply needs to be ignited. We humans have a tenderness within which is sometimes dormant, but can be awakened under the right circumstances.

While on the topic of good souls, I was very touched when I heard Anuttama Das from Washington D.C., was coming to spend four days on the trail. One of my great moral supporters, Anuttama was committed to participating in an ultimate pedestrian experience. It took him a few hours to get used to the pace, but he adapted quickly and enjoyed his time with us.

"We're using different leg muscles now," Anuttama remarked as we trudged up a narrow passageway designed for walkers near East Port. "This is a steep climb; something I don't get to do very often back east in Washington."

Suddenly, we startled a pair of well-camouflaged deer—one of them a big buck with crowning antlers, put his head down and moved quickly toward us. But he was as scared of us as we were of him, and in a moment of panic, desperately looking for an escape route, he made an abrupt turn and impulsively burst through a fence, frantically fleeing into the shelter and safety of the forest. We stood there stunned, realizing we had been seconds away from being gored and trampled.

MY DEAR FRIEND, ANUTTAMA, JOINED ME FOR FOUR FANTASTIC DAYS.

That incident caused us to have a momentary feeling of diffidence which became our theme for the day. Meek moments of a different kind arose as we wandered along through the giant redwoods which appeared now and then in clusters along the trail. We were in awe of the opposing ecosystems divided by the trail. On the one side, there was intense sun exposure, and on the other, a shaded coolness, each having different effects on the flora and fauna.

We continued following Huckleberry and East Bay Trail where the pathways once again narrowed. With no phone reception, and in a more remote area featuring dynamic switchbacks, we laboured on, not quite knowing where we were, and inevitably got lost. It was another humbling experience on this day to remember. We reminded ourselves that we were on an adventure and the stunning vistas we witnessed from the higher elevations gave us hope.

The good thing about being lost is getting found. Eventually, the two *brahmachari* monks, concerned about our safety and whereabouts, sought us out and finally found us. I must say we, and they, were equally grateful and relieved.

Anuttama spent four precious days with us, and during that time also experienced a firsthand encounter with the police. Three officers quickly descended upon us in the pre-dawn hours only to discover we were a false alarm.

Adios, Anuttama!

By now it was mid-September, Wednesday the 13th, to be precise, and all was well. I figured it would take just a couple days to complete the mission of walking across the United States. A dense fog had set in, which was a far cry from the many weeks we had spent in the high and dry altitudes. The world before me revealed a completely different universe as I made an incremental descent to sea level.

My health had been good for the entire trip, but on the 14th, I experienced dizzy spells, broke into a sweat, and turned pretty pale. It sure seemed peculiar for symptoms such as these to occur when the finish line was almost in sight. In his combined enthusiasm and innocence, Hayagriva wanted to show me an online video of some Sufi Dervish. He thought it might present a possible approach we could adapt in a future *kirtan* dance, but I clearly declined to look, as the timing couldn't have been worse. More vertigo was not what I aspired for at that particular moment. My personal diagnosis was that my condition had been caused by the jolting change in weather, from dry heat to damp coolness. My prescription was to lie down and rest.

After an uneasy sleep, I was anxious to complete the final six miles so I could say I had done them. But on second thought, I soon realized it was God and *guru* who had allowed me to complete this task. And so, after a sensational trek over the almost two-mile expanse of the Golden Gate Bridge, I was finally on the home stretch, ready to take the last few steps to the Pacific Ocean.

My dear friends, Vaisesika and Nirakula from San Jose, came to join us for the final four miles, from Masonic and Page, to Irving and the Lower

Great Highway. It was the same route where the hippies had paraded with the Hare Krishna devotees fifty years before in an historic re-enactment of the ancient chariot festival, *Ratha Yatra*.

Gurudas, a lawyer from Honolulu, Mandala from Ottawa, and two artists from Vancouver also came to participate. Our toes soon sifted through the sand before being immersed in the Pacific Ocean where we ritually sprinkled water upon our heads under a kind San Francisco sun.

Coast to coast, the trip was 3,550 miles, which works out to 5,713 kilometres. I finished the final steps of the trek across the United States of America with fewer pounds of flesh, and fewer ounces of *karma*.

It was September 15th, 2017. The trip was a blessed blast, and in my meditation on my teacher, His Divine Grace A.C. Bhaktivedanta Swami Prabhupada, I dedicated the following words:

TOUCHDOWN AT THE PACIFIC! RELAXING, BEADS UP!

Leaving home behind
A new comfort to find
It was in 1965
The ocean you did survive
On ship with beads and books
There were stares and looks
When you landed upon the shore
And made that big score
In the city of fashion
Of darkness and passion
There was snow and cold
But you were so bold
There was noise and heat
You said, "No!" to defeat.

From the above description
I learned a great conviction
In going step by step
A stride to be kept
For around every bend
There's definitely a friend
A touch of magic
Making life less tragic

AFTERWORD
MY WALKING COMPADRES

"The strongest people make time to help others, even if they are struggling with their own personal demons."

–Author Unknown

Everyone with integrity and experience knows it takes a team to make a project successful. It would be a case of bad karma to not give credit to the many entities who contributed to these marathon walking endeavours. Those entities include the stars, the moon, the sun, and all that is beneath and above them.

I really want to share my gratitude to all the *compadres* who have supported my walking mission. I like the sound of '*compadre*', a Spanish word that could mean 'buddy', 'chum', 'comrade', 'mate', or 'confidant'. Although *compadre* is a reference to male friends, I would be remiss not to mention that I received much encouragement from many *comadres*, the female equivalent of *compadre*.

I also had various encounters with wild and tame animals. The most notable was a ravishing beauty in the form of a blue-fronted Amazon parrot. She is a true *comadre* and goes by the name of Billie Jean. She is a passionate creature and very much in love with her 'boyfriend', Daruka, who is human, by the way.

When Daruka joined me on my third Canadian walk, Billie Jean came along, too. It was not my intent to interfere with their strong bond, but since we were going to be travelling companions, I thought I would offer a gesture of friendship by petting her head. My attempts failed and I became a regular beneficiary of serious 'kisses' from her sharp beak. My attempts at having her perch on my shoulder were also met with defeat as the darling usually gifted me with her posterior blessing.

I forgave the aggressive behaviour because she played a key role in our efforts to share the message of simple living and high thinking. Whenever we came into a new town, folks would see a walking monk and an actual talking parrot with her skipper friend resembling a pirate. We were quite a sensation and soon discovered a new way to promote the pilgrimage.

It all started in Mine Centre, a small town in Northwestern Ontario. The school there, attended mostly by children from the Ojibwe First Nation, invited us to give a little talk about the walk. The kids were enthralled by Billie Jean who blurted out her standard, "Hello." My presentation of talking, chanting, and dancing was clearly upstaged by the parrot.

From Ontario to the Alberta border, from town to town and school to school, even in the more conservative communities of Mennonites and Hutterites, we were a breath of fresh air. Daruka would drive ahead, visit the school in the next town and ask the principal if we could drop in. The principal would almost always say they had heard we visited the school in the last town and invite us to his or her school. The principal would tell us the students were interested in hearing about the monk's walk, but don't forget to bring the parrot!

One day after completing my day's walking quota, Daruka drove us down an endless dirt road that eventually led to a Manitoban Hutterite community. The students and three teachers were anxiously waiting for us, but as soon as we got out of the van, an elder rode up on his all-terrain vehicle. "What's going on here?" he demanded in a loud farmer's voice. "We are here to talk about my walk across Canada, and this is my support team, Daruka and Billie Jean, the talking parrot," I explained.

"Hello!" said Billie Jean.

The middle age man looked at the children who were eager to meet us and then asked me a question.

"You're not here to…" and then he stopped seemingly searching for an appropriate word.

"Proselytize?" I asked.

"Yeah, that," he said.

"No sir, we are simply speaking about the joys of the outdoors and the benefits of walking," I replied.

He hesitated and looking again at the enthusiastic bunch, said, "Alright."

He climbed on his ATV and rode away. Then it was show time once again for Billie Jean, Daruka and me.

Most small-town schools included students from grades one to twelve, and when we arrived they would gather in their gym or auditorium to check us out. Teachers often told us they loved our program, not only for talking about the challenge of walking across a big country, but for the positive message it left with the students.

"You are opening up the world for them," one teacher said. "We discourage them from playing with electronic devices and encourage a more active life outdoors, and now you show up and demonstrate how to do it." So many thanks to Billie Jean, who often helped us get a foot in the door and always stole the show. I hope she can appreciate that I put her at the top of my list of supporters, or as I like to say, at the top of the pecking order.

Although Billie Jean was the 'showstopper', Daruka, a selfless and adventurous man from Winnipeg, Manitoba, always demonstrated a spirit of service and devotion. Despite one of his legs being in great pain, he agreed to be the support driver for my walk. Driving was a challenge, but by some little miracle natural healing took place. He put a lot of trust and faith in the transcendental sound vibration of chanting the Hare Krishna *mantra*, and within a week or two the pain was gone for good!

Daruka loved driving and showing off Billie Jean. He found many venues including schools, yoga studios, libraries, churches, community centres, service clubs, and people's homes. Daruka was also a very good photographer, and one of the iconic images he captured was a close-up of mating grasshoppers. With their humungous eyes directed at the photographer they seemed to say, "Do you mind?"

All thanks to Daruka, because service is the

SUPPORT PERSON AND FANTASTIC PHOTOGRAPHER, DARUKA, AND HIS FAMOUS SIDEKICK, BILLIE JEAN.

dharma of his soul, or in other words, service is at his soul's core.

David, who was my *compadre* for part of the first Canadian walk, expressed enthusiasm in his decision to follow the wandering mendicant. I didn't know about 'the stuff' he was going through in his personal life, but his paradigm shift to the ways of a pilgrim proved fruitful. It was he and I who first tested the waters of this power walking project in 1996. Speaking of water, on a day in our tradition called *nirjal*, David felt inspired to fast, fully abstaining from all food and water. I normally walked approximately nine hours a day while chanting sixty-four times around my strand of 108 *japa* beads, but on *nirjal*, David inspired me to trek for a few more hours and I ended up doing fifty kilometres on an empty stomach. As the old Vedic phrase goes, "Austerity is the wealth of the holy person."

David had to leave part way through the first walk, but Brian Gonsalves gave us his assistance from Quebec to the end of the '96 trek. He and I had some good chats walking in the land of Anne of Green Gables in Prince Edward Island. I believe the fresh ocean salt air did both of us good, especially Brian. He was tired of living in the city, and I believe walking, particularly in rural areas, was a good way to clear the cobwebs from his mind. It is also a great way to boost *bhakti*.

Madhai, from the United Kingdom, joined our team midway through that first walk. His arrival resulted in a huge improvement in our culinary program because he has the knack of producing great curries, and his sandwiches are phenomenal too. He also contributed much laughter to our small group and raised our morale on several occasions. Madhai had been living in the temple *ashram*, and needing a change, brought his unique brand of *bhakti* (devotion) to our little team.

SUPPORT PERSON, MADHAI, COOKING UP A STORM.

Tattva Darshan (aka Tim Hitchner from Vancouver), Devadatta from Toronto, and Benjamin Barnes from the UK joined me for the second Canadian walk. Benjamin, who happens to be one of George Harrison's son's best friends, had some interesting stories to tell. What a blend of *bhakti* this group was, but we learned that three's a crowd, especially when there is a fourth one—me.

Another stalwart trooper was Garuda, whose life-long companion, Krishna Karuna, passed away from cancer. Garuda needed a way to address his grief, and the services he rendered did wonders getting his mind

GARUDA VAHAN AND HIS SON, TULSI.

off his loss.

Every morning Garuda would drop me off to continue from the point where I had stopped walking the previous day. He then drove into the next town and visited the local newspaper, as well as radio and television stations to arrange interviews. He introduced himself as Garuda from Wiarton, the home of Wiarton Willy, the famous groundhog. Everyone knew about the friendly rodent who pokes his head out of the ground predicting an early or late spring. If Willy saw his shadow, there would be another six weeks of winter remaining. These connections were Garuda's way of making his own *compadres*.

SUPPORT AND PHOTOGRAPHER EXTRAORDINAIRE, VIVASVAN.

I must also acknowledge the *compadres* and *comadres* who supported my trek across the United States in 2015. Vivasvan, a young Ukrainian man, certainly shed light on the walk with his expert navigational skills through some hilly sections of New England, New York, New Jersey, and Pennsylvania. By the way, *vivasvan* is a Sanskrit word meaning 'the sun'. His guidance was a blessing because he directed us through some of the most scenic landscapes in the Appalachian Mountains during the time when autumn colours matter most. Vivasvan, who is generally good natured, was fighting some demons when Tre'von came on board. The juxtaposition of a reserved, stern but kind Eastern European and a much younger and more extroverted Tre'von, caused some minor misunderstandings. I believe all three of us grew from this experience because after all, we are not these bodies, we are spirit souls.

SUPPORT PERSON, TRE'VON, IN THE CORN FIELD.

Vivasvan drove the vehicle while Tre'von walked along with me. I

291

taught Tre'von Sanskrit *mantras* which he incorporated into his spontaneously composed raps. I'm sure many motorists saw us as an odd duo—two suspects, or perhaps even a couple of criminals. I could have been mistaken for an escaped Caucasian convict dressed in prison orange, while he could have been racially stereotyped as a drug dealer from the inner city. Late one sunny morning I grew so tired that I laid down to rest in the grass next to the road near Harrisburg, Pennsylvania. Tre'von watched over me like a loyal guard, but soon a concerned motorist stopped and wanted to know if everything was alright.

SUPPORT TEAM, UTTAMANANDA, ABHIMANYU ARJUNA, AND GOPAL KELLER (L-R).

"This is my *guru* and I am watching over him. He is walking across the entire United States, and sometimes he gets tired." That was thoughtful of Tre'von, who had quickly picked up the spirit of devotional service becoming my friend, hero, and *compadre*. I like what heavyweight champion, Muhammad Ali, was once quoted as saying, "Service to others is the rent you pay for your room on Earth."

Gopal, from Texas, joined me through the Midwestern states. It was a golden opportunity for this bright talented man who was struggling with his own demons. Gopal was grappling with illusion, something many of us call 'maya'. Maya often wins life's battles, but we have to keep fighting it, because even though life is not easy, we should get stronger as time goes on.

There were other notable folks who provided support during the American walk, and I want to mention their glorious names. Anuttama, Rajasuya, Karuna Sindhu, Uttamananda, Hayagriva, Mandala, Marshall, Curtis, and Abhimanyu Arjuna all accompanied me for some sections of that walk across the 'land of the free and the home of the brave!'

SUPPORT TEAM, HAYAGRIVA, CURTIS, AND MARSHALL (L-R).

292

All of them were, and are, practitioners of *bhakti* yoga. While connecting (yoga) with the bigger picture through service (*bhakti*), each of them was dealing with various life issues. And all of them admitted having a rather awesome time with a mixture of adventure, therapy, and introspection.

I must also honour and give thanks to all of the motel owners from India who so graciously hosted us in the United States. Most nights during my walks across Canada, we roughed it by sleeping in a tent. But in America, Indian motel owners gave us free rooms for our comfort and protection from the elements. But their *bhakti* also burst forth in another way. "Oh, we must also cook for Swami-ji!" they would say. *Compadres* and *comadres* indeed!

SUPPORT PERSON, MANDALA RAMA.

Kind strangers, especially those in vehicles on long and lonely stretches of highway, often offered kindness and connection. Though I couldn't always accept their offers of a ride or certain foodstuffs, they were much appreciated. Drivers would often pull over at just the right moment for an enthusiasm-fuelling chat, or fruit and a beverage to fuel my parched and weary body. Even some friendly toots on the horn and a wave as they whizzed by offered encouragement.

These marathon walks built up leg muscles and spirit, hopefully bringing me a few steps closer to the Creator. Chapter eighteen of the *Bhagavad-gita* sums it up nicely by informing us that devotional service helps us better understand life.

A HUGE SUPPORT ON LONELY HIGHWAYS ARE FRIENDLY MOTORISTS STOPPING TO SAY HI.

When I was a teen, I was as thin as a rail and quite hopeless at most sports. Football and wrestling, which required brute strength, were totally out of the question, but I was a pretty fast runner when I set my mind to it. Determination came from the chores I had to do on the farm where I grew up. My summers were marathons in the barn, the field, or the orchard, and that experience taught me endurance. I developed a love for the sport of walking, which I believe is the pace a body is meant to go. Walking not only enhances our sensitivities, it takes us to the place where gratitude can be found.

"Your name, Bhaktimarga Swami, actually translates as 'The Walking Monk'," said a wise listener at one of my talks.

I agreed and added that my Sanskrit name was provided by my *guru*, Srila Prabhupada. Even though I never spoke to him personally, I learned all I know from his books, lectures, and students. Prabhupada and his c*ompadres* and *comadres* are responsible for setting my heart and feet on the trail of *bhakti*.

The roughest part of life is dealing with people. People can be quite nasty, and gossip is a lethal weapon. Animals may bite, sting, and pounce, but they don't gossip. Like many, I've been the target of tall and hurtful tales, but I chose to forgive the instigator because, in one sense, they did me a favour by inspiring me to take to the trail. I guess you could say he or she is also my *compadre* or *comadre*!

Life is like a journey on the road of rough patches. Yes, rough and tough times come at us in waves. They don't last long, but tough people do.

My advice to all:

    Open your mind
    Open the door
    Open the world
    Walk on
    You're a pilgrim

May the Source be with you!

ABOUT THE AUTHOR

A shy Canadian farm boy turned monk, John Vis (now Bhaktimarga Swami) stepped his way into the moniker of "The Walking Monk" one stride at a time after finding a path forged by saintly Indian scholar and spiritualist, the founder and preceptor of ISKCON, A.C. Bhaktivedanta Swami.

The Walking Monk joyfully shares the wisdom of India's ancient and inspiring texts worldwide through upbeat musical mantra meditation and dance, his vibrant and original live community theatre productions, and of course, marathon walking! These marathons have been covered in two Canadian film documentaries and numerous international media outlets.

Bhaktimarga Swami is based in Toronto, Canada. When not tending to the more administrative side of his leadership duties, he eagerly sets the rhythm of his feet far and near, by tree and by tower, to honour the practice of history's greatest pilgrims. He details his experiences promoting connection to nature, to each other, and to the Divine in his daily blog and on his Instagram page.

thewalkingmonk.net
@thewalkingmonk

Manufactured by Amazon.ca
Bolton, ON

39286521R00179